75171

A. v. Humboldt

Douglas Botting

HUMBOLDT
and the Cosmos

Harper & Row, Publishers
New York · Evanston · San Francisco · London

This book was designed and produced by
George Rainbird Ltd,
Marble Arch House, 44 Edgware Road,
London, W.2, England

House Editor: Curigwen Lewis
Designer: Michael Mendelsohn
Maps: Tom Stalker-Miller

Photoset by BAS Printers Limited, Wallop, Hampshire
Printed and bound by
Dai Nippon Printing Company Ltd,
Tokyo, Japan

Library of Congress Catalog Card Number: 76-186774
ISBN: 06-010412-0

First published 1973

Contents

Color Plates

Acknowledgments

I should like to thank Daphne Bryant and Norman Isaacs for their invaluable help with the translation of German source material. I should also like to thank Dr Hanno Beck, the leading authority on Alexander von Humboldt, for reading my manuscript and putting me right on several points; Bud Young for helpful comments about Humboldt in Venezuela and Mexico; Francis Busson for his help with Humboldt in Paris and David Attenborough for his help in locating Humboldt texts. I am grateful to the Royal Geographical Society, the Royal Society, the British Museum (Natural History) and the London Library for both books and illustrations and to all those persons in Britain, Germany, France, Italy, Spain and the USA who have kindly assisted this book in various ways. I thank Lynette Dibden and Ilse Pedroza, who typed my manuscript, and Curigwen Lewis, of George Rainbird Limited, for her patience and thoroughness in preparing the book for publication. Finally, I am grateful to my wife, Louise, for many valuable suggestions and unshakable coolness under fire.

Preface

I first became aware of Alexander von Humboldt and his achievements during a journey along the Casiquiare canal and the Upper Orinoco of Venezuela on which I followed very much in his footsteps. Though it was more than a hundred and fifty years since he had passed that way during his great journey of scientific exploration in South America, I was forcibly reminded of him at every turn in the river, every cataract and forest clearing. So when the idea of writing a biography of Humboldt was first suggested by Tony Birks, formerly of George Rainbird Limited, it seemed that this was a timely opportunity to reintroduce to the public a very great man whose memory in some quarters has been undeservedly neglected. It has been difficult, in the space of one volume, to do justice to Humboldt's range of achievements during an unusually long and active life, but if it stimulates interest it will have served its purpose.

Douglas Botting
London
December 1971

CHAPTER I

The Little Apothecary

Baron Friedrich Wilhelm Karl Heinrich Alexander von Humboldt—scientist, explorer, liberal and last great universal man—was born in the Berlin of Frederick the Great on 14 September 1769, the same year as his future friends and acquaintances Napoleon, Wellington, Canning, Chateaubriand and Cuvier. His father, who had heaved his cutlass alongside the Duke of Brunswick in the Seven Years War and afterwards become Chamberlain to the King, later married Elisabeth von Colomb, a wealthy widow. From this uneasy union the couple produced two sons—Wilhelm, born in 1767, and Alexander. Both boys passed their formative years at Schloss Tegel, the family estate among the pine woods and sand dunes twelve miles north of Berlin, and here they learnt that happiness is not necessarily the product of privilege.

Alexander did not have an enjoyable childhood and there were times when he was positively wretched. As far as parental love was concerned he might just as well have been an orphan. His father, who seems to have been a warm and amiable character, died when he was only nine. His mother, who controlled the household after her husband's death, was aloof, cold, self-sufficient, puritanical. Ordinary maternal warmth seems to have been beyond her and though she had her children's future at heart, and arranged the best education she could for them, she showed them little actual love and in return received none. The brothers were brought up in an emotional waste land where work and achievement were substituted for love and play; deprived of the ordinary things of boyhood, they turned their gift for friendship on each other and grew up like twins. To Alexander especially, a boy of natural exuberance and vitality, the repressive atmosphere of his mother's home was anathema.

Both boys were privately educated at home under the supervision of a tutor. Their first tutor was a pedantic young man called Joachim Heinrich Campe, a writer of books for the young, who taught the three R's. More important was his successor, Gottlob Christian Kunth, the son of a poor pastor who first arrived at the Humboldt household when he was barely twenty and stayed there until his death fifty years later. Kunth seems to have been a well-educated, well-mannered young fellow and Frau Humboldt placed great trust in him; ultimately he was made responsible not only for the education of her sons but for the management of her estates as well. He was an admirer of the liberal ideas of Rousseau, gave the boys a

Alexander at the age of fifteen

grounding in history and mathematics and placed great emphasis on languages. When they were older he arranged for specialists to give them more advanced lessons in their town house in Berlin—a scholastic regimen of unremitting toil.

But Alexander's private pursuits were more important than his formal instruction. From a very early age he showed a marked interest in natural history—so much so that at home he was nicknamed 'the little apothecary'. Flowers, butterflies, beetles, shells and stones were his favourite playthings, and he took to wandering alone through the woods and among the dunes of Tegel in search of them, and arranging and labelling his collections in the room he shared with his brother. He found in this solitary intimacy with the natural world some sort of refuge from the constraints that human society imposed on him, and in the books he read in his leisure hours he found an even more effective escape in the daydream world of foreign travel and adventure.

He grew up in an age of daring exploration and discovery. La Condamine had sailed down the Amazon, Carsten Niebuhr had travelled through unknown Arabia, James Bruce had reached the source of the Blue Nile, and by the time Alexander was ten, Captain James Cook, in the company of men like Banks and the two Forsters, had explored the whole extent of the Pacific Ocean. The books that Alexander read

Alexander's mother, Elisabeth von Humboldt—'aloof, cold, self-sufficient, puritanical'—and his father, Major Alexander Georg von Humboldt, framing Schloss Tegel, the Humboldt country home near Berlin

about these enterprises filled him with a 'secret fascination' that at times was 'almost irresistible'. In particular, Georg Forster's vivid account of the South Sea islands, together with a painting by Hodge of a scene on the Ganges, and a gigantic dragon tree in an old tower of the Botanic Gardens in Berlin, gave him a romantic fondness for the tropics, idealized in the works of Rousseau, Buffon and Bernardin de St-Pierre.

By their early teens it was clear that the two brothers were developing in very different directions. Wilhelm was the idol of the household and showed such outstanding ability at his lessons that his mother decided he ought to be trained for high public office. Alexander was more of a problem. He was a slow learner and quite frequently so frail and ailing that he was almost prostrate, and could only master his daily tasks by dint of extraordinary effort. He was a restless child and visitors to the house described him as a *petit esprit malin*. He wanted to be a soldier but his only talent seemed to be as an artist—the walls of his mother's bedroom were hung with the portraits and landscapes he had drawn in his free time. Frau Humboldt seems to have had less confidence in her younger son's prospects; for him she chose a less ambitious career in the Prussian bureaucracy and a humdrum training in economics. As for science, Alexander neither received any lessons in the subject nor showed the slightest interest in it.

His ignorance of science in the Berlin of those days—a philistine and provincial place of 140,000 people—was hardly surprising. It was not a recognized part of a schoolboy's syllabus, it was not an established part of the cultural environment, it had no status and received little encouragement. The average German savant had barely heard of Kant and preferred hypotheses of the wildest kind to the routine discipline of experiment and observation. The Berlin Academy of Science was a joke. One learned Academician gave a lecture on the sun in which, with supposedly incontrovertible reasoning, he came to the conclusion that the sun was a kitchen stove and sun spots were heaps of soot. Another Academician announced that he had discovered how to make gold out of a volatile salt, while another decided that the pyramids (which he had never seen) were really volcanoes. But there were exceptions to the general level of mediocrity and it was Alexander's good fortune, when he was only sixteen, to be introduced to one of them—the Jewish physician, Marcus Herz. Herz was a devoted disciple of Kant and had organized at his home a popular course of lectures on physics and philosophy which he illustrated with remarkably elaborate scientific experiments. These were the first experiments Alexander had ever seen and they had such an effect on him that from this moment forward his inclination turned him more and more towards a scientific career.

Marcus Herz's scientific soirées had two more immediate results, however. First, after watching a demonstration of the principles of Benjamin Franklin's lightning conductor—a device which many clerics condemned as a direct interference with the divine will—Alexander arranged to have one installed at Schloss Tegel: probably the first appliance of its kind ever put up in Berlin. Secondly, and what was of far greater importance to him, he met Marcus' wife, Henriette Herz.

Henriette was twenty-two at this time—seventeen years younger than her husband. She was a woman of great charm and wit, and famous throughout Berlin for her beauty. 'If you haven't seen the Theatre Royal and Henriette Herz,' the Berliner used to say, 'you haven't seen Berlin.' She was also a flirt and made a practice of collecting young and whenever possible brilliant men around her, so that before long both Wilhelm and Alexander had been added to her clever and dazzling circle. Alexander probably came nearer to this dark-eyed Jewess than he ever came to any other woman in his life. 'She is', he said, 'the most beautiful and also the cleverest— no, I must say the wisest woman I know.' They seem to have shared the same kind of gaiety and sense of humour, the same bubbling, outgoing temperament, and the same quick intelligence. For Alexander, brought up in the emotionally arid company of a cold mother and impersonal tutors, this was the first taste of female warmth and comfort he had ever experienced.

Henriette herself—part mother, part sister, part friend to her young protégé— allowed herself to be carried along by his enthusiasm. He was a witty, amiable, good-looking boy, with a reputation as a graceful dancer—he was the first to teach Henriette the steps of the new 'Minuet à la Reine'—and he sent her many amusing and dreadfully long letters, which he wrote in English if he wanted to show off or in Hebrew if he had anything confidential to say. Often when he wrote to Henriette from Schloss Tegel he headed his letters *Schloss Langweil*—'Castle of Boredom'.

It was not the done thing for a Berliner to be seen to prefer the company of Jews, who had no civil rights whatsoever, but they offered almost the only intellectual life there was in the city. The small brilliant circles of Herz and Moses Mendelssohn and his sons, with their emancipated women, modern science and avant-garde poetry, were for both Wilhelm and Alexander like oases on a long desert crossing.

In October 1787, the two Humboldt brothers, accompanied by their ever-watch-ful and conscientious guardian, Kunth—he had been deputed by their mother to keep an eye on their moral welfare—began their university education at Frankfurt an der Oder, a benighted place which had been chosen for its nearness to the maternal home at Tegel, only a day's coach drive away, rather than its academic virtues. The town itself was small, drab and provincial, and the university was not the kind of institution to set the young intellects of Germany alight. The student body consisted of little more than two hundred boys, mostly sons of Pomeranian noblemen, and the teaching faculties were composed of a mere handful of dull and undistinguished professors. There was no science course, the library was very badly stocked and there was only one small bookshop in the town. At his mother's insistence, Alexander started to read political economy as a preparation for entering the Prussian Civil Service, but this subject was regarded with some derision by the students, since it required little work yet inevitably led to a degree and high office, and the teaching of it was appalling. They learnt to draw plans for a brandy distillery, a tar-kiln, or

Karl Ludwig Willdenow, who first introduced the young Humboldt to botany.
'From then on the subject became a passion.'

a flour mill; they learnt the requisite number of threads in the warp and woof of linen and taffeta; they learnt how to make cheese and to smelt iron, and how to destroy caterpillars and noxious insects; but of the higher principles of political economy they did not have the faintest conception.

The only apparent result of the winter this eighteen-year-old boy spent by the ice-bound banks of the Oder was the sudden blossoming of the first of his numerous intense friendships with other men—in this case with an obscure young theology student named Wegener, to whom he wrote interminable and often sentimental letters full of expressions of eternal brotherly love and descriptions of dreams that symbolized his longed-for union with his friend. Transitory though it was, this relationship seems to have fulfilled some kind of desperate need on Humboldt's part and in it one can detect the future pattern of his unsatisfactory and ultimately inexplicable private life: the enigma of the warm, passionate, unattached and probably chaste adult he was to be.

In the spring of 1788 the Humboldt brothers turned their backs on Frankfurt, after only six months' residence. Wilhelm, whom his mother continued to regard as the more promising of her sons, went direct to Göttingen University to read law, but Alexander spent the next year at home where he studied manufacturing processes and ancient Greek with private tutors and formed an increasing interest in botany— a highly esoteric pursuit in the Berlin of those days.

Until he was eighteen Alexander had never even heard of botany, but his interest was fired by his friendship with a young man of twenty-two, Karl Ludwig Willdenow, who had just published a Flora of Berlin. He never actually had any lessons but Willdenow used to classify the plants he brought him and from then on the subject became a passion. The mere sight of an exotic plant, even a dried specimen in a herbarium, thrilled him so much that he longed more and more to see the tropical vegetation of southern lands with his own eyes.

In the spring of 1789 Alexander joined his brother at Göttingen University, then the foremost university of Germany. Here he shared digs with the young Count Metternich, studied a wide variety of subjects under outstanding teachers like C. G. Heyne, one of the founders of classical philology and archaeology, and set out on his first geological field trip which resulted in a learned little paper on the basalts of the Rhine. Already he seems to have worked out a principle for conducting his life which he adhered to for the rest of his days. He would never be overwhelmed by any passion, he said. 'Hard work and the quiet pursuit of natural history will preserve me from the temptations of life.'

Alexander's university course at Göttingen lasted no longer than a year but by the end of that time he had laid the solid foundations of a knowledge of physics and chemistry and begun to see in what direction his real inclinations lay. More important still, it was at Göttingen that he teamed up with Georg Forster, his 'guiding star', and the greatest single influence on his future life.

Henriette Herz. 'Alexander probably came nearer to this dark-eyed Jewess than he ever came to any other woman in his life.' Painting by Anna-Dorothea Therbusch

The two men were introduced by Heyne, whose daughter Forster had married. Forster was thirty-six years old at the time of this meeting and famous throughout Germany. The instant affinity the two men felt for each other was hardly surprising, for in many ways Forster—as an explorer, naturalist, geographer, linguist and famous author—was Alexander's prototype. He had been born near Danzig in 1754, the son of Reinhold Forster, a tempestuous clergyman and brilliant amateur scientist of Scottish descent. In 1766, when he was twelve, the young Georg emigrated to England with his family, and in 1772, at the age of eighteen, was invited (with his father) to accompany Captain James Cook on his second voyage round the world as natural history draughtsman. Georg Forster's account of this journey, *A Voyage Round the World*—a work of travel, science and literature all in one—was first published in London in 1777, and in a German version, *Reise um die Welt*, in Berlin a year later. In Germany at least the book instantly established his fame. It revealed him as one of the most accomplished stylists in the German language and had a profound influence on German scientific and literary writing.

Forster had returned to Germany in 1778 and was university librarian at Mainz when Humboldt met him—a gentle, humane, charming man, but erratic, unsettled and discontented. In the spring of 1790 he decided to make a return visit to England to find a publisher for his proposed new geography of the South Seas and obtain redress from the English Government for some real or imaginary wrong done to his father. In the last week of March, in the company of Humboldt, he set out.

They travelled by boat down the lower Rhine to Holland and Belgium and thence to England. For Humboldt the journey was a revelation. With Forster for a guide nothing escaped the closest scrutiny—art and nature, past and present, the living and the dead, politics and economics, factories and docks, parks and observatories, all were prodded and poked, so to speak, with meticulous attention. And the more Forster saw of his young disciple the more he found to admire in him.

At Dunkerque Alexander had his first sight and smell of the sea and fell in love with it for ever. In Lille he witnessed the civil insurrection. In London he attended the trial of Warren Hastings, listened to the music in Westminster Abbey, heard Burke, Pitt and Sheridan speak in Parliament on the same evening, met Cavendish, William Herschel, John Sibthorp and Sir Joseph Banks (Captain Cook's companion on his first journey round the world) and was shown Bank's magnificent herbarium, the largest in the world, and his vast botanical library. He travelled as far north as the Peak district of Derbyshire (where he spent a whole day below ground exploring the Peak Cavern, Eldon Hole and Poole's Hole) and as far west as Bristol, industriously filling his notebook wherever he went with the bald facts of the island's economy— the price of English wool, the quality of English beer, the rotation of English crops— in a kind of mercantile five-finger exercise.

On their way back to Germany the two travellers passed through revolutionary Paris. It was the eve of the first Quatorze Juillet and the streets were full of jubilant

Georg Forster, naturalist, writer and revolutionary, who sailed the South Seas with Captain Cook and first inspired Humboldt to become an explorer. Painting by J. H. W. Tischbein

crowds; the atmosphere, after a year of political liberty, was fantastic, and the enthusiasm of the people and their sense of unity and purpose had a lasting impact on both of them. In 1790 the Revolution had not yet gone sour and its ideals were still intact; it still seemed possible to hope for a free and equal brotherhood of man. Humboldt, already a confirmed liberal, described those few days he spent in Paris as the most instructive and the most memorable of his life and for ever after accounted himself a man of the Revolution. Forster went even further; he became an active participator in it, and only four years later he died for it. On 11 July he and Humboldt returned to Mainz and parted, never to meet again. Two years afterwards, when Mainz fell to the French, Forster joined the revolutionaries and became a leading member of the provisional republican government. In 1793 he went to Paris to negotiate on behalf of that government and in his absence the Germans recaptured Mainz. Unable to return, publicly reviled as a traitor in Germany, and disillusioned by the turn the Revolution had taken in France, Georg Forster died in miserable circumstances in January 1794. He was forty years old.

Humboldt's journey with Georg Forster was one of the most profoundly important events of his early life. For it was with Forster, the circumnavigator of the world, the companion of Cook, that Humboldt had set eyes on the sea for the first time, and it was under his influence, too, that his vague, barely conscious wish to travel the earth and explore the world of nature became a concrete, conscious plan. His life had suddenly taken a positive step towards a definite goal.

His mother and Kunth, however, in their mundane wisdom, arranged for Alexander to attend the Hamburg School of Commerce as soon as he returned to Germany so that he could acquire a practical knowledge of commercial office routine. Alexander—aware that a qualification in practical science was more useful on an expedition than a qualification in book-keeping—wished to apply for a place at the famous Freiberg Mining School, but in deference to his mother's wishes, he duly enrolled at the School of Commerce in the summer of 1790 and plunged at once into his habitual frenzy of curricular and extra-curricular studies.

He had the undisturbed use of a small room in a secluded garden where the only interruption was the dinner and supper bell and he spent long hours in his study. He seems to have indulged in few, if any, of the more ordinary diversions of student life—no play ever distracted him from his remorseless, self-imposed programme of work. His leisure hours were taken up with geology and botany and he had started to learn Danish and Swedish. He was almost manic about learning. It was as though there was a demon in him. 'I can't spare myself', he told Wegener. 'There's a drive in me which at times makes me feel as if I'm losing my mind. But I've just got to work hard if I'm going to achieve anything.'

The frenetic imbalance which seemed to characterize Alexander's personality at this period, the hyper-activity of mind and body that pushed him almost to the brink of insanity, did not pass unnoticed by others. Forster's wife, who did not like him, had described him as a sick and nervous companion, and Forster himself put his condition down to overwork. Caroline von Dachröden, Wilhelm's fiancée, actually believed he might lose his reason. 'I honestly think he's nutty,' she wrote to Wilhelm, 'and he may go mad any time.' Alexander was shaping in a way that caused Wilhelm some anxiety. 'He has a lovable nature, but he maintains very peculiar ideas for which I really don't care. . . . He is a busybody, full of enterprise that to others must necessarily seem like vanity. He peddles the wares of his knowledge with much ado, as if he desperately needs either to dazzle people or to beg for their sympathy. All this wanting to impress others really stems from a desire to impress oneself.' And again: 'Alexander is undoubtedly vain and has his own way of seeing and admiring greatness in others where he believes he can find it. I can't discern anything really significant in him, yet he has more than average warmth, a capacity for sacrificing himself for others and for forming quick attachments. I don't think he'll ever be happy . . .'

At Easter 1791 the academic interlude at Hamburg came to an end and Humboldt wrote out an application for a position in the Prussian Ministry of Industry and Mines which he addressed to the Minister, Baron von Heinitz. At the end of May he received his reply. He was to undertake his course of training at Freiberg Mining Academy: when he had completed it, he would be appointed to a suitable position in the Department of Mines. Thus he began a career he never intended to follow for a day longer than he could help.

The Mining Academy at Freiberg in Saxony—the first school of its kind in the world and one of the foremost scientific institutions in Europe—had been founded by Heinitz in 1766 and now attracted students from all over the world on account of the reputation of its director, Professor A. G. Werner. In those days Werner, who supported the Neptunist theory of the aqueous origins of the earth's rocks, was to geology what Linnaeus had been to botany. He was regarded, in Germany at least, as the founder of the science, and a gifted teacher.

Humboldt's reputation as an interesting young student of science had preceded him to Freiberg—throughout his life, wherever he was, he always made sure that it did—and his *Basalts of the Rhine*, which supported the Neptunist theory, ensured for him a warm welcome from the great Werner. Alexander's studies began with a descent into the neighbouring mines. His guide was a young instructor in surveying, Karl Freiesleben, two years his senior, with whom he soon formed one of those intense and exclusive male relationships which had already become a marked feature of his emotional life.

The training at Freiberg was thorough and exhausting by any standards. The mornings from six or seven till midday were spent down at the pit face studying the practical problems of mining and mineralogy. The afternoons were taken up with theory—geology and the classification of rocks, surveying, essaying, mathematics and law—and often Humboldt found himself attending as many as six lectures crammed between lunch and dinner. The rest of his time was his own but he chose to spend it, as ever, in additional work—either botanizing for mosses and lichens or teaching himself chemistry and palaeontology in his room.

During his many private expeditions through the sunless labyrinth of the Freiberg mines he became fascinated by the mosses and other plants that still managed to produce a green pigmentation in nothing but the feeble light of a miner's lamp. This prompted him to carry out research in his small subterranean garden into the effect of light on plant growth, the results of which were incorporated into his later work on the physiology of plants, *Florae Fribergensis*.

It was an almost crippling programme he set himself and it left little time over for social life and his friends—he did not bother to answer even Forster's and Wegener's letters and excused himself from attending his brother Wilhelm's wedding. Such a self-imposed burden of activity took its toll, especially as the winter months drew on. 'I have never been so busy in my life. My health has suffered in consequence, though I am on the whole very happy. I am in a profession that must be followed passionately to be enjoyed.'

In February 1792, however, Humboldt formally celebrated the successful end of his studies at Freiberg with his classmates. It was the end of his student days, the end of a major phase in his life. Under Werner's intensive tutelage he had, in only eight months, obtained every qualification necessary for his future profession. From Berlin he received a letter stating that 'on account of the valuable knowledge, both theoretical and practical, possessed by him in mathematics, physics, natural history, chemistry, technology, the arts of mining and smelting, and the general routine of business', he was to be appointed Assistant Inspector in the Department of Mines. His professional life had begun—and the first step towards the realization of his innermost dreams.

Humboldt's interest in the cosmos began early. Recently discovered drawings of the New World and the Copernican planetary system, done by Humboldt in 1783 when he was fourteen

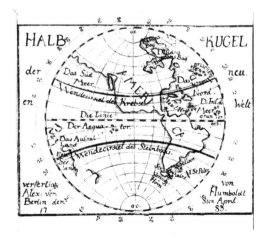

CHAPTER 2

Gold Miner

'I feel quite ashamed for being elated at such a trifle', Alexander wrote to Freiesleben when he heard he had been appointed Assistant Inspector of Mines without having to serve the usual probation as a cadet. 'It seems unfair to make me an Assistant straight away over the heads of a whole troop of cadets and ex-students, etc. I have openly expressed this opinion here, but I have been told that in this department no one had a better claim than myself, and this', he added with characteristic modesty, 'is very likely true.'

But even Humboldt himself was aware he started with a great deal in his favour. He came from a privileged aristocracy for whom preferment in State employ was virtually automatic. He had a private income, which not only enabled him to survive on his Civil Service salary—a pittance of less than 8 thalers a week—but freed him to pursue his own independent line of action at the mines. He was already a compelling personality, with the kind of charisma it was difficult to ignore even in a crowded room. He was good looking, attractive to both women and men, and a remarkable conversationalist. He was popular in society, and though his manners were not always impeccable, he was almost always gay and entertaining company. He was ambitious and drove himself unsparingly. He had immense enthusiasm for things that interested him, an extraordinary appetite for work and a range of knowledge so encyclopedic it struck dumb all who came near it. He was, in short, a quite exceptionally talented eighteenth century Prussian whizz-kid, and the Mining Department was only too anxious to secure his services, for in the public life of Prussia at that time men of his calibre were rare.

Indeed, under Prussia's weak and indolent king, Frederick William II, the efficient bureaucratic machine set up by Frederick the Great had run down and virtually seized-up altogether. After nearly a decade of corrupt misrule, Prussia was sliding steadily towards bankruptcy and the military catastrophe of Jena. In his marble palace at Potsdam the King planned his inglorious campaigns, squandered huge sums borrowed from abroad, and passed his leisure hours in the pursuit of the occult. The surest way for an official to get on in public service now was to be a Rosicrucian, an alchemist, an astrologer or a quack—or pretend to be. In almost every department of the Civil Service, ability and a knowledge of one's subject were considered unnecessary, and scientific or literary interests embarrassing. One of

Inside the salt mine at Wieliczka, Poland, which Humboldt visited on his 3,000-mile fact-finding tour

Humboldt's superiors at that time, Baron von Stein, used to tell the story of a Minister who was so diffident about literature of any sort that when his staff presented him with a printed address on his birthday he refused it. 'You know I don't read anything in print,' he scolded them, 'let me have it in handwriting.' Government had degenerated to an unheard of level, and files of useless information piled up in offices, unread by anyone. Besides, the pay was so poor that recruitment of first-class men was difficult and corruption was everywhere rife.

What is surprising, under such circumstances, is not that Humboldt joined the service at all—he had never made it much of a secret that he always regarded the job merely as a useful stepping stone to greater things—but that he stuck it so long. In general, he hated bureaucracy and had little in common with his colleagues. The job had its compensations, however. The Mining Department's jurisdiction covered a wide area from Franconia in the south to the Baltic coast in the north and Prussia's Polish possessions in the east; it included stone quarries, peat and soft coal in Brandenburg, hard coal and iron in Silesia, salt mines by the sea, copper and gold in the Fichtel mountains. It therefore provided Humboldt with an unparalleled opportunity for travel and original scientific field work, and he had need for greater experience of both.

From the start, the new recruit was both headstrong and outspoken—he knew what needed to be done, and he had no hesitation in saying so. When he was told he was going to be given a desk job in Berlin he turned it down flat. When one of his directors insisted that he was *too* preoccupied with the practical details of mining and reminded him that he wasn't born to be a common foreman, Humboldt retorted that in his opinion mining officials who dealt in generalities got nowhere. Berlin, he reckoned, was as inappropriate a place for a Department of Mining as it was for a Board of Admiralty. In any case, he loathed the city—even the Academy of Science was like a leper house, he said, where you couldn't tell the healthy from the sick.

At the end of June 1792 Humboldt had his way and was finally despatched from Berlin to make a report on the geology and the state of the mines in the wild Fichtel mountains and the Franconian hills, part of the newly acquired territory around Bayreuth. It was his first opportunity to distinguish himself in official life and he didn't waste it. By the end of August he had submitted his 150 page report. It caused a sensation. Von Heinitz was delighted, spoke warmly of Humboldt's 'indefatigable activity', 'sound judgement' and 'judicious application of scientific principles' and ordered the report to be circulated among all the officials of the department. A day or two later he promoted Humboldt from Assistant to Chief Inspector of Mines and at the special request of Count von Hardenberg, Governor of Ansbach-Bayreuth, seconded him to Bayreuth where he was to take over the mining establishments of the surrounding district.

'I am intoxicated with joy', Humboldt wrote to Freiesleben when he heard the news. 'It is only a year ago that I was asking you what a "winze" was, and now I am Chief Inspector. What wonderful progress I have made! Think how much I shall learn in such a position.'

His secondment to Bayreuth, however, was not to become effective until March of the following year. In the meantime he was requested to make a 3,000-mile fact-finding tour of the foreign salt-processing works of Austria and Poland, and by 23 September, with barely enough time to gather his things together, he was on his way.

The roads Humboldt travelled over on this first official tour of his—from Bayreuth to Munich and thence through Austria and what is now Czechoslovakia, Poland and East Germany, back to Berlin—followed precisely the same course as they do today, but they wound through a vastly different landscape. If we could have accompanied him on his way to the salt-works of Hallein and Berchtesgaden and Tarnowitz and Wieliczka that autumn and winter of 1792, sat next to this quick-eyed and tireless young man in that clattering-carriage, our ears full of the thud of the horses hooves and the squeak of the iron-rimmed wheels, the physical world would have struck us as a marvellously pristine one compared with our own—a perfect, unravished ruritania. The Industrial Revolution had not yet reached the continent of Europe. There were no modern factories belching smoke, no clank and hiss of steam machinery, no proletarian slums. Outside the infrequent big towns the views remained unrelievedly bucolic. Across the sandy marshes of Brandenburg, among the mountains of Austria and Bavaria and over the rolling grasslands of Bohemia and the endless forests and steppes of Poland, Humboldt could have travelled for hours on end without passing another carriage or setting eyes on another soul.

Before many miles, though, the extraordinary squalor and uncouthness of a large part of the human world of that time would have dominated all other impressions—the wretchedness of the peasants and serfs; the maimed and the diseased begging for alms through the carriage window; the streets full of flies and animal dung and human slop; the pigs rooting in the gutters; the smells. For the central European countryside that Humboldt travelled through then was still a largely medieval world of timeless inertia—and, in the age of the discovery of electricity and manned flight, the gentry and the peasantry alike maintained an existence that had hardly changed since the time of Horace.

It was winter by the time he reached Vienna. He was cold and exhausted after a long journey through heavy snow in the Austrian Alps, but within a day or two he was off again, out across the drifts of the Moravian uplands and the frozen Polish plains, through Waldenburg and Kupferberg and among the Riesengebirge, never longer than two days in a place, travelling in the midst of extreme cold and far into the night, preparing his elaborate reports and his plan-drawings of the salt-works, hissing over the ice in a sleigh among the wintery hills—perpetual motion itself.

It was the end of January before he was back in Berlin. It was June before he assumed his duties in Bayreuth as Chief Inspector of Mines.

*   *   *

In the district under his charge Humboldt was confronted with a number of mines in a bad state of neglect and dilapidation; in that respect the wild region of the Fichtel mountains was a depressed area, and some of the workings had not been mined for nearly three centuries. To put such mines back on their feet again was a task that might have daunted the average official, especially one as young and in-experienced as he was. But he approached the problem with confidence. From the State archives in the fortress at Plessenburg he removed three chests of sixteenth century documents containing detailed records of the old workings in the mines, and from a careful study of these, backed up by first-hand inspection of all the abandoned galleries, he obtained the vital clues to the location of the gold seams that his predecessors in office had lacked.

Throughout that scorching summer he rode alone on horseback from mine to mine, often over considerable distances. For days on end he would be down the pits by half-past four in the morning and stay there till ten at night, analysing and as-saying the ores in spite of the unbearable heat and the enervating atmosphere. Within two weeks the preliminary organization was almost complete; the main office was open, the estimates of cost drawn up, the necessary buildings in course of construction. 'Everything is making satisfactory progress' Humboldt wrote. 'I possess the confidence of the men, who think I must have at least four arms and eight legs—which is just as well in my position among so many lazy officials.'

Bad Steben in the Fichtel mountains where Humboldt opened his Free Royal Mining School. 'On this side of the ocean, no place would ever seem to me its equal.'

By the winter the redevelopment of the once defunct mines was more spectacular than even Humboldt had hoped.

> An expenditure of 14,000 florins in eight years has produced barely 150 tons of gold ore, while I have procured from this mine alone in one year, and with the labour of only 9 men, 125 tons of gold ore at a cost of less than 7,000 florins. . . . You see, my dear friend, I am becoming quite a boaster.

Gold, iron, vitriol, cobalt, tin, antimony, copper, alum—the yields soared. He had never been fitter in his life. The constitutional frailty and nervous hypertension of his youth seemed to have gone. 'Don't worry yourself about my health,' he told Freiesleben, 'I've kept extremely well throughout the summer, and my delicacy seems to be leaving me. I consider that the improvement in my health is entirely due to my work in the mines.'

*   *   *

When he first arrived in the district Humboldt had been amazed at the ignorance of the ordinary miners. They were quite unable to tell one rock from another, let alone spot even the commonest mineral of commercial value; and superstition and prejudice affected every aspect of their work, from the danger of choke-damp to the search for ore-bearing seams. To remedy this situation Humboldt decided, against everyone's advice, to open a school for the common miners.

Secretly, without the knowledge of his superiors or any charter from the Government, Humboldt inaugurated his free mining school in November 1793 at a small mining village called Steben, high up in the Fichtel mountains. He paid for this pioneer venture in adult education—the first workers' training school ever started in Germany—entirely out of his own pocket, and personally trained its first instructor, a local lad who was familiar with local conditions and the dialect spoken by his mates. Attendance was purely voluntary and anyone over the age of twelve could go, but to avoid friction with the village school, the Free Royal Mining School only held its classes on Wednesday and Saturday afternoons. There the pupils were taught the rudiments of geology and mineralogy, the phenomena of the water table and the course of rivers, mining law, local geography and the sort of mathematics that was useful in the maintenance of the mines. The interest these lessons excited was so great that they often went on far into the night.

Though he does not say as much, it is evident that Humboldt was very much loved at Steben. For his part, he appears to have been very emotionally involved with the working folk of the district and his work among them. Years later he described his feelings:

> Steben had such a strong influence on my ideas, I worked out so many of my greatest plans there and abandoned myself so completely to feeling that I almost dread the impression it would make on me if I ever saw it again. During my stay there, especially in the autumn and winter of 1793, I

was kept in a state of such nervous tension, that I could never see the lights of the cottages at Spitzberg shining through the evening mist without emotion. On this side of the ocean no place would ever seem to me its equal.

Minister von Heinitz was delighted when he heard of the school. From Berlin he sent a sum of money to defray Humboldt's expenses. Humboldt refused it. 'It would be laying myself open to the charge of pecuniary motives, from which I am quite free' he said. It would please him more if the money could be distributed amongst the most deserving miners in the coming winter, and if a pension could be provided for the families of miners who had fallen on hard times as a result of accidents or sickness down the pit.

For a Prussian of that period Humboldt had an extraordinarily developed social conscience; he also had a highly practical talent for implementing it. Mining was a notoriously dangerous occupation and pitfalls and disastrous explosions were events of almost daily occurrence. Even more destructive in the long run were the insidious

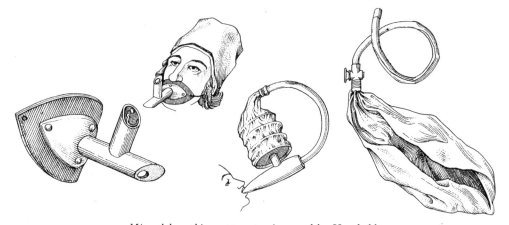

Miners' breathing apparatus invented by Humboldt

diseases that work down the mines often entailed—asthma, palsy, jaundice, inflamation of the glands and diseases of the skin and bone, to name a few. To find ways of reducing these risks to his miners' lives and health, Humboldt embarked on an exhaustive programme of research. It was arduous and dangerous work and on one occasion he was nearly killed by choke-damp in the disused cross-cut of an alum mine. In spite of such risks, however, he was able to analyse the chemical composition of the various gases in the mines and on the basis of his discoveries he devised a respirator and four kinds of safety lamp which were often used down the mines until they were replaced by Davy's improved version some years later.

* * *

Humboldt's star continued to wax brightly. In 1794, after only two years in the mining service, his chief, Heinitz, offered him promotion to a desk job in Berlin at

Humboldt at twenty-six. He was then a Prussian mining official. Drawing by François Gérard

1,500 thalers per annum, four times his current salary. And in the following year, Count von Hardenberg, administrator of Ansbach-Bayreuth, took him on a secret diplomatic mission to the King's headquarters at Frankfurt am Main, where the Allied German States and the French revolutionary army were conducting the preliminary negotiations that were to lead to the Peace of Basle. Humboldt's precise rôle during his four-month secondment to Hardenberg's staff was never made clear, but his appointment on such a crucial and delicate matter of state was evidently an immense distinction and a year or two later he was put in charge of a diplomatic mission of his own at Hohenlohe. It seemed the highest positions in science and government were already within his grasp. And yet he had barely had time to unpack his bags on his return from Frankfurt before he had officially announced his intention of throwing it all up for a dim and embryonic vision of his private destiny.

Humboldt had never made much of a secret that his only real ambition was to become an explorer and carry out original scientific field work in the remoter corners of the earth. After his previous promotion he had confided to Freiesleben: 'My former plans remain undisturbed. I shall resign my post in two years, and go to Russia, Siberia, and I don't know where.' Heinitz may have got wind of his impending resignation—it had always been built in to his original contract anyway—because he wrote him an extraordinarily flattering letter in February 1795 and tried to induce him to stay in the service by offering him the exalted post of Director of Mines in Silesia, Prussia's south-eastern province. Humboldt was forced to come clean.

He could not accept the post, he said, because he was contemplating a complete change in his mode of life and intended to withdraw from any position within the state. Heinitz, however, refused to accept Humboldt's resignation. He repeated his inducements in almost pressing terms and Humboldt became even more explicit in refusing them. He had postponed his resignation because of his mother's illness, he said, but he was determined to leave public service in the spring of 1797 whatever the circumstances. As soon as he had formulated firm plans and a suitable opportunity arose, he would be off. In the meantime he would continue to fulfill his miscellaneous duties as usual.

CHAPTER 3

Goethe and Galvanism

At the age of twenty-six Humboldt was one of the busiest men in Europe. What with dashing from one mine to the next, or half way across Europe on errands of international diplomacy, it is remarkable that he found time for his private work, let alone his private life. But he was one of those fortunate men who had learned how to defeat time. No matter how long his official working day had been, he still managed to conjure up a few more hours in which to conduct experiments and write books. His energy was quite phenomenal, and exhausted any of his contemporaries who tried to keep pace with it.

He managed this terrific activity at the expense of the ordinary time-wasters of life; sleep, mealtimes, recreation. He never spent long in bed, never lingered at table, and made full use of every spare second of the day. In an age of increasing specialization, he remained a scientist with universal interests. During his mining days in Bayreuth he worked on subjects as divers as the geological stratification of Europe, the effects of various gases on animals, subterranean climatology and the geography of plants. He developed a highly original system of shorthand notation for use in chemistry and physics, which he called pasigraphy, and became interested in terrestrial magnetism after discovering a serpentine rock with a polarity opposite to that of the earth. 'You're aware that I'm quite mad enough to be tied up with three books at once', he wrote to a friend. 'The fact is I can't exist without experiments.' When he was criticized for working in too many fields at once, his reply was 'How can you stop a man wanting to find things out and understand the world around him? In any case, a wide variety of knowledge is vital to a traveller.'

His *principal* obsession during his years at Bayreuth was a series of experiments into the nature of so-called animal electricity. Galvani had already demonstrated that if you applied two different metals in contact to the nerves and muscles of a frog's leg, the leg would convulse. This, he claimed, was because of the electricity contained in the animal's nerves. Volta, on the other hand, disagreed. According to him, it was not animal electricity that caused the convulsions but electricity produced by the contact between the two metals. Humboldt's hypothesis was somewhere between the two: the metals intensified the convulsions but were not the cause of them. His experiments continued on and off for months and then for years, and he did not confine himself to frogs but tried other animals, plants, and even his own body. It was in an effort to determine the effect of an electric current on the secretion of serum and blood that he first applied electrodes to himself—in the best traditions of experimental medicine but with dire results.

> I raised two blisters on my back, each the size of a crown-piece and covering the trapezius and deltoid muscles respectively. Meanwhile I lay flat on my stomach. When the blisters were cut and contact was made with the zinc and silver electrodes, I experienced a sharp pain, which was so severe that the trapezius muscle swelled considerably, and the quivering was communicated upwards to the base of the skull and the spinous processes of the vertebra. Contact with silver produced three or four single throbbings which I could clearly separate. Frogs placed upon my back were observed to hop.
>
> Hitherto my right shoulder was the one principally affected. It gave me considerable pain, and the large amount of lymphatic serum produced by the irritation was red in colour and so acrid that it caused excoriation in places where it ran down the back. The phenomenon was so extraordinary that I repeated it. This time I applied the electrodes to the wound on my left shoulder, which was still filled with a colourless watery discharge, and violently excited the nerves. Four minutes sufficed to produce a similar amount of pain and inflammation with the same redness and excoriation of the parts. After it had been washed my back looked for many hours like that of a man who had been running the gauntlet.

When Humboldt repeated the experiment later his back was so badly skinned that he and his attendant doctor became very frightened and had to wash the wounds with luke-warm milk. On another occasion Humboldt applied the electrodes to a cavity in his jaw where a tooth had been pulled out—he wanted to find out whether pain could be deadened by the over-stimulation of the nerve, but the pain actually became so violent he had to end the experiment.

Altogether he carried out 4,000 experiments and published the results in his *Experiments on the excited muscle and nerve fibre with conjectures on the chemical process of life in the animal and vegetable world* (1797), which he called his great work in physical science. At the time it appeared it caused some stir in the scientific world, but its reputation did not last long.

In 1795 Volta had shown how to produce electricity without any animal tissues at all by putting two different metals together with liquid or a damp cloth between them. He had, in effect, invented the first electric battery. It seemed he had also finally discredited the concept of animal electricity and Galvani's and Humboldt's work along with it. Humboldt himself felt deeply humiliated when Volta's results were made known. He felt ashamed that he had not made sufficient distinction between purely physiological and purely electrical phenomena, and he was profoundly saddened when he realized how near he had come to inventing the electric battery himself—it had just never occurred to him to try out his combinations of metal plates and liquids without the presence of physiological tissues. He never forgot the bitterness of this failure.

However, in spite of this setback, Humboldt was already commanding the serious attention of the scientific world. One of his earliest books, *Florae Fribergensis*, which he wrote in Latin and published in Berlin in 1793, had received a very favourable recep-

tion. Princes and scholars in numerous capital cities loudly acclaimed it. A Swedish botanist named a new Indian laurel after its author. The Elector of Saxony sent Humboldt a huge gold medal 'to serve as a public testimony of the pleasure your work has afforded me', while Goethe made enquiries about Humboldt in the hope that he might meet him and discuss his own studies on the metamorphosis of plants. This was the beginning of Humboldt's long association with that great man and with his exclusive coterie at Weimar and Jena, the twin cultural capitals of Germany.

Goethe was not only an outstanding poet—and critic, statesman, painter, theatre manager and educationalist—but a considerable scientist as well. Apart from his book on the morphology of plants he had published a work on optics and made the important discovery that in the human jaw bone there was a part very similar to the intermaxillary bone in apes—a discovery that preceded Darwin by more than half a century. There were times, in fact, when he rated his scientific work higher than even his poetry, and few men were more aware of the mental process involved in scientific research than he was.

It was not until March 1794, however, that the two men were able to meet in Jena. They were introduced by Wilhelm von Humboldt, whom Goethe already knew well, and they took to each other at once. This was no mean feat on Alexander's part and speaks a lot for his personableness and intelligence. For by this time Goethe was a positively Olympian figure in Germany, godlike, aloof and cold; he was difficult to approach and almost impossible to know, and he did not suffer even clever men gladly. Even his closest acquaintance, the poet and dramatist Schiller, had failed to penetrate through the outward reserve to the inner man. Visitors described him as completely cold towards every person and thing on earth, a man who no longer admired anything, not even himself, a god who had cut himself off from the stirring events of his time. 'There is something unsettled and suspicious in his whole de- meanour', wrote one such visitor, the actor Iffland, 'which prevents anyone feeling at ease in his presence. I have the feeling I cannot sit still on one of his chairs. Out- wardly he is the most fortunate of men. He has genius, he is honoured, he lives in comfort, he can enjoy the arts. And yet I would not be in his position even for an income of three thousand thalers.'

Goethe was at a strange stage in his life—a sort of lofty but lonely altiplano where he seemed unsure which way he should turn. Behind him was the passionate period of *Sturm und Drang* and a host of love affairs, the twenty years of service as a Court official at Weimar, the years of prolific creativity. Ahead of him was his masterpiece, *Faust*, and the final confirmation of his place as greatest poet and master of classical literature Germany had ever known. Schiller, then Professor of History at the University of Jena, had already rekindled Geothe's literary enthusiasm. It was left to Alexander von Humboldt to stimulate his lapsed interest in science.

Humboldt seems to have left no record of his first encounter with Goethe. It must have been an exciting moment but it may well have been a disappointing one too. Goethe was now forty-six years of age and his physical presence was no longer as magnetic as it had been. In middle age he had become heavy, massive and gloomy. 'His gait is exceedingly slow,' an acquaintance described him at this time, 'his stomach pendulous, like that of a woman in the last stages of pregnancy, his chin drawn right down onto his neck and tightly enveloped in a roll of fat; his cheeks are too fat and his mouth is half-moon shaped; only his eyes are turned heavenward, though his hat is even more so. His whole expression conveys a kind of complacent indifference, but he does not look really happy. He moves me to pity, this fine man, who once expressed himself so nobly in his body.'

It was only among intimates, or small groups of two or three people—especially if he could relax in his dressing gown—that Goethe revealed the depth and range of his genius. Alexander's great fortune was to be included among the chosen few who were admitted into this exclusive company. Both men had a number of things in common, not least their efforts to probe the secrets of a universe they conceived as a unity.

From 1795 until his departure from Europe, Alexander's visits to Jena and Weimar never failed to rouse Goethe's interest in natural science. In Goethe's house, the only one in Weimar decorated in the Italian style, and full of collections of rocks and plants and reproduction antique statuary, they discussed problems of geology, Goethe's theories of anatomy and the metamorphosis of insects, and almost every aspect of nature. 'He is a true *cornu copiae* of natural science', Goethe reported to his friend Karl August, Duke of Saxe-Weimar. 'His company is very stimulating and interesting indeed. You couldn't learn as much from books in a week as he teaches you in an hour.' Humboldt, for his part, acknowledged Goethe as one of

View of Jena

Wilhelm von Humboldt. Marble relief by Martin Klauer, 1796

the great influences in his life, and as a talented scientist whose descriptions of nature he ranked with those of Forster, Buffon and Bernardin de St-Pierre. Being with Goethe, he said, was like being equipped with new organs.

One man who had reservations about the younger Humboldt, however, was Schiller. He was a physically unprepossessing man, haggard and ill-looking and constantly hard up; he smoked and sniffed snuff incessantly and kept such awful hours that he was forced to resort to 'stimulants' like punch, coffee and rotten apples which he kept in a drawer and stunk the house out. He was a marvellous poet but he saw things—nature, especially—in a completely different way from Alexander von Humboldt.

Alexander had been one of the first people he had asked to contribute to his new philosophical journal, *Die Horen* (The Hours)—the only scientist, in fact, to be asked at all. Alexander was flattered and in due course his essay, *The Life Force, or The Genius of Rhodes*, was published. It was an impossible subject treated in an impossible way—a biochemical hypothesis stated in the form of high-flown poetical allegory—and Schiller was quick to describe Humboldt's uncharacteristic effort to define the nature of the secret of life, the so-called life force, as 'rubbish'. Within a year or two Schiller's doubts had hardened considerably and in August 1797, in a letter to his friend Körner, he delivered the most damning judgement ever passed on Alexander.

> I am afraid that despite all his talents and restless activity, he will never accomplish anything truly great in science. A trivial, restless vanity is the main-spring of all his actions. I have not been able to detect in him a single spark of purely objective interest; and absurd though it may sound in view of his wealth of knowledge, it seems to me he shows a poverty of intellect that is quite disastrous to a man in his profession. His mind is that cold, dissecting kind that wants all nature to be shamelessly exposed to scrutiny; and with unbelievable impertinence he uses his scientific formulae, which are often nothing but empty words and narrow concepts, as a universal standard.

Alexander had no imagination, Schiller went on. His powers of understanding were too limited. The world of nature—which could never be fully comprehended anyway and should always be held in respectful awe—ought to be contemplated with more feeling and reverence than Alexander ever displayed. 'Alexander imposes upon many people and exploits them. He has the gift of the gab and knows how to blow his own trumpet. As to absolute worth, I cannot compare the two, for I consider Wilhelm so much the more deserving of esteem.'

This was an exceedingly harsh judgement by one great man on another, and though it contains a kernel of truth it reflects poorly upon Schiller himself. Schiller belonged to that school of natural philosophy which regarded nature as others regarded God. The investigation of natural phenomena was a completely subjective process, he argued, a matter of intuitive perception and revelation. To coldly measure and analyse nature and reduce it to symbols, as Humboldt did, was sacrilege. Schiller was quite unable to comprehend the methodology of a totally modern scientist like Humboldt, or to see that Humboldt's systematic accumulation of verified facts and observations was the only kind of groundwork upon which the new science could be built.

The kind of sensitive perception Schiller went in for Humboldt called sentimental sloppiness. Science had not yet completely separated itself from metaphysics and myth, and many general philosophers reckoned they could turn their hand to a theory of the universe or a scientific hypothesis or two when occasion demanded. To a rigorously empirical scientist like Humboldt such amateur conjecturing was anathema. Facts, mere facts, were what he was after. 'In every branch of physical knowledge', he wrote from Bayreuth in 1796, 'there is nothing stable and certain but facts. Theories are as variable as the opinions that gave them birth. They are the meteors of the intellectual world, rarely productive of good, and more often hurtful to the intellectual progress of mankind.'

In essence the difference between the two men was the difference between a romantic poet and an empirical scientist—the kind of difference which persists even today between the Arts man and the Science man. But it seems the intellectual

Schiller entertaining his friends in his garden in Jena. The men in the back row include Goethe (left), Wilhelm von Humboldt (third from left), and Alexander, leaning on the balustrade

difference was compounded by some personal rancour on Schiller's part—envy perhaps, or incompatibility of temperament. Alexander's personality certainly could be a trying one if you were not first won over by his effervescent warmth and charm. His close friends sometimes remonstrated with him, as gently and tactfully as they could, about his vanity and constant need to impress, and at the end of 1796 Freiesleben felt compelled to warn him that his arrogance was arousing considerable antagonism in certain scientific circles. It was an innocent sort of vanity, though; not narcissism so much as an ingenuous attempt to communicate the excitement he felt about his work to others; and it was tempered by a self-deprecatory irony that usually deflated his more bombastic self-appraisals. Nor was Humboldt really selfish; though he was a go-getter he never consciously did anybody down and in later life his generosity was to be proverbial.

LEFT Some of the 4,000 experiments Humboldt made into the nature of so-called animal electricity. He did not confine his researches to frogs' legs but tried other animals, plants and even his own body. RIGHT During these experiments in galvanism Humboldt came near to inventing the first electric battery but failed to recognize his apparatus as such. He never forgave himself this failure

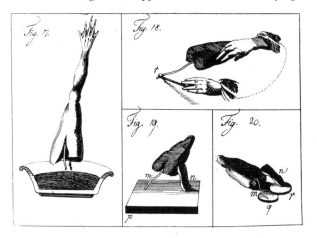
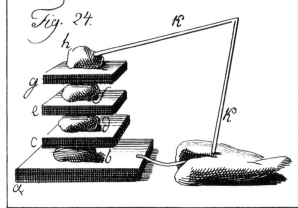

CHAPTER 4

An End to Loving

Schiller's onslaught was fortunately unknown to Humboldt until a long time later. But if he *had* known about it it is doubtful if it would have made much difference to his self-esteem. For outwardly at least it seemed his life was careering along in exactly the direction he wanted it to go and by his twenty-seventh birthday, in the autumn of 1796, he was one of the most successful young men in the country. But for all that, Humboldt would have been envied by few who knew the real state of his affairs. For his public success concealed a bitter and private failure, and by the end of the year—possibly the unhappiest he had ever known—a stage in his life was behind him. Any emotional ties that might have kept him in his job and home a little longer had been severed for ever, and he was free to wander the face of the earth.

The most immediate cause of Humboldt's unhappiness was an obscure young infantry subaltern called Reinhard von Haeften, an officer in the Grevenitz Regiment at that time stationed in Bayreuth. No portrait of him exists and little is known about him except that he was a pleasant, well-educated young man with a bent for science, four years younger than Humboldt. Humboldt had met him in Bayreuth towards the end of 1794, and they soon became intimate friends. They often lived together under the same roof, and Humboldt wrote numerous long letters in enthusiastic praise of his friend—letters which were later discreetly edited by their recipients. People chose to explain Humboldt's close association with Haeften—a man socially and intellectually his inferior—to the fact that he was really courting either Haeften's divorcée fiancée, Cristiane, or his sister, Minette. But from the few letters that have survived from this friendship, there seems to be a quite different explanation: what Humboldt felt for Haeften can only be described as an agonizing sexual passion.

Humboldt had had these warm friendships with other men before—that in itself meant nothing, the eighteenth century was full of such sentimental attachments. He had written passionate letters to men before, too—but in the Germany of that period the public inflation of emotions of any kind was a common social practice and expressions of regard often took extravagant forms. Nor had Humboldt's life been devoid of women. The delightful Henriette Herz remained a lifelong close friend. In Berlin he had at times dallied with the occasional dancer and actress in the company of his brother and their libidinous and gonorrhoeal playboy friend, Friedrich von Gentz[1], and in the spring of 1797 it was even rumoured that he was planning to marry Amalie von Imhoff, a beautiful, clever and worldly thirty-one-year-old he had met at Schiller's house in Jena. Things had got to such a pass that his sister-in-law, Caroline, had sent an engagement present to Amalie, while Amalie's aunt had publicly announced that she would welcome Alexander as a nephew. But that was as far as it ever went. There is no record that Humboldt had any strong feelings for Amalie, and in any case marriage was hardly the obvious course for a man who planned shortly to set off to the other end of the earth. Whether he liked women or not, it must already have been clear to him that the dedicated pursuit of his chosen vocation would inevitably make his life increasingly lonely and isolated. 'A man should get used to standing alone early on in his life', he had told his former tutor, Campe, in anticipation of this. 'Isolation has a lot in its favour. It teaches you to search inwardly and to gain self-respect without being dependent on the opinions of others.' His nature was a restless one and he had led the life of the uprooted for some years now. He had been constantly on the move ever since he had left home, and he was destined not to have a permanent abode until he was a very old man. He seems to have had none of the ordinary instincts for domesticity—family, property, roots—and when all is said, it is doubtful if he had any real instinct for women either.

Caroline von Humboldt, with her perceptive nose for such things, seems to have realized this early on. 'Alexander will never be inspired by anything that does not come through men', she wrote to Wilhelm. Wilhelm himself agreed. 'He will hardly ever be happy, and never at peace, because I can't believe that he will ever form a real relationship. He will never be satisfied with himself because he seems to sense his incapacity to develop into a full personality. Now and then he admitted that much to me, though generally a veil hung over our innermost feelings which neither of us dared lift.'

This veil hung over his private world throughout his life. It was parted in a few letters to a few intimates, and some of these revelations have survived the ravages of time and well-intentioned censorship—scattered potsherds in the archaeology of sex. One of the longest and most remarkable of these letters was one he wrote to Henriette Herz in April 1796, half-way through his 'affair' with Lieutenant von Haeften. It is remarkable not only as a brilliantly detailed record of a dream, but as a shrewd analysis of his own sexual ambivalence.

> If all dreams were as sweet as the one I had yesterday, then I'd like to spend my whole life dreaming.
> I was reading an old Greek philosopher—don't be put off by my erudition, it was only a French translation this time—and I came across these words by Alcibiades: 'Reason and Virtue ought

---

[1]Gentz, later one of Germany's leading reactionaries and Secretary to the Congress of Vienna, and Wilhelm von Humboldt and their girl friends used to share the same bed until Gentz got the clap and Wilhelm pubic lice.

44

Caroline von Humboldt. Painting by Gottlieb Schick

to be respected in a man but in a woman they ought to be treasured.' I shut the book and thought about this as best I could—and gradually my mind wandered and I drifted off. Suddenly, there in front of me stood a splendid old man. He shook my hand in a friendly way and said, 'Follow me, young fellow, I'll show you people.' I followed the old man and he led me into a marvellous town full of people who were all wearing long cloaks and had their faces covered up so that you couldn't tell what sex they were.

Almost immediately I saw three figures and though I couldn't quite make out who they were, they filled me with a strange feeling of longing and desire. Everything that I heard them saying was so sensible, so beautiful in a masculine kind of way, that I thought first of all that these were three young men who were repeating some of the wise things their tutors had taught them. Anyway, after we had done a day's work we decided to look for something amusing to do.

Well, everything was set and we began to get ready—and what do you think, dear girl?—two of these long-cloaked souls got up all of a sudden, laughed and ran off in a great hurry. Then I started laughing as well—at myself and the mistakes I had made. For I realized I was in the company of three women, and that these three women were ten times more interesting than the three boys had been.

One of the women, Alexander went on, was dressed in a white cloak and was as tall and majestic as Minerva. The second was dressed in a wonderful lilac-blue cloak. The third, who walked with her head bent, was dressed in a black cloak; when Humboldt lifted a corner of it he found it was pink inside—'Just like all the rest of her sex who never turn their coats round and show us what they really are like on the inside.'

On the road a few steps in front of us lay an unfortunate girl who had been raped by robbers. She was naked and covered in wounds. Suddenly the three women took off their cloaks and started squabbling as to which one of them was going to give her cloak to the girl. The tallest of the three women was the winner and now she stood in front of me without her cloak on. I wanted to look at her but some invisible power made me avert my gaze and all at once I saw beside me my old guide sitting on the grass bank. 'I *have* found people!' I shouted to him in a frenzy of delight.

We were both silent for a while. Then my guide looked at me and said: 'If you want to see the woman who gave her cloak away again, have a look at this picture. Nature wanted to make a man, but she made a mistake with the clay and modelled a woman instead.'

I looked at the picture and what did I see? No you're not going to find out, my love. I looked up again and lo and behold! the old man had turned into a beautiful boy. A golden light played about his head, I wanted to embrace him—but the vision had faded.

ALEXANDER

PS. People who don't think and feel and speak the way we do are going to find it hard to work this puzzling dream out. But this wasn't written for those people. . . .

Humboldt was right. It is a puzzling dream and the key is now lost. Was the woman in the white cloak Henriette Herz herself, one of the few women with whom he ever had a close relationship? Was the dream an elaboration of his affection for her? Is it significant that the only person to whom Humboldt made any actual gesture of affection was the beautiful boy at the end? What seems clear is that in this dream Humboldt gave expression to his yearning for what some psychologists would now called The Significant Other; that this yearning was at times wrapped up in erotic symbolism; and that the sexual polarity of the mysterious love object was sometimes male and sometimes female and sometimes both male and female at the same time.

The letters he wrote to Reinhard von Haeften, which were not discovered until more than fifty years after Humboldt's death, are less obscure. To put it in the most

Humboldt as a young man. Charcoal drawing by Daniel Caffe

reserved and considered way possible, he seems to have gone beyond the conventional proprieties that exist between one man and another. Haeften appears to have aroused a profound emotion in Humboldt—an emotion he never reciprocated to the same degree—and caused him, in the end, an agonizing grief. In this sad and unsatisfactory relationship Humboldt's ailing sexuality seems to have fought its last struggle for life—a struggle that ended in a death rattle and one of the most unhappy *cris de coeur* in all of his voluminous correspondence.

At first all went well. At the start of the Christmas holidays in 1794 Humboldt wrote to Haeften in the first flush of their friendship:

47

I always keep my promise, my dearly beloved Reinhard. In a few hours I leave and will ride to Lavenstein tomorrow, and on the 21st to Steben, so that I may embrace you on Christmas Eve . . . Goethe insisted on my returning with him to Weimar, where he was wanted by the Duke. Much as I like to be with Goethe (he really is my favourite here), I would have lost the holidays. It would have meant seeing you six days later, and such a loss cannot be made up by anything in the whole world. Other people may have no understanding of this, I know only that I live through you, my good precious Reinhard, and that I can only be happy in your presence.

Haeften and Humboldt spent that first Christmas together and in the following summer set out on a tour through the Tyrol to Venice and the Italian Alps. Humboldt had invited the faithful Freiesleben to join them, at the same time warning him that: 'This tour is planned more for Haeften than for myself. I am, as you are aware, under some obligation to him, therefore I would rather neglect some of my scientific aims than not be entirely at his disposal during the first part of the journey.' Freiesleben chose not to undergo this experience and for a short spell his place was taken by— of all people—the Minister for War and the Interior, who was no less than Humboldt's former boss, Count von Hardenberg. Freiesleben only joined Humboldt for the second half of his tour—through Switzerland and the Bernese Alps to Lucerne— after Haeften had returned to barracks at the end of his army leave. Haeften's departure prompted Humboldt to write a curious letter to his friend's fiancée:

Nothing could really have happened to our dear Reinhard, but you know yourself how deep is my indescribable and wonderful attachment to this precious person, sufficient for me to worry over the merest possibility of mischief . . . I can well imagine the feeling of bliss you must have felt when you saw him again, I have felt the same myself . . . Tell Reinhard how much I loved the lakes of Lucerne and Sarnen. For me they make the most wonderful scenery in the whole of Switzerland, and if we can't go to America, that's where we should go, removed from all so-called educated people, to live a happy life in harmony together.

The reaction of the bride-to-be to this proposed *ménage à trois* in some cosy hide-away in the New World (or the Old) has not been recorded. It does not seem to have affected the wedding plans, however, and in November of that year, as soon as Humboldt was back from his Swiss tour, Reinhard and Cristiane became man and wife. To celebrate the event, Humboldt held a grand ball in the old castle in Bayreuth, and for the next year he was never very far from the newly-weds' side. Such a situation could not last and Humboldt knew it. When, in January 1797, he sensed that the inevitable break was not far away, he sat down and wrote a letter to Haeften in Bayreuth. It was winter, it was cold, it was night and it was dark, and Humboldt was alone and *in extremis*. This letter is not couched in any formal extravagance of style; the man's anguish breaks through every line.

Two years have passed since we met, since your fate became mine. I still bless the day when you confided for the first time in me, telling me how comforting it was for you. I felt better in your company, and from that moment I was tied to you by iron chains. Even if you feel you must turn me down and treat me coldly with disdain, I would still like to be with you, and I can thank heaven that before my death I was granted the great experience of knowing how much two human beings can mean to each other. With each day my love and attachment for you increase. For two years I have known no other happiness on earth but your gaiety, your company, and the slightest expression of your contentment. My love for you is not just friendship, or brotherly love—it is veneration, childlike gratefulness, and devotion to your will as my most exalted law. I will vow to die if on this festive night an untrue word should flow from my pen.

It was what they call the dark night of the soul. It was the last love letter, in the ordinary sense of the word, he ever wrote in his life. It was as though with the departure of Haeften—from his emotional life at least—something had died in him. Was it simply coincidence that he had filed his last will and testament at the Municipal Court in Berlin not long before? Had he conceivably contemplated suicide? Certainly his private life had rarely reached such a low ebb and his despair over Haeften had not been made any easier to bear as a result of another loss. For at the end of November, after a long and painful illness, his mother had died, in agony, of cancer.

A page of Humboldt's letter to Haeften, written at the start of the Christmas holidays of 1794

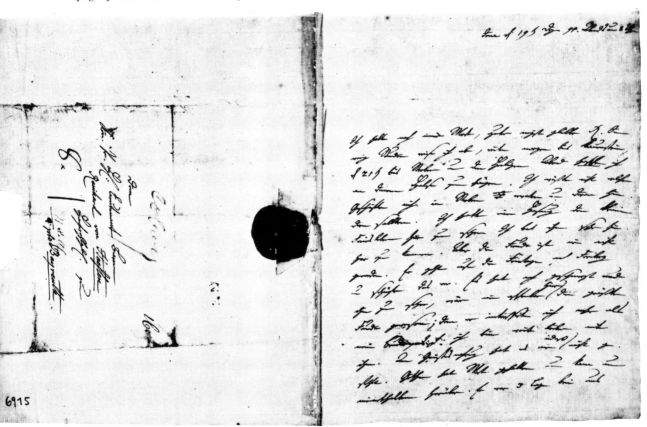

49

CHAPTER 5

Frustrations of an Explorer

It was the intensity of his mother's suffering rather than the fact of her death which upset Alexander. As early as the previous spring of 1796 he had hurried to Berlin to join his brother Wilhelm at her bedside when it looked as though she would not last much longer. She was fifty-five and had cancer of the breast. Beyond administering laudanum there was little anyone could do for her and the pain was unbearable, but during the summer she appears to have rallied—at any rate Alexander seems to have felt free to return to his work. It was not until the end of November that he received the news of her death. He felt relieved that her sufferings were at last at an end, but otherwise the event left him unmoved, for they had always been strangers to each other.

His mother's death was a crucial event in Alexander's life. It freed him emotionally of any last ties with home, severed once and for all the childhood complexes and the filial obligations he had taken with him into manhood. Even more important, it freed him financially of any need to earn a living or worry about money in the future, for by his mother's will he inherited a large estate and various mortgages valued, after settling debts, at 85,375 thalers, which provided an average income of 3,476 thalers a year, or six times the salary of a Superintendent of Mines. This was an enormous sum for those days. Alexander had become a millionaire overnight. In practical terms it meant he was now free to put his long-cherished plans into action and embark on his scientific exploration of the earth.

In February 1797 he finally resigned from his mining job. He was free at last.

*   *   *

Humboldt's first move was to join his brother and his family in Jena. His plan was to travel with them to Italy in order to study volcanoes, then to go to Paris to obtain scientific instruments, and finally to spend some time in England before catching an English ship to the West Indies. But nothing had really gone right from the start. Caroline has not recovered her health after the recent birth of their third child and Wilhelm and the children had gone down with fever, so their departure for Italy (via Dresden and Vienna) was very delayed. It was not till the beginning of June that the entire Humboldt family, together with Reinhard von Haeften and his wife and two children, set off on their great journey in what Goethe, who had declined to join them, in amused disbelief called their caravan—a ménage of two mothers, two fathers, five children, two maids, a manservant, and Alexander, all crowded, infants and convalescents alike, into two hot rattling coaches which were already overloaded with the Haeften's excessive baggage and Alexander's instruments.

This odd assortment of voyagers had barely got to Dresden before Caroline suffered a relapse and the onward leg to Vienna was delayed still further. 'It's likely to prove an agreeable journey,' Schiller wrote to Goethe at the end of the month, 'when they've used up their time before they've even set off!' But the enforced stay in the Saxon capital was not wasted. Humboldt's social standing had provided him with an entrée into official circles and one day he made the chance acquaintance of the brother of a certain Baron von Forell, Saxon Ambassador to the Spanish Court in Madrid. It was only a tenuous contact but it was to prove a most crucial one.

By now Alexander was growing impatient. He was losing sight of his first aim, and events in Italy, where Napoleon's armies marched and counter-marched amid a hubbub of political manoeuvres, were growing daily more confused. On 25 July he set off alone to Vienna by way of Prague. He would wait for Wilhelm's family and the Haeftens to catch up with him there.

While he waited to see how events across the border would turn out, Humboldt

Vienna at the end of the eighteenth century

continued his intensive self-tuition in useful expeditionary disciplines. For several weeks he studied the magnificent herbarium of rare and exotic plants in the Imperial Gardens at Schönbrunn, and he made the acquaintance of several outstanding scientists working at that time in Vienna, a few of whom seemed to resemble prototypes of those endearing figures of modern mythology, the mad scientist and the absent-minded professor. One of the more eccentric among them was Professor Franz Porth, a very rich medical man who had first gained fame as Emperor Joseph II's eye specialist and whom Humboldt considered to be the most genial man in Vienna.

> As he resides near the Botanic Gardens, I was able to visit him very frequently, in his *one* room, in which he lives surrounded by a heterogeneous collection of foreign plants and animals, statues, dried specimens, and coins. Everything around him bears the impress of his peculiarities. For example, he wears a waistcoat provided with sleeves and terminating in breeches and stockings, and looks as if he is standing in a sentry box. He eats only once a day, and that at ten o'clock at night, in order, so he says, not to carry food about in the body, which is very fatiguing and burdensome. One of his treasures is an antique statue of one of the sons of Niobe, for which he paid 15,000 florins. It stands in the same corner of the room in which he carries on his chemical experiments and where he hatches chickens. He is now contriving a hat for his own wear which will expand into an umbrella three feet in diameter when he pulls a string. In short, it is impossible to find united in one person more genius, learning, and practical ingenuity than he exhibits, combined with which is an amount of eccentricity bordering upon madness.

By now any possibility of touring Italy to study volcanoes was out of the question. In the late autumn Wilhelm drifted off to Paris with his family and Alexander proposed to spend the winter in Switzerland with the Haeftens and wait there for the trouble in Italy to clear up. But one day he bumped into a friend from his Freiberg days, the geologist Leopold von Buch, and as a result changed all his plans.

Buch was rich and eccentric like Porth, but he was also terribly shy and so unsociable that he was almost impossible in company. Humboldt took him round to see some friends but Buch behaved as if he had come from the moon. He would put on his spectacles and become entirely absorbed in the study of some cracks in the stove-tiles in the furthest corner of the room, or else slink round the room like a hedgehog, looking at the skirting boards. On his own, though, he was a very interesting and charming person and it soon became clear to Humboldt that he would profit a lot from his friend's extensive geological knowledge. So, with the lack of consideration typical of some single-minded men, he suddenly abandoned the Haeftens and their ailing children and left Vienna with Buch to spend the winter of 1797–98 in Salzburg and Berchtesgaden. The Haeftens tagged along behind him later, but they could have seen little of him.

That winter, high among the snow-covered Tyrolean mountains, Humboldt led an austere life of almost priest-like devotion to scientific observation. He wished to learn as much as possible from Buch and the two of them spent their time in an unremitting programme of magnetic, geographical and meteorological measurements. Humboldt practised constantly with his twelve-inch sextant, a beautiful instrument

A sextant similar to the one used by Humboldt high among the snow-covered Tyrolean mountains

but a cripplingly heavy one to carry around the mountains, and discovered that the latitudes on existing maps were everywhere wrong by as much as 5 to 6 minutes. He was out all day—and sometimes all night—in total solitude and all kinds of weather, measuring at predetermined hours the barometric pressure, the temperature, the humidity, the oxygen and carbon-dioxide content and the electrical charge of the air—a programme of readings that was to become the universally accepted procedure for meteorological observations all over the world.

At the beginning of that winter Humboldt had received a surprise invitation from an Englishman, the notorious Lord Bristol, Bishop of Derry, to join an expedition up the Nile. He seems to have kept very quiet about this invitation and clearly he had grave reservations about it. For one thing, it was in complete conflict with his own plan for the West Indies. For another, Lord Bristol, 'half mad and half genius', was not the kind of expedition leader in whom he had absolute faith. Humboldt had only seen him once, during one of the journeys the 'mad old Lord' made on horseback between Pyrmont and Naples, but he was fully aware of his peculiar character. He was the eccentric of eccentrics. He had an income of £60,000 a year— an unimaginable sum in those days—and a prominent position in fashionable society. In spite of his high rank in the church he was an outspoken free thinker, a playboy, a lavish patron of the arts, and the lusty admirer of King Frederick William II's former mistress, the Countess of Lichtenau. His plans for the Nile expedition were themselves unusual, for apart from himself, Humboldt and an archaeologist called Hirt, two women were to accompany them—Madam Dennis, the respectable wife of an artist and close friend of Lady Emma Hamilton, and Lord Bristol's own *chère amie et adorable* Countess of Lichtenau herself, to whom he sent raving letters full of gallantries and double meanings. '*Jamais un voyage ne sera plus complet tout pour l'âme que pour le corps*', he promised her. And again: '*Quant aux femmes, il faut que vous passiez pour la mienne, et que pour n'être pas violée, vous soyez voilée, et*

The eccentric Lord Bristol, Bishop of Derry, who invited Humboldt on an expedition up the Nile to Aswan

alors votre personne est plus sacrée que la mienne.' The death of Frederick William II, however, had made the Countess's position at Court rather precarious, and she was eventually forced to deny the good Bishop the pleasure of her person on the Nile.

Lord Bristol proposed that this oddly composed team should put out from Naples and spend eight months sailing and rowing along the Nile and looking at ancient monuments as far as Aswan in Upper Egypt. The two private yachts would carry armed crews and a team of artists and sculptors—not only for the ruins and views, but also for the costumes—together with a kitchen, a well-stocked cellar, and every kind of luxury.

It was not quite Humboldt's style but it was better than nothing. He had failed

54

to reach Italy and it looked as though he would fail to reach the West Indies too, for the English navy had now established a blockade of the continental coast. By the end of the winter he had reluctantly come to the conclusion that he would do best to accept Lord Bristol's invitation. He realized that the somewhat scandalous company of his Lordship might prove difficult, but by travelling at his own expense, Humboldt reckoned to preserve his independence and if things became too difficult he could always leave. 'Besides, he's a man of genius and it would be a pity to let such a wonderful opportunity pass—I might be able to do something in meteorology.'

On 24 April 1798, Humboldt said goodbye to Salzburg and set out for Paris where he aimed to equip himself with all the scientific instruments he needed and take leave of his brother Wilhelm. But he travelled without very much hope. There had been a massive build-up of French troops and transports in Toulon. Everywhere it was rumoured that Napoleon was on the point of invading Egypt. If he did, then Lord Bristol's expedition would certainly not be allowed to set foot there as well. 'Thus our most cherished plans are scattered in the wind', Humboldt lamented. Before he had even reached the French border, Napoleon had set sail for Alexandria with a crack force of veteran troops and a huge expedition of some 160 of the leading scholars and scientists of France in the rear. Lord Bristol was arrested in Milan and thrown into prison as a suspected British secret agent. Humboldt arrived in Paris with his plans for the future in ruins.

Italy, the West Indies, Egypt; the explorer was stimied at every turn. More than a year had passed since he threw up his job and set out, and he had not yet arrived in any place he had not seen before.

> I am so hampered in all my projects that I daily feel inclined to wish I had lived either forty years earlier or forty years later. There is only one advantage to be gathered from the present state of things, and that is the extermination of the feudal system and of all the aristocratic privileges which have so long pressed upon the poorer and more intellectual classes of mankind.

All was not lost, however. He still had youth on his side—he was only twenty-eight when he got to Paris—besides wealth, station, reputation and experience in almost every conceivable branch of field research. And Paris at the time of Napoleon's greatness was the finest city on earth in which to plan a scientific expedition. It was the intellectual capital of the world. Its streets and salons were crowded with scientists and artists of international distinction. Its learned institutions focussed the foremost ideas and discoveries of the age. Money and men and even ships were instantly available for the most ambitious scientific ventures. After the dead hand of the Terror, Paris was in a cultural ferment, and Humboldt, living in his brother's house, loved it. He loved French things anyway, and the sophisticated social life and the international concourse of first-class minds, and he was welcomed everywhere he went. Great men like the chemists Chaptal, Vauquelin, Thénard and Fourcroy, the botanists Jussieu, Desfontaines and Lamarck, the zoologist Cuvier, and the astronomers and mathematicians Delambre, Lalande, Laplace and Borda—

Georges Cuvier, founder of the studies of comparative anatomy and palaeontology

the man who first turned Humboldt's attention to the problems of the magnetic field of the earth—discussed their research with him and advised him on equipment and methods. He studied at the Jardin des Plantes and the Observatoire, lectured at the famous Institut de France, and for a few glorious days of summer plied his sextant in the countryside between Melun and Lieursaint where Delambre and his geodetic survey team were completing the measurements of the northern portion of the famous Dunkerque-Barcelona meridian line through Paris—measurements which later served as a basis for the length of the standard French metre (one forty-millionth of the Paris meridian).

Louis Antoine de Bougainville, circumnavigator of the globe

It was in the course of this historic episode that Humboldt first met an old boyhood hero, the French navigator and explorer, Louis Antoine de Bougainville.
Bougainville had returned from his great voyage of discovery in the Pacific Ocean
a few months before Alexander was born, and his account of it had been one of
Alexander's favourite childhood books. The old salt was seventy now, and an
admiral, but he still hankered for the high seas, and a short time after their meeting
he made a proposition that set Alexander's mind in a whirl.

The French government was planning a new expedition round the world. It was
to last five years and entail scientific work both on land and at sea. In the first two

years the expedition was to concentrate on South America, Mexico and California. In the third year they were to explore the Pacific Ocean and try and reach the South Pole. In the fourth year they would be based on Madagascar, and in the fifth on the West African coast. The venerable Bougainville had been put in charge of this ambitious venture and he asked Humboldt to join the scientific staff. Humboldt, not unnaturally, was beside himself at the prospect.

'I was busy with magnetic research at the time,' he wrote, 'so it seemed to me that an expedition to the South Pole might be a lot more use than a trip to Egypt.' Many of his friends tried to put him off—five years at sea was a long time, they said— but it was too good an opportunity to miss: circumnavigations were not common events, and he could never hope to see so much of the world at his own expense. He began to have some doubts about the enterprise, however, when the French authorities replaced the ageing Bougainville with a sea captain of dubious personal character called Baudin in whom Humboldt had little confidence. But he was too preoccupied with preparations to have serious second thoughts. Time was short and the ships were already rigged. He ransacked the government stores for instruments and helped choose the personnel and equipment. He met the men he was to share a ship with for five years and found them well-chosen, well-qualified, young and strong. He arranged to take Bougainville's fifteen-year-old son under his wing for the voyage. Within a fortnight his preparations were complete, he had received orders to embark, the ships were ready to sail—many of his friends in Paris thought they *had* sailed—when at the last minute his dreams were shattered again.

A new war was breaking out with Austria; under the circumstances, the Directory felt it could no longer afford the 300,000 livres the Baudin expedition entailed; accordingly they had decided to postpone it indefinitely.

Humboldt took the blow philosophically. 'A man can't just sit down and cry,' he wrote to Willdenow, 'he's got to do something.' The disappointment seems to have filled him with a desperate decisiveness: if he couldn't go on somebody else's expedition he would go on one of his own. And almost immediately he announced his intention of starting out on a private journey through North Africa in the company of a young Frenchman whose name was to become inseparably linked with his own in the history of exploration.

CHAPTER 6

At the Court of Aranjuez

Aimé Bonpland was twenty-five years old. Like Humboldt he had been a member of the Baudin expedition—its botanist, in fact—and both he and Humboldt had put up at the Hotel Boston in the Rue Colombier during the final days of preparation. It was there that their famous partnership began. Humboldt used to bump into him on the stairs when he was handing in his key—a breezy young man who always carried a battered satchel of botanical specimens around with him like a badge of office.

Humboldt liked Bonpland. He was a first-class botanist with a useful grounding in comparative anatomy, who had studied medicine in Paris during the Revolution and served in the navy as a ship's doctor under Baudin. He was a cheerful, level-headed character with a good sense of humour and an amusing affection for women, fit, capable, and courageous. He shared the same political views as Humboldt, the same scientific bent, the same wanderlust, and now—stranded in Paris—the same predicament. Soon the two men had become very good friends and by October 1798, in the greatest good humour, they were on their way in a diligence bound for Marseille and a sailing ship to Algiers. 'I was very cut up when he left,' Wilhelm wrote a few days after his brother's departure, 'but I don't think it will be long before we see him again.' As it turned out, this was a very wrong assumption indeed.

Humboldt's plan was to join up with the scientific retinue in the rear of Napoleon's conquering army in Egypt. To do this he proposed to sail for Algiers in a Swedish packet-boat carrying gifts for the Dey, winter in the Atlas Mountains, and then meet up with the pilgrim caravan that crossed the desert between Tripoli and Cairo on its way to Mecca. The Swedish frigate had not yet docked in Marseille but was expected hourly and Humboldt and Bonpland settled down to wait. But the hours turned into days, then into weeks and finally, to Humboldt's consternation, into months. They were packed and ready to leave at a moment's notice but no sail appeared and the number of endorsements in their passports rose till there were more than twenty.[1] To while away the time they made an excursion to Toulon, a town packed with prisoners-of-war, and Humboldt was amazed to see in the outer roadstead of the harbour the frigate in which Bougainville had made his great round-

---

[1]According to Humboldt's passport issued in Paris he was 5 feet 8 inches tall, with light brown hair, grey eyes, large nose, well-formed chin, rather large mouth, and open forehead marked with smallpox.

the-world voyage more than twenty years before—*La Boudeuse*, the very same ship that had filled his childhood daydreams at Tegel. Though she was on the point of sailing Humboldt insisted in rowing out to have a look over her.

> The whole ship was astir, and all hands on deck to work the sails. I felt incredibly happy as I watched the preparations going on around me, but when I went down into the cabin, a spacious suite, I thought about Baudin's voyage and became terribly depressed. I lay by the window for a good ten minutes, staring out at the bright mirror of the sea. In the end they came down looking for me. I could almost have wept at the thought of my shattered prospects.

Aimé Bonpland, after he and Humboldt returned from South America. Humboldt wrote of him: 'I could never have hoped to meet again with such a loyal and brave and hard-working friend.'

Christmas had come and gone when the news came through that the Swedish ship had been damaged off Portugal and had limped into Cadiz for repairs. She would not reach Marseille till at least the spring.

Undeterred, Humboldt and Bonpland then booked their passage on a small barque bound for Tunis, but while the main cabin was being cleared of livestock to make room for them, they learned that the Tunisian authorities were throwing all passengers arriving from French ports into a dungeon, and they therefore wisely

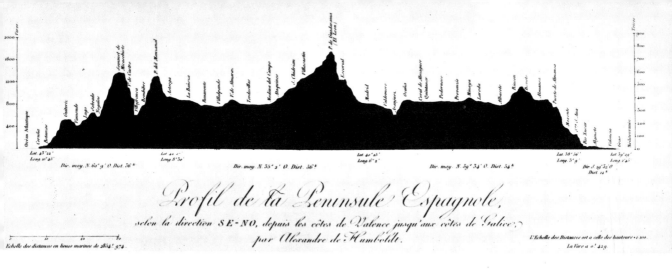

Humboldt's novel profiles of the Spanish Peninsula. ABOVE *South-east to north-west, from Valencia to Galicia;* BELOW *South-west to north-east, from the Pyrenees to the Sierra Nevada in Grenada. He was the first to observe that the interior of Spain was a high plateau*

allowed the vessel to sail without them. Any hope of reaching Egypt was now gone.

The travellers' next move seemed purely arbitrary—they decided to walk to Spain and catch a boat from there to Smyrna in the spring. So, in the last few days of 1798, they set out on foot along the Mediterranean coast, crossed the Pyrenees at the eastern end and made their way through Catalonia towards Madrid.

The journey to Madrid took six weeks, almost every day of which Humboldt was busy with his observations. Among the superstitious and isolated inhabitants of the small country towns he cut a curious figure as he squinted at the heavenly bodies through his various instruments. Crowds would gather in the streets and boo at him, so that often he was afraid to unpack the instruments until the sun was way past the meridian. In the end he was forced to make his readings at night and even then he found himself surrounded by spectators who kept shouting to each other that he was worshipping the moon. But he persisted, and in the wild and un-inhabited region between Barcelona and Valencia, so poorly mapped that Valencia's geographical position varied by as much as two minutes, his astronomical fixes

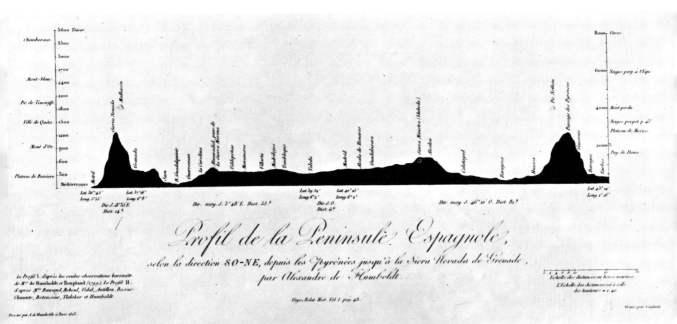

became the only established points in these vast ocean-like plains. Even more important were his measurements to determine altitude by means of barometric pressure, which he recorded all the way from Valencia to Galicia. Starting from scratch he had by the end worked out a sectional elevation right the way across Spain from the south-east to the north-west which revealed—astonishingly, for the first time—that the interior of Spain was one high continuous plateau. This pioneer field work not only made an important contribution to the geographical knowledge of the day but showed that Humboldt was already one of the most meticulous and well-trained travellers of his time. His setbacks and delays had not been a total waste of time, for he could now handle almost every kind of complicated scientific instrument, under all sorts of conditions. His apprenticeship was over.

It was mid-February, and very cold, when the two travellers reached Madrid. Humboldt thought vaguely of making for Cadiz to board the damaged Swedish ship being repaired there; he still hankered after the West Indies; yet in less than a month he had been accorded unlooked-for privileges that were unique in the history of exploration of his day.

The principal agent in the events that so rapidly overtook Humbolt in Madrid was the Saxon Ambassador (not the Prussian one, who had been no help at all), Baron Philippe von Forell. In those days—and especially in the petticoat court of Carlos IV of Spain—influence and nepotism were as important in getting on as rank and station: who you knew as much as who you were. It so happened that Humboldt had met Forell's brother in Dresden. Forell, who was keen on science and intrigued by Humboldt's plans, had the ear of the Prime Minister, Don Mariano Luis de Urquijo. Urquijo, it was widely rumoured, was the paramour of the Queen, the coarse and sensual Maria Luisa de Parma. And what the Queen advised, the King, who was so stupid he was nearly imbecile, usually did. There was only one logical conclusion to this neat chain of contacts and in March 1799 Humboldt was duly presented to the King and Queen of Spain at the Court of Aranjuez.

Humboldt made the best of his opportunity. He told the King of his desire to visit the Spanish-American colonies and formally handed over a memorandum on the advantages to the Spanish government of his doing so. The King was impressed that a Prussian had enough wit to speak Spanish. He was also intrigued with the thought that a mining geologist of Humboldt's distinction might discover new mineral deposits or new ways of reworking old ones. He agreed to Humboldt's request.

Humboldt and Bonpland, whose occupation was described as 'companion and secretary', each received two passports under the royal seal—one from the Secretary of State and another from the Council of the Indies. The passports assured the travellers of the assistance of every governor and magistrate they would ever come across and access to any place they ever wanted to visit. For Humboldt, a Protestant, they were as good as letters of recommendation from His Catholic Majesty himself.

Detail of a painting by Goya of Carlos IV of Spain and Queen Maria Luisa and their children, with Humboldt's passport to South America issued by the Secretary of State in Madrid (inset)

It is not difficult to imagine Humboldt's state of mind during those first halcyon days. Everything he had asked for had been granted. After two years of frustration the world—the New World and its unknown interior—suddenly lay open before him. He wrote that he thought he was living in a fairy story. 'Never before has a traveller been granted such unlimited permission, and never before has a foreigner been honoured by such marks of confidence from the Spanish Government.' Bonpland, who only ever stood in Humboldt's shadow, was infected with the same rapturous enthusiasm. The two friends were too impatient to delay their great adventure any longer. By May they were on the road through Old Castile en route for Corunna and a ship for the Americas.

Their position was unique. The Spanish American colonies to which they were bound covered an enormous area of the earth. They stretched from California to Cape Horn and included most of the West Indian islands, all of Central America, all of South America (except for Brazil, Patagonia and Tierra del Fuego), and nearly one-third of the present-day territory of the United States. This vast empire, parcelled out into kingdoms and administered by viceroys, was under the direct rule of the Spanish government in Madrid and almost completely sealed off from the rest of the world. Trade with any country except Spain was strictly forbidden and foreigners themselves were as unwelcome as their goods (and their ideas). In three hundred years of Spanish rule there had been barely a dozen expeditions to Spanish America and even these had for the most part been limited to surveys of the coast. The last of them had been led by the unfortunate Marqués de Malaspina, an admiral in the Spanish fleet, who on his return to Spain in 1795 had been arrested on suspicion of political intrigue and thrown into prison without trial, never to be heard of again. Not surprisingly, therefore, the interior of Spanish America was in many places *terra incognita* and no foreign scientist had set foot there since the expedition of the Frenchman, La Condamine, in 1735—sixty-four years previously. Geographically it was virgin territory; it was the privilege of Humboldt and Bonpland to make the first real scientific exploration of it in history.

They reached the port of Corunna at the end of May. The next ship to sail was the corvette *Pizarro*, a packet-boat bound for Havana, and the harbourmaster urged the travellers to take passage on her. She was not a fast ship but she was generally considered a lucky one, and her skipper, Captain Manuel Cagigal, was known to be particularly reliable. Humboldt and Bonpland went on board at once to arrange accommodation for themselves and their baggage and two days before they were due to sail they brought their personal effects, books and scientific instruments on board. No traveller had ever been so well equipped as Humboldt was. To feel the pulse of heaven and earth, so to speak—to study the formation of rocks and strata, analyse the atmosphere, measure its pressure, temperature, humidity and electrical charge, observe the influence of the climate on the distribution of plants and animals, the strength of terrestrial magnetism, the blueness of the skies and the temperatures of the oceans, and to synthesize these phenomena into a single point of view, these were the aims he had set himself. And to fulfil these aims he had fitted himself out with some of the finest apparatus you could find anywhere in the world at the time, including sextants and quadrants, balances and compasses, telescopes and microscopes, hygrometers and barometers, cyanometers, eudiometers, thermometers, chronometers, magnetometers, a Leyden jar and a *lunette d'épreuve*. The practical difficulties of finance—he was going to pay for the whole expedition out of his own pocket—had been solved by the personal kindness of banker friends in Berlin and Madrid who were prepared to honour his bills of exchange for an indefinite period without any kind of security. No detail had been overlooked. He had made his will, made arrangements for the shipment of their specimens home. No contingency had not been foreseen—except for the three British warships that lay hove-to beyond the harbour mouth.

For a few anxious days it looked as though Humboldt's plans could be balked again at the very last moment. A strong on-shore north-westerly at last forced the British ships to bear off, but it also prevented the *Pizarro* from weighing anchor. For two days, however, a thick fog covered the horizon and indicated a change of weather, and by June 5 a favourable north-easterly wind was blowing. Captain Cagigal informed Humboldt they would be sailing on the tide that afternoon, and while the sailors on deck made the ship ready Humboldt sat down and wrote his last farewell letters to his friends, including one to Freiesleben in which he outlined his aims in South America. It was not personal adventure he was after, or the indiscriminate collecting of data and specimens, but something much more visionary.

> In a few hours we sail round Cape Finisterre. I shall collect plants and fossils and make astronomic observations. But that's not the main purpose of my expedition. I shall try to find out how the forces of nature interreact upon one another and how the geographic environment influences plant and animal life. In other words, I must find out about the unity of nature.

At 2 pm the *Pizarro* weighed anchor. The British squadron had been sighted from a watch-tower a few hours previously but nobody seemed worried and in a short while the ship was moving slowly down the long and narrow passage leading from the port to the open sea. The passage widened at the seaward end and the *Pizarro* made a series of ineffectual tacks against the wind. For a moment it seemed that the current might drive her on to the rocks, but then she was clear and soon her decks were heaving on the open Atlantic swell.

Standing on deck, watching Europe fall away, Humboldt's eyes were glued for a very long time on the castle of St Antonio, one of the last landmarks on the coast of Spain. St Antonio was a state prison and inside it lay the doomed Malaspina. But by evening the castle had vanished from sight and the wind was rising and the sea running high. As darkness fell on the land and the ocean, Alexander saw far away the light of a fisherman's hut at Sisarga—the last object he set eyes on in the Old World. Then he went below, amongst the swinging lamps and creaking timbers, for his first night at sea on the great ocean crossing.

View of the port of Corunna, from where Humboldt and Bonpland set sail for South America

CHAPTER 7

Voyage Out

The captain of the *Pizarro* had been instructed to put in at Teneriffe in the Canary Islands so that Humboldt and Bonpland could spend a few days exploring its great volcano, the Pico de Teide. But there was a moment, only three days out from Corunna, when their plans seemed in jeopardy yet again. From the masthead the look-out spotted the unmistakable outlines of a British convoy heading down the coast in a south-easterly direction, and the *Pizarro* was obliged to alter course to avoid it. Thereafter, in accordance with Spanish naval standing orders, the captain imposed a strict blackout on board and every night Humboldt had to read his instruments by the feeble light of a dark-lantern in the great cabin—a handicap that became increasingly irksome to him as the strong nor'-easter drove them towards the more southerly latitudes of Africa and Madeira and the sun set earlier each day.

Humboldt seems to have taken instinctively to the sea. He never once suffered

Santa Cruz de Teneriffe—'a great caravanserai on the road to America', with (inset) a dip circle similar to the one used by Humboldt to observe the inclination of the magnetic needle during the voyage

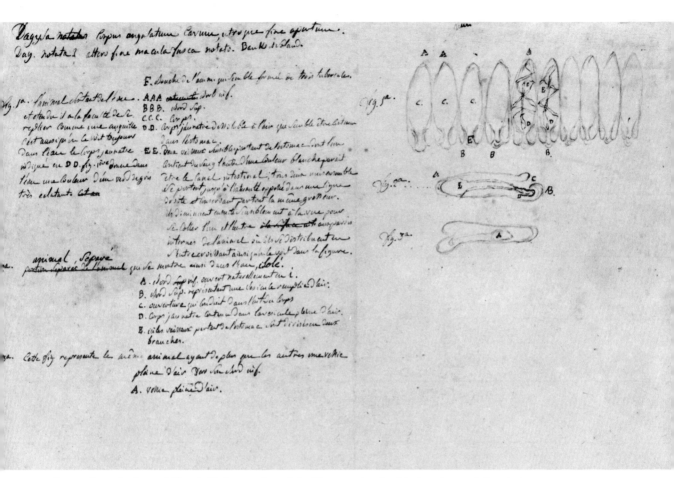

A page from the journal Humboldt kept on board the Pizarro, *showing his drawings and descriptive notes of the rare marine organism* dagysa

from the sea-sickness that troubled Darwin so much and the sea air redoubled his appetite for work. Part of the after-deck was kept clear for him and here, under the cracking sails and the whining rigging, he and Bonpland were busy all day with astronomical and meteorological observations, measuring the temperature of the sea, analysing its chemical constitution and examining the marine life that was dragged up in the nets.

They were in the Gulf Stream now, alone with the dolphins and sea-swallows that followed the ship. When they were almost becalmed they were overtaken by a vast mass of jellyfish travelling south-east at four times the speed of the current. These curious purple and violet and yellow and brown creatures covered the ocean as far as the eye could see and it took nearly an hour before the last straggler had floated by. Amongst them Bonpland found a rare kind of organism called a *dagysa*[1]—a

[1]In all probability this was a marine animal that now bears the name *Cyclosalpa pinnata* (of the class Tunicata).

small, gelatinous, transparent, cylindrical bag, open at both ends and hanging vertically down in clusters like organ pipes. Humboldt tried his galvanic experiments on these creatures without much success. But he did find that if he put a jellyfish on a pewter plate and struck the plate with any metal implement, the jellyfish emitted a phosphorescent light.

At night Humboldt was entranced by the phosphorescent glow of the ocean beneath him and the beauty of the African sky above. 'The nights were magnificent; in this clear, tranquil atmosphere it was quite possible to read the sextant in the brilliant moonlight—and then the southern constellations, Lupus and Centaur! What splendid nights!'

Sea fogs and contrary winds and currents, together with some odd notions Captain Cagigal had culled from an out-of-date Portuguese pilot, caused the *Pizarro* to lose herself temporarily among the many rocks and islets of the Canaries. On one occasion they mistook a rock of basalt on one island for a military fortress on another, saluted it by raising the Spanish flag, and sent a boat with an officer to ask the Commandant whether he had seen any British ships cruising in the roads. Eventually, on 19 June, the *Pizarro* edged into Santa Cruz, Teneriffe—a great caravanserai on the road to America.

They anchored after several soundings, for the mist was so thick that they could barely pick anything out at a few cables' distance. But as soon as they began to salute the place, the fog lifted. The peak of Teide appeared in a break in the clouds, and the first rays of the sun shone on the summit of the volcano. They all rushed to the ship's bow to watch this magnificent spectacle and at that precise moment saw four British warships lying-to very near their stern. They had passed right under the nose of the Royal Navy without being spotted and the fog that had hidden the peak from view had also saved them from being captured and taken back to Europe.

For safety's sake the *Pizarro* anchored as close as it could below the fort at Santa Cruz, and Humboldt and Bonpland wasted no time in getting ashore—the same shore, incidentally, on which Admiral Nelson's arm had been carried off by a cannon-ball only two years previously. This was the barren and rocky end of the island and they found the streets of the little whitewashed town of 8,000 people suffocatingly hot and blindingly bright. The light on the pumice-stone summit of the volcano towering 12,300 feet above them was of such a dazzling white that the travellers thought at first it was still covered in snow and doubted whether they could ever reach the crater in the four or five days available. They were happy to push on as quickly as possible through the beautiful Orotava valley to the cooler and greener western end of the island, where they hoped to find guides for their ascent of the Peak. It was from the foot of the Peak that Alexander wrote his first letter home to his brother Wilhelm on 20 June 1799:

> I'm really quite ecstatic at finding myself on African soil at last, surrounded by coconut palms and bananas . . . I'm in excellent health and I get on splendidly with Bonpland. We are invited

'When they were almost becalmed they were overtaken by a vast mass of jellyfish, travelling south-east at four times the speed of the current. It took nearly an hour before the last straggler floated by.' Portuguese man-of-war illustrated by Louis Choris

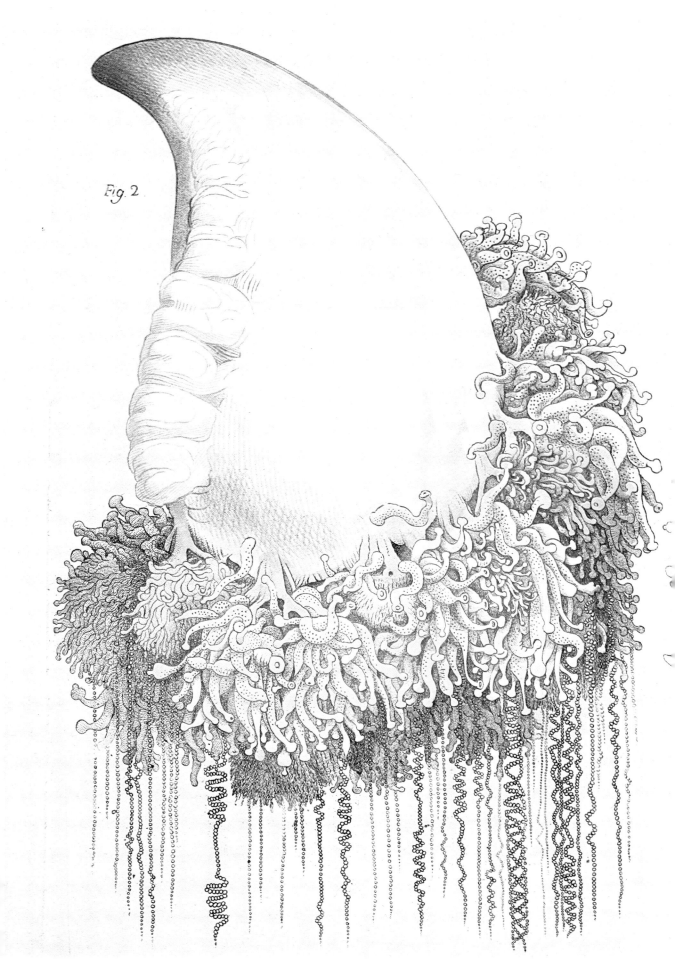

Fig. 2

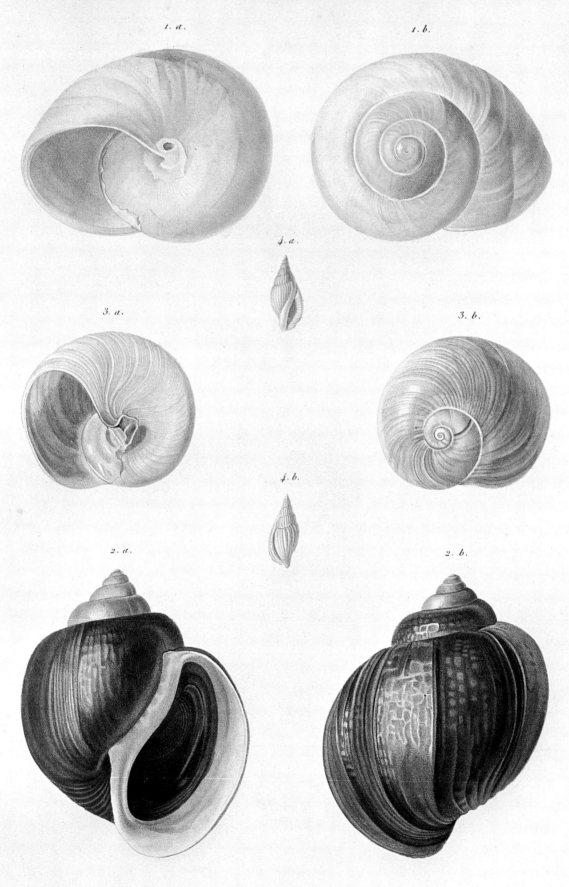

Pl. LVII.

1. a.

1. b.

4. a.

3. a.

3. b.

4. b.

2. a.

2. b.

J.C.Werner pinx:

Ch: Schnetz sculp:

everywhere, with or without introduction, merely for the sake of hearing the lastest news from Europe; and the royal passport works wonders.

The next morning he set off up the volcano, which had recently spewed lava for the first time in ninety-two years, in the company of Bonpland and three local guides—the French vice-consul, his secretary, and an English gardener. Three days later he wrote again:

I got back last night from a trip up the Peak. What a fantastic place! What a time we had! We climbed down some way into the crater, perhaps further than any previous scientific traveller. There isn't much danger in the ascent, you just get rather done up by the heat and cold; the sulphurous vapour in the crater burnt holes in our clothes while our hands were frozen numb.

It's really quite a sight at a height of 11,500 feet! The dark-blue vault of sky overhead; old streams of lava at our feet; on either side this scene of devastation. . . .

The crater we climbed down into emits only sulphurous vapour. The lava stream breaks out at the sides of the mountain. Fire and water rage below the surface—I noticed steam escaping all over the place . . .

PS. In the district of Orotava there is a dragon tree (*Dracaena draco*) measuring forty-five feet in circumference. Four centuries ago the girth was as great as it is now.

I could almost weep at the prospect of leaving this place; I should be quite happy to settle here, and yet I am barely out of Europe. If only you could see these luxuriant fields, these centuries-old laurel forests, these vines and roses! They actually fatten the pigs on apricots here. The roads swarm with camels.

We weigh anchor on the 25th of this month.

The Spanish sailors called the 3,000 miles of ocean between the Canaries and the coast of America '*El Golfo de las Damas*' (Ladies' Gulf) on the grounds that it was such an easy stretch of sea that even women could navigate it. This was Columbus' route, and the *Pizarro*'s voyage across it was swift and uneventful until the last few days. The flying fish flopped on to the deck; the sun grew hotter; the familiar constellations of the northern hemisphere sank progressively from sight and on the night of 4 July the Southern Cross appeared clearly for the first time low on the horizon—a sight which moved Humboldt deeply, for it was the realization of one of the dreams of his early youth.

By 6 July they were sailing off the coast of Brazil and Humboldt was as busy as ever. He wrote to his brother later:

I was very preoccupied with measuring the temperature of the ocean and finding out its specific gravity by means of one of Dollond's excellent balances. The idea put forward by Franklin and Jonathan Williams of taking soundings with a thermometer attached to the lead is an ingenious one and will eventually become very important to navigation. I carried out several experiments on board with Hadley's mirror sextant. I have an eight-inch one with a silvered arc divided to 20 seconds. I also have a two-inch sextant by Troughton, which I call my snuff-box sextant: it is really incredible what you can do with this little instrument. A single set of observations taken by it of the altitude of the sun when passing the prime vertical will give the correct time within two or three seconds. Even if this accuracy is purely accidental, I must admit that it happens very frequently.

I systematically kept an astronomical journal, and whenever the weather and the calmness

South American snail shells. From Recueil d'observations de zoologie *by Humboldt and Bonpland*

Humboldt and Bonpland in the crater of the Pico de Teide on Teneriffe. 'The sulphurous vapour in the crater burnt holes in our clothes while our hands were frozen numb.'

of the sea allowed I made observations of the latitude and longitude of the ship or the places where we landed; I also observed the inclination of the magnetic needle, which can be found to within 20 minutes by means of Borda's new instrument.

The chronometer I have with me is one of Louis Berthoud's, No. 27: it has frequently been made use of by travellers, and its excellence is well known to Borda; it has kept its usual regular good time with me.

I must admit it takes a remarkable amount of patience to make astronomical observations with sufficient accuracy in this heat, and to do one's work *con amore*. But you will notice that however overpowering the heat may be, it does not seem to make me less active.

Between decks the *Pizarro* was very overcrowded with crew and passengers travelling steerage, and as the vessel neared the Antilles and the shade temperature

'In the district of Orotava there is a dragon tree measuring forty-five feet in circumference. Four centuries ago the girth was as great as it is now.'

soared to 36°C this small congested space became as hot as an oven. An eighteenth century Spanish sailing ship at the end of a month's voyage was not very sanitary accommodation at the best of times, but under these conditions, and in the tropics, it was doubly unhealthy. The worst happened, and by 8 July it was clear to all on board that the *Pizarro* was in the grip of an outbreak of typhoid fever of epidemic proportions. Two sailors, several passengers, two negroes from the coast of Guinea and a mulatto child were the first to go down, and by the next day the strongest of them were in delirium. The ship's medical facilities were worse than inadequate. Humboldt complained that no attempt was made to fumigate the ship and that there was no quinine bark on board—neither he nor Bonpland had brought any with them, never dreaming that a Spanish ship would be without it. The ship's surgeon—an ignorant and phlegmatic Gallician—attributed the fever to what he called 'heat and corruption of the blood' and ordered useless bleedings. The fatal effect of his purgative remedies soon became evident, for by the time the *Pizarro* had sighted land one of the negroes had gone mad and the youngest European passenger—a nineteen-year-old Spanish lad, the only son of an impoverished widow who had sent him on this voyage against his will in the hope that he might make his fortune in the colonies—had died.

> We were assembled on the deck, lost in melancholy thought. There was no longer any doubt that the fever which raged on board had taken a fatal turn in the last few days. Our eyes were fixed on a hilly and desert coast on which the moon shone fitfully through the clouds. We could hear nothing but the monotonous cry of a few large sea-birds flying towards the shore. There was a gentle swell and a pale phosphorescent glow on the sea. About 8 pm they started tolling the dead man's knell. As soon as they heard this mournful sound the crew stopped work and threw themselves on their knees to offer a momentary prayer. They brought the body of the young Spaniard up on deck during the night, but the priest asked them not to commit it to the waves until after sunrise, so that he could perform the last rites according to Roman Catholic practice. Every single person on board was deeply upset by the death of this young man who only a few days before had been so full of health and spirits.

Under these appalling circumstances the *Pizarro* could no longer hope to continue as far as Havana. On 14 July Humboldt and Bonpland, who had luckily escaped the epidemic, came to the decision—a momentous one, as it turned out—to alter their plans once again and leave the ship along with the other passengers at the first port they came to on the mainland of South America.

But it was one thing looking for a harbour and another thing finding it. The best nautical charts of those days were wildly, even dangerously inaccurate; they included islands—and even a maelstrom—that did not exist, but ignored rocks and reefs that did; the Spanish, French and English charts on board *Pizarro* all differed from one another and in any case showed the coast of Venezuela 15 miles further south than it actually was. Humboldt found that the discrepancy between his astronomical fixes and the pilot's dead reckoning was sometimes more than a degree of longitude and on one occasion the estimate of latitude was wrong by almost 40 miles. It is hardly surprising that the *Pizarro*, edging along the nondescript eastern coast of Venezuela with its ailing and panic-stricken complement, had difficulty in discovering Cumaná, the nearest port. The captain decided to send a pilot ashore, and the crew were preparing to get the long-boat out when they saw two canoes sailing along the coast. They fired a gun to attract their attention, and hoisted the Spanish flag, but understandably the canoemen were very suspicious and drew nearer only with considerable caution.

There were eighteen Indians in each of the two dug-out canoes. They were Guayquerias—a civilized and highly privileged tribe from the neighbourhood of Cumaná whom the Spanish regarded as one of the finest race of men in Terra Firma. They were naked to the waist, tall, muscular and copper-coloured. From a distance, standing motionless in silhouette against the horizon, they reminded Humboldt of bronze statues. They climbed on board when they were confident that the *Pizarro* was a Spanish ship—a lot of English cruisers frequented this in-shore channel, they said—and Humboldt's eyes boggled when he saw the simple produce they had brought with them: fresh coconuts and exquisitely coloured fish, bunches of plantains, calabashes, the cuirass of an armadillo. 'In our eyes they were riches', he wrote afterwards. 'They served as proof that we had at last achieved the goal we have been striving for and dreaming about for so long.'

The Indian in charge of one of the canoes volunteered to remain on board the *Pizarro* and pilot her into Cumaná but there was little wind and the captain decided to stand off until daybreak. On the eve of setting foot in the New World, Humboldt took the opportunity to talk with the Indian—the Prussian and the Guayqueria had Spanish in common—and long after the sun had gone down they sat on deck while the Indian told of the cool mountains inland and the crocodiles on the plains, of boas, electric eels and jaguars, and of creatures whose names Humboldt had not even heard before—*bava, cachicamo, temblador*. And thus he spent the night—squatting with an American-Indian on the deck of a Spanish ship off the scented coast of Terra Firma under this vast and brilliant tropic sky!

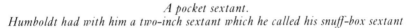
A pocket sextant.
Humboldt had with him a two-inch sextant which he called his snuff-box sextant

CHAPTER 8

The Tropic Earth

At 9 am on 16 July 1799, the *Pizarro* anchored in the port of Cumaná and even the surviving typhoid victims managed to drag themselves up on deck to have a look. After three weeks on the high seas, the land seemed breathtaking. The high mountains of New Andalusia, half veiled by mist, lined the horizon; the town and its fort glimmered between tall coconut palms along the banks of a river; rose-coloured flamingoes, snowy egrets and huge brown pelicans the size of swans foraged along the shore at the edge of a motionless green sea; even at that early hour, the light was dazzling. Humboldt and Bonpland hurried ashore and looked around them. The place bowled them over, instantly and totally. In the first flush of his enthusiasm, Alexander wrote to his brother:

> What a fabulous and extravagant country we're in! Fantastic plants, electric eels, armadillos, monkeys, parrots: and many, many, real, half-savage Indians.
>
> What trees! Coconut palms, 50 to 60 feet high; *Poinciana pulcherrima* with a big bouquet of wonderful crimson flowers; pisang and a whole host of trees with enormous leaves and sweet smelling flowers as big as your hand, all utterly new to us. As for the colours of the birds and fishes—even the crabs are sky-blue and yellow!
>
> Up till now we've been running around like a couple of mad things; for the first three days we couldn't settle to anything; we'd find one thing, only to abandon it for the next. Bonpland keeps telling me he'll go out of his mind if the wonders don't cease soon.

In this exotic new world the explorers seem to have experienced a kind of sensory ecstasy. Nothing—no shape, no form, no voice, no colour, no smell—was familiar to them. Nothing would readily fit into their existing pattern of memory and experience, therefore everything seemed to demand equal attention. The Indians—*naked*! Their huts—*bamboo and palm leaf*! Their chairs—*branches of coral washed up on the shore*! Their plates—*half a coconut shell*! This way and that they charged, confronted at every turn with brilliant and startling new visions, like men in a mescalin trance—here a *quama* tree loaded with silvery blossoms, there a castle moat full of crocodiles. It required some effort of will to turn their attention to more mundane but necessary matters. For first they had to present their passports to the Governor, and then they had to find somewhere to live.

Don Vincente Emparan, the popular and enlightened Governor of Cumaná, who was later the last Spanish Governor of Venezuela, could not have been more welcoming. He placed everything at their disposal, showed them cottons dyed with local plants and fine furniture made exclusively from the wood of the country, and astonished them with highly technical questions of a scientific nature, for he was himself a lover of science. As for a house, the two travellers did not have to hunt far in a town that had been almost razed by an earthquake less than two years before. They rented a pleasant, spacious new house of white cinchona and satin-wood for 20 piastres a month, and since the windows had no glass in them—nor even the paper panes that were used as a substitute for glass in Cumaná—the place was deliciously cool whenever a breeze blew. An old ex-navy quartermaster, who had spent many years in Paris, St Domingo and the Philippines, looked after the house for them with the help of two negroes and a negress to do the cooking—foodstuffs were plentiful but Humboldt complained at the lack of flour to make bread or biscuits —and they began to settle into their tropical home.

They spent their first few weeks in South America testing their instruments and botanizing in the surrounding plains. They were staggered at the prodigious rate of growth of the trees and shrubs—they found a cactus with a circumference of 4 feet 9 inches, for example, and a silk cotton tree, only four years old, with a diameter of two and a half feet. 'You can imagine how completely unexplored this country is,' Humboldt wrote to his brother, 'when I tell you that a new genus, first described by Mutis only two years ago, here grows as a wide-spreading tree, sixty feet high. So what a huge number of smaller plants must have escaped detection as yet!'

From a scientific point of view they were confronted with such an *embarras de richesses* that at first they could not work out a research programme to cope with it. Nor was this their only problem. The local people were as fascinated with the travellers' scientific instruments as the travellers were with the local natural history. Their house was constantly crowded with visitors who clamoured to peer at moon spots through Dollond's telescope or watch the effects of galvanism on the motions of a frog. They were forced to answer an endless stream of questions, many of them of a most obscure and recondite nature, and to repeat the same experiments for hours on end. But the most popular curiosity of all was the microscope, especially among the elegantly dressed ladies of Cumaná, who loved to look through this instrument at the greatly magnified images of the lice and other creatures they found in each other's hair-do's. 'I'm often amazed,' Humboldt wrote in a letter home, 'to see the many different kinds of lice there are that lodge in these curly hairstyles. Each different kind has its own Indian name.' In return for such treats, Humboldt was invited to dances almost every day. He learned the stiff old Spanish dances and partnered the coloured girls of Cumaná in modern dances with predominantly negro rhythms—the samba, the *animalito* and the Congo minuet. But most of the time he was busy with his work.

Humboldt's main preoccupation in Cumaná at this period was continuous meteorological observation—the tropics, with their regular rise and fall of the thermometer and barometer, were ideal for this—and to this end he was often up half the night. At the beginning of September he wrote to his astronomist friend in Jena, Baron von Zach:

I wish I could give an adequate idea of the exquisite beauty of the nights here, or some sort of notion of the fabulous translucency of the air; quite often I have been able to read the vernier of my little sextant by the light of Venus, using a magnifying glass! Venus plays the rôle of the moon here. She shows big, luminous haloes and the most beautiful rainbow colour, even when the air is quite clear and the sky is perfectly blue. I don't think you'll ever find such splendid skies as the ones in these particular latitudes. . . .

Another remarkable and surprising phenomenon is the atmospheric tide, which I observed

'Humboldt partnered the coloured girls of Cumaná in modern dances.'

straightaway on the second day I was here. The thermometer is constantly on the move. From 9 am to 4 pm the mercury falls. Then it rises until 11 pm, falls again until 4.30, rises until 9 am again. It doesn't matter what the weather is—rain, wind, hurricane, storms, the moon, etc.— nothing changes this process. It seems that the sun alone has an influence on the rise and fall. I have collected hundreds of these observations and before long I shall have thousands of them.

Humboldt's house in Cumaná was very well situated for making astronomical observations and had a convenient veranda on which to set up instruments, but it overlooked the main square of the town and sometimes he found the activities there very upsetting indeed. A part of the great square was surrounded with arcades and above them there was a long wooden gallery. This was the place where they sold the slaves shipped over from Africa—mostly young men between fifteen and twenty years of age. Every morning they were given palm oil which they had to rub on their bodies so that their skins would have a shiny black polish. From his house Humboldt could see the prospective buyers force the Africans' mouths open and examine their teeth in order to determine their age—a daily ritual that sickened him.

Humboldt was on the whole remarkably tolerant of ordinary human foibles and seems always to have been above petty rancour and malice. He seldom quarrelled, always apologized, always forgave and never made any permanent enemies. In South America he later endured extreme privation with patience and as far as we can tell never had a cross word with Aimé Bonpland, even under the most trying

The only thing that made Humboldt lose his temper was slavery. Slave market in South America

circumstances, throughout the duration of their long expedition. He was a passionate man, but only one thing ever really made him lose his temper, and that was the slave system, for which he had nothing but absolute loathing. He was the first to admit that slaves in the Spanish possessions were better off than slaves elsewhere but everything in his nature made him revolt against tyranny and injustice wherever he saw it and under whatever guise. When a Spanish priest tried to persuade him that the slave trade was necessary and that all negroes were innately wicked and derived much benefit from their state of slavery among the Christians, Humboldt was disgusted. Throughout his life he never saw any reason to change the beliefs that had crystallized during his stay with Georg Forster in revolutionary Paris.

Before long Humboldt and Bonpland were venturing further and further into the countryside around Cumaná. Sometimes they were forced to seek shelter for the night wherever they could find it, and from the simple mulatto peasantry of the district, who had never even heard of Prussia, they received extraordinarily kind hospitality. It was during one of these field trips that they first heard the remarkable story of Francisco Loyano, a Creole labourer whom they met later.

> This man suckled a child with his own milk. When the mother was ill, the father took the infant into bed with him to quieten it and pressed it to his breast. Loyano, then thirty-two years of age, had never previously mentioned that he had milk but the nipple was irritated when the baby sucked it and this caused the milk to accumulate. It was thick milk, and very sweet. The father was surprised at the increase in the size of his breast and suckled his child two or three times a day for five months thereafter. This attracted the attention of his neighbours, but he never thought—as he probably would have done in Europe—of making any money out of people's curiosity. We saw the certificate which had been drawn up on the spot to confirm this remarkable fact, and some of the eye-witnesses are still alive. They assured us that during this suckling the child had no other nourishment than the father's milk.

Bonpland's subsequent medical examination of Loyano appeared to confirm all that the travellers had been told about him.

*   *   *

On 4 September 1799, after seven weeks on the coast at Cumaná, the two explorers felt sufficiently acclimatized and *au fait* with local conditions to venture out on their first extensive foray. Their goal was the Missions of the Chayma Indians among the highlands that backed Cumaná to the south.

They had been told that the roads up into the mountains were very difficult and that they should cut their baggage down to a minimum, and in the end they set off with no more than could be carried on the backs of two mules—provisions, paper for drying plants, and a case containing a sextant, a dipping-needle, an apparatus to measure the magnetic variation, a few thermometers and Saussure's hygrometer.

As they toiled higher into the deliciously cool and refreshing air of the uplands they entered the great tropical rain forest of South America for the first time. The track crossed mountain streams and wound along the edge of ravines from which soared gigantic trees covered in lianas; it passed beneath festoons of low-hanging creepers and through thickets of bamboo and giant fern; once it narrowed to a mere fifteen inches, with a precipice on one side. For hours they walked in the green gloom beneath the matted forest canopy, pursued by the cries of the brilliantly coloured orioles and macaws high overhead; the majestic trees and luxuriant vegetation that shut out the sky entranced them, though they were vexed that the exotic leaves and flowers and fruit grew so far beyond their reach. Occasionally they came to a clearing from which they could look back the way they had come, and they saw at their feet this immense forest stretching to the edge of the ocean, a vast carpet of greenery, intertwined with lianas and crowned with long wreaths of flowers.

'*They entered the great tropical rain forest of South America for the first time. The track crossed mountain streams and wound along the edges of ravines from which soared gigantic trees covered in lianas.*'

The headquarters of the Capuchin Missions among the Chayma Indians was at a place called Caripe, high up in the mountains, and for a week Humboldt and Bonpland used it as a base for their excursions into the surrounding hills. It was a delightful spot and reminded Humboldt of the valleys of Derbyshire and the Muggendorf hills in Franconia. The climate was cool, there were no noxious insects, and numberless springs of sweet water gushed from crevices in the sheer, thousand-foot-high rock face that backed the monastery. It was here that Humboldt celebrated his thirtieth birthday.

The building had an inner court surrounded by an arcade, like the monasteries in Spain, and Humboldt found this a convenient spot to set up his instruments and make his observations. The monastery itself was quite full. There were young monks who had recently arrived from Spain and were getting ready to settle into the various missions, and there were old, ailing monks who had come to convalesce in the fresh and salubrious air of the mountains of Caripe. Judging from the books he found in the monastery it seemed to Humboldt that the progress of knowledge was ad-

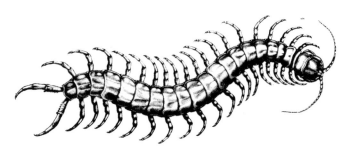

A centipede of tropical America

vancing even in the forests of America. The youngest of the Capuchin monks, for example, had brought with him a Spanish translation of Chaptal's *Treatise on Chemistry*, and he intended to study this work in the solitude in which he was destined to pass the remainder of his days.

The travellers were welcomed with great hospitality by the monks of Caripe and Humboldt himself was given accommodation in the cell of the Superior of the monastery. He was surprised at the absence of any religious intolerance towards him. The monks knew perfectly well that he came from the Protestant part of Germany but no indiscreet question, no hint of distrust, no attempt at controversy ever spoiled their sincere and generous welcome.

In this beautiful and peaceful place the days passed quickly by. From sunrise to sunset Humboldt and Bonpland tramped through the forests and over the hills to collect plants. If it was raining they spent the day with the Chayma Indians, compiling a vocabulary of their language or watching the children devour eighteen-inch-long millipedes which they drew out of the ground like worms. They only returned when they heard the sound of the monastery bell summoning them to refectory—a sound they came to dread when they discovered that the monks were doing without their slender ration of wine and wheaten bread in order that *they* might have enough. Every evening after supper they wrote up their notes, dried the plants they had collected and made drawings of the ones they thought formed new genera. The thick mist in the valley usually prevented any observation of the stars, though Humboldt stayed up most nights in the hope that the sky might clear. On evenings when it looked like rain the valley echoed with the weird roar of the howler monkeys—like the distant sound of wind when it shakes the forest. It was a wild and idyllic location.

Sometimes, very early in the mornings, Humboldt and Bonpland accompanied the missionaries to church to attend the *doctrina*, the religious instruction of the Indians. Humboldt wrote:

> It was rather a difficult task to explain dogmas to the neophytes, especially the ones who only had a very imperfect knowledge of the Spanish language. The similarity of sounds in Spanish confuses the poor Indians and puts the most whimsical ideas into their heads. For example, I saw a missionary labouring with great earnestness to prove that *infierno* (hell) and *invierno* (winter) were not one and the same thing but as different as heat and cold. The Chaymas know no other winter than the season of rains, so consequently they imagined that the 'hell of the white man' was a place where the wicked are exposed to frequent showers. The missionary harangued in vain; it was impossible to efface the impression caused by the similarity between the two consonants.

On the whole, Humboldt did not think very highly of the Mission System. Although the Indians of the Spanish colonies were protected in law, many of them lived lives that were more wretched than the openly enslaved negroes and it was to shore up the ruins of this Indian society after nearly two centuries of oppression that the Mission System was adopted. Its purpose was to settle the nomadic tribes—scattered like the remnants of a vast wreck—into stable communities (called Missions), protect their rights and, of course, give instruction in the Catholic faith. 'It was the privilege of religion', Humboldt commented dryly 'to console humanity for some of the evils committed in its name.'

Humboldt gave the system credit for preventing tribal wars, for giving the Indians subsistence and security and for enabling their numbers to increase (they were mothers at twelve), but he was quick to see that the rigid discipline and dull monotony of the missions were producing communities of zombies, tribes stultified by inertia and devoid of any corporate soul. By erasing the traditional beliefs of the tribes, and banning nakedness and such harmless customs as the painting and tattooing of the skin, the missionaries had, without realizing it, knocked away the infrastructure of Indian society. At the same time, they had failed to substitute any acceptable new beliefs in place of the ones they had destroyed. The majority of the Indians, as Humboldt was quick to perceive, paid little more than lip-service to the Christian faith. The result was a sort of shocked condition of permanent torpor—a condition only too familiar to anthropologists in South America today. 'They show by their morose and diffident looks,' Humboldt noted, 'that they have not sacrificed their freedom for their security without regret.'

Not far from the Mission of Caripe, in the wildest and most rugged part of the mountains, was a cave that formed an endless topic of conversation throughout Venezuela. Locally it was called 'the mine of fat' and large colonies of a curious nocturnal bird called the guacharo or oil-bird lived there—a species apparently unknown to science. One day before they returned to Cumaná, Humboldt and Bonpland, accompanied by some Indian guides and most of the population of the monastery, set out to explore this cave and found that it far exceeded their expectations. Its entrance, pierced in the vertical profile of a huge rock, was over seventy feet high and surmounted by trees of gigantic height; gold-coloured orchids grew in

The guacharo or oil-bird, Steatornis caripensis. *After a sketch by Humboldt*

the dry clefts of the rock and a thick canopy of creeping plants hung down in festoons over the cave mouth.

Inside, the cave formed a single continuous passage that led straight into the mountainside for nearly 500 yards before it narrowed and changed its direction; the daylight therefore penetrated a long way into the interior and they had gone almost 150 yards before they needed to light their bark-and-resin torches. It was at this point that they first heard far off the horrendous noise of the guacharos, hoarse cries and castanet-like clatterings that grew louder as the party stumbled on into the darkness, splashing clumsily along the stream that poured down the middle of the cave and ducking under the masses of great stalactites that hung from the roof high above. It reminded Humboldt of a descent into Tartarus. The shrill and piercing cries of the thousands of birds disturbed from their nests were answered by a similar din from other colonies in other parts of the cave. Occasionally, when one of the Indian guides held up a torch on the end of a long pole, they caught a

The expedition reaches the entrance to the cave of Caripe.
After a sketch by Humboldt

brief glimpse of a momentarily dazzled bird, but in order to have a closer look and procure a few specimens for science they were forced to discharge their guns into the darkness, aiming vaguely in the direction of the loudest noise.

From an examination of two specimens shot by Bonpland, Humboldt could see that the guacharo was a completely new species. It was the size of a crow, with a three-and-a-half-foot wingspan and an enormously strong, corn-cracking beak. Between the legs of the younger birds lay a thick cushion of edible fat. This fat was highly prized by the locals and once a year, towards midsummer, the Indians entered the caves armed with long poles and killed several thousand of the young birds. The fat they procured from them, melted down into oil, would keep for a year or more without turning rancid and the monastery kitchen at Caripe used no other kind in its cooking.

The Indians normally never went any further into the cave than the end of the first great chamber. They believed that beyond the waterfall which separated it from the inner recesses slept the souls of their ancestors who had 'gone to join the guacharos'. It required all the authority of the monks to persuade them to venture on into the lower and narrower passage beyond, thick with mud underfoot and even noisier overhead, where the acrid smoke from their primitive torches made them all cough and weep. Here, to everyone's astonishment—Humboldt's and the Indians' not least—they came across strange forms of subterranean vegetation sprouting weirdly in the darkness. Seeds dropped by the guacharos had germinated in the fine mould covering the rocks, and the blanched stalks, with a few half-formed leaves, had risen to a height of two feet, their form and colour changed beyond all recognition by the absence of light. Humboldt himself was fascinated—it reminded him of his research into photosynthesis below ground during his Freiberg days—but the Indians contemplated these pale and deformed plants in nervous silence, evidently believing that they were phantoms banished from the face of the earth. Though the cave clearly continued on its course for a considerable distance, nothing could persuade these superstitious animists to proceed any further. 'We were obliged to yield to the pusillanimity of our guides,' Humboldt recorded with regret, 'and trace back our steps.'

*   *   *

Humboldt and Bonpland returned to Cumaná at the end of September. It seems they had already abandoned any idea of keeping to their original schedule and instead of looking for a ship to take them on to Havana they began to make plans for a more ambitious journey of exploration into the little-known region of the Upper Orinoco. They now looked on the circumstances that had forced them to disembark in Cumaná in the first place as a piece of rare good fortune, though in the ensuing month a series of quite extraordinary incidents occurred which must have made them wish that they had changed their minds.

Humboldt in Venezuela, plant press on his lap, top hat and barometer behind him. Painting by F. G. Weitsch

ALEXANDER
von HUMBOLDT

First came the incident of the crazy half-breed. Humboldt and Bonpland had gone down to the beach about eight o'clock on the evening of 27 October to catch a breath of fresh sea-air—it was a hot, overcast night. They had just crossed the beach when Humboldt sensed that somebody was walking immediately behind them and turned in time to see a tall, nearly naked half-breed in the act of swinging a great wooden club in the direction of his skull. Humboldt avoided the blow by leaping to his left, but Bonpland saw the man too late and was struck a violent thwack on the temple and knocked unconscious. Instead of clubbing Humboldt as well, however, the half-breed ambled off to pick up Bonpland's hat, which had fallen on to the sand a few feet away. During this incongruous manoeuvre, Bonpland regained his senses and staggered to his feet. Incensed with pain and anger, he immediately leapt at his assailant and chased him into a cactus thicket—mainly composed, the ever-observant Humboldt took the opportunity to note, of arborescent avicennia. Here the half-breed slipped and fell, and Bonpland grabbed him, whereupon the half-breed drew a long knife and would undoubtedly have stabbed him had not a group of European traders rushed up to help. The half-breed ran off again and was eventually caught, exhausted, in a cowshed where he had tried to lay up and rest.

Under interrogation the half-breed gave such confused and dotty answers that the reason for the attack never became clear. Poor Bonpland had a gash stretching from his temple to the crown of his head and during the night developed a fever. The next morning, with characteristic cheerfulness, he insisted on getting up to work but every time he bent down to pick a plant he became so giddy that Humboldt was afraid he was developing an internal abscess. These fears were fortunately unfounded, but it was three months before the symptoms of Bonpland's concussion vanished altogether. All told it had been a lucky escape for both of them.

The very next day after Bonpland's injury, Humboldt spent all morning on the terrace of their house observing the eclipse of the sun through his instruments. The heat had been oppressive and almost unbearable—the metal of one of the instruments had reached a temperature of $124°F$—and his face was so badly burnt that he was forced to go indoors and lie down. It was two days before he felt well enough to get up again and when he did finally go outdoors the atmosphere over Cumaná had turned very peculiar and the local inhabitants were pointing out all the infallible prognostics of impending disaster.

At every sunset the sky had been covered in an unusual red mist. 'After the 28th October,' Humboldt related, 'the reddish mist became thicker than it had previously been. The heat of the nights seemed stifling. The breeze, which generally cooled the air from eight or nine o'clock in the evening, was no longer felt. The atmosphere was burning hot, and the parched and dusty ground was everywhere cracked. On the 4th November, about two in the afternoon, large clouds of peculiar blackness enveloped the high mountains of Brigantine and the Tataraqual. They extended by degrees as far as the zenith. About four in the afternoon thunder was heard over

The guacharo or oil-bird and chick, nocturnal creatures found by
Humboldt in the cave of Caripe

our heads, at an immense height, not regularly rolling, but with a hollow and often interrupted sound.' The thunder was followed immediately by a violent blast of wind and electric rain falling in huge drops. Humboldt, who was observing this with his usual methodical precision, tested the electric charge in the atmosphere and found it had reversed its polarity from positive to negative. The blast of wind was followed by a dead calm. A few seconds later, it happened.

> At the moment of the strongest electric explosion, at 4.12 pm, there were two shocks of earthquake, which followed each other at fifteen second intervals. The people ran into the streets, uttering loud cries. M. Bonpland, who was leaning over a table examining plants, was almost thrown on the floor. I felt the shock very strongly, even though I was lying in a hammock. Slaves who were drawing water from a well more than eighteen or twenty feet deep near the river Manzanares heard a noise like the explosion of a strong charge of gunpowder. The noise seemed to come from the bottom of the well.

This was Humboldt's first experience of an earthquake. It was not an undulation, he noted, but a positive movement upward and downward, and it was the novelty rather than the fear of danger that made it so unforgettable. 'It is like waking up. . We feel that we have been deceived by the apparent stability of nature; we mistrust for the first time the soil we have so long trod with confidence.' Humboldt was not totally unnerved, however, and during the tremors was sufficiently cool-headed to notice that the dip of the magnetic needle was reduced by more than $1°$—a remarkably phlegmatic observation, under the circumstances.

The people of Cumaná, who had seen their houses destroyed by earthquake not long before, were not unnaturally thoroughly alarmed at these latest tremors, which they blamed on the eclipse. But no one had been hurt and no damage had been done, and after a few more subterranean rumbles and one more sunset of extraordinary magnificence, the atmospheric conditions gradually reverted to normal.

Or almost normal. Only a week after the earthquake the travellers were treated to one last spectacle in Cumaná. Aimé Bonpland was the first to notice it. At about half-past two in the morning of 12 November he had got up—'to enjoy the freshness of the air', so Humboldt said—and was astonished to see that the clear night sky was raining fireballs. Thousands of meteorites with brilliant white nuclei and long luminous traces were rocketing through the sky and exploding one after the other like gigantic fireworks. There were so many in the sky at once that there was never a space bigger than three diameters of the moon that was not filled with them every instant, and they continued to rain down incessantly until a quarter of an hour after sunrise. The apprehensive inhabitants of Cumaná, who had left their houses before four o'clock to attend early morning mass, viewed this display of heavenly pyrotechnics as yet another ill-omened phenomenon and started worrying about earthquakes all over again. Not till much later did Humboldt discover that this meteor shower—now a celebrated event in the history of astronomy—had been witnessed not only by the people of Cumaná but by missionaries in Brazil, an exiled French count in Cayenne, the United States astronomer off Florida, eskimoes in Labrador and Greenland, and a vicar in Weimar! In all, this extraordinary phenomenon had been seen over an area of nearly a million square miles of the earth's surface, but Humboldt's precise observation of it was the starting point of astronomers' researches into the nature and periodicity of asteroids.

* * *

On the night of 16 November, Humboldt and Bonpland left Cumaná by sea for Caracas, the capital city of Venezuela, where they proposed to spend the rest of the rainy season before setting out for the unknown regions of the Orinoco. For Humboldt, as the little coaster edged away from a shore sparkling with fireflies into a sea crisscrossed with the phosphorescent wakes of porpoises, it was a sad occasion. He felt that Cumaná had been his home for years, and in later life he recalled:

> This was the first spot we set foot on in a land I had been dreaming about since I was a boy . . . In my mind's eye it is not to all the wonders of the Cordilleras that I return most often, but to Cumaná and its dusty soil.

Leaf of an Amazonas palm

CHAPTER 9

The Llanos

Humboldt and Bonpland rented a large and comfortable house in Caracas. It was situated in the highest and most fashionable part of town and overlooked the Plaza de la Trinidad at the front and the misty peaks and valleys of the Caracas mountains at the back. Here, in a mild upland climate of perpetual spring and ever-blossoming flowers, they settled down to wait for the end of the rainy season before continuing their expedition into the interior.

The Caracas of Humboldt's time—it was destroyed by a great earthquake in 1812—was a fine city. The 40,000 people that lived there were, for the most part, cultivated, well-informed and noted especially for their appreciation of music. Humboldt, who loathed music and thought it a social calamity, was unable to avoid the occasional musical soirée. Thus we find him among the company assembled in a garden at Chacao listening to the latest modern music—Mozart, Haydn, Pleyel—under the orange trees, or sitting in the open-air pit of the city's theatre, looking not at the stage but at the night sky where he hoped to observe an eclipse of the satellites of Jupiter. Humboldt, who never ceased to be gratified by the hospitality and kindness of the Spanish Americans, was instantly welcomed into Caracas society. And though he was careful never to involve himself too obviously in politics, he was inevitably made aware of the toughening of attitudes among the Creole intellectuals of the city and the gradual gathering of the forces of the revolution with which his own name, rightly or wrongly, was to be for ever associated.

The Spanish Empire in America had survived 300 years of direct rule from Madrid and at the beginning of the nineteenth century still remained intact from California to Cape Horn. But among the majority of Creoles, who were denied any right to participate in foreign trade or the government of their own country, the tide of resentment was rising. Revolutionary ideas secretly imported from France sowed notions of liberty and republican government. The success of the United States in throwing off British rule encouraged them. And the British naval blockade of the Spanish American ports further weakened the hold of the royalist government in Madrid. Nowhere throughout this immense territory was there greater political awareness than in Caracas. It was here that Francisco Miranda and Simón Bolívar and many other leading figures in the future struggle for independence were born. It was here that the first premature rebellion was crushed, less than three years before Humbolt's arrival in the city. And it was here, ten years later, that revolution and independence were first proclaimed in Spanish America. In 1800 the underground movement in Caracas was still only a movement of ideas among the educated élite (Rousseau and *The Rights of Man* hidden in private houses and reprinted on illicit presses) but Humboldt was well aware of the currents of change and in his realistic way he was sympathetic to them. However, he counted both *Criollos* and *Peninsulares* among his acquaintances—not least the Captain-General of Caracas himself—and preferred to remain an uncommitted witness to the decay of Spanish authority in its last decade of rule over the biggest empire on earth. His only total committment in Spanish America was to its geophysical phenomena.

Incapable of inactivity for long, and frustrated by the cloudy weather which had prevented him from making any astronomical sightings for twenty-seven consecutive days, Humboldt one day made the first recorded climb of the Silla, the highest of the peaks dominating Caracas. Accompanied by Bonpland and preceded by eighteen uproarious slaves carrying their baggage, he climbed up to the summit, approximately 8,000 feet, and down again non-stop in fifteen hours, viewed through telescopes by the incredulous citizens of the capital far below. For most of the time they had neither food nor water—the slaves seemed to have consumed everything but the olives—and by the end their feet were bleeding.

Finally, on 7 February 1800, after a stay of two and a half months, the explorers left Caracas for the interior. It was like travelling through time as well as space, for their route took them through regions whose inhabitants lived at widely different stages of human progress. The people of the coastal towns, for example, enjoyed most of the advantages of eighteenth century civilization. But further inland, beyond the coastal mountains, the half-wild cattlemen of the great river plains (the *llanos*) lived the life of a far more ancient and pastoral culture. And further inland still,

The llanos. '*All around us the plains seemed to reach to the sky, and this vast and profound solitude looked like an ocean covered with seaweed.*'

beyond the *llanos*, lay the unexplored forests of the Orinoco, where tribes of savage Indians, under the tentative rule of a handful of Franciscan missionaries, dwelt in a primordial state unchanged since Columbus' discovery of the New World. This huge and primitive extremity of Venezuela was the goal of Humboldt's and Bonpland's expedition. In the headwater region of the Orinoco they proposed to investigate one, possibly two, major geographical problems. Firstly the existence of an extraordinary natural canal called the Casiquiare, a unique and controversial phenomenon that was supposed to link the Orinoco with the Amazon basin—though some geographers did not believe it; secondly if possible, the whereabouts of the source of the Orinoco itself.

Their route was not a straight one. First they headed west, crossing the fertile valleys of Aragua, rich in sugar cane, coffee, bananas, and orchards of peach trees

Lake Valencia, Venezuela

covered in blossom, en route to Puerto Cabello. Here they stayed a short time before finally heading south. At Lake Valencia they drank copious draughts of the remarkable vegetable milk of the aptly-named cow-tree, *Brosimum utile*, and lived in the manner of the rich of the country, bathing twice a day, sleeping three times, and eating three meals in the twenty-four hours. Then, a month after their departure from Caracas, they turned their backs on the comforts of the civilized world and started out for the Orinoco.

On 12 March the party descended the southern slopes of the mountains and entered the great *llanos* of South America—a vast plain, bigger than France and almost as big as Texas, stretching without a break from the Andes to the Atlantic and from the Caracas mountains to the Guiana forests. Huge herds of cattle and horses, nearly two million head in all, ranged freely over this lonely wilderness. Many of them died of thirst during the long dry season, or drowned in the widespread floods that followed the rains. It was an inclement country, infested with snakes, alligators and vampire bats, and except for some scattered ranchers and a few bandits and cattle rustlers it was almost uninhabited.

It was noon when they first reached the plain and the sun was nearly at its zenith. Under the burning sky the earth was cracked and scorching—the ground temperature was 50°C when Humbolt measured it. There was not a breath of air and nothing stirred but the dust devils whirling across the desolate and arid spaces. The extreme flatness of the plains was depressing—as far as the eye could see (and there was no telling how far that was) there was not a single bump or hillock more than a foot high. 'All around us,' Humboldt recorded, 'the plains seemed to reach to the sky, and this vast and profound solitude looked like an ocean covered with seaweed.'

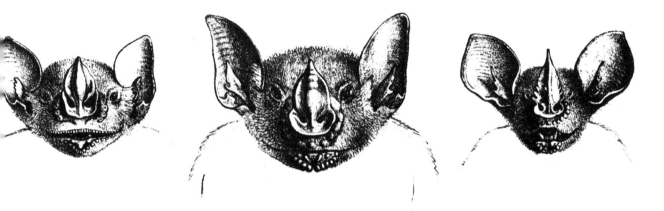

Vampire bats attacked the horses and cattle of the llanos *and hovered over Humboldt's hammock during the night*

In the suffocating heat they turned their mules towards the south-east, resigned to the rigours of a long trek across a hostile land where one horizon looked like the next and never seemed to get any nearer.

They travelled by night beneath an immense sky, starry but moonless, while a cool breeze blew across the plain and stirred the grass like a sea swell. At daybreak it was not one sun but two that rose over the horizon, the effect of refraction; and as the day progressed the mirages of hills and trees and large shimmering lakes sprang up on the plain ahead of them. The temperature rose to 41°C and they filled their hats with leaves to keep their heads cool. They tried to rest during the heat of the day but there were never any trees big enough to provide shade from the sun and their skins became burnt and thickly caked in dust. Once they came across a thirteen-year-old Indian girl stretched naked and half-dead from thirst beside a water-pitcher full of sand; they refilled the pitcher but she would accept no other help and in the end they had to leave her to her own stoical and solitary devices. They suffered greatly from thirst themselves but at the infrequent ranches of the rude and inhospitable *llaneros*—the wild mulatto cowboys who spent their lives in the saddle—they were given not milk but stinking yellow puddle water which they had to drink through a linen filter. Once, hoping to bathe, they were chased out of a waterhole by an alligator. Another time they got lost and wandered aimlessly for hours across the darkened and featureless plain. The *llanos* were not a nice place to be and they were glad when they reached the relative comforts of Calabozo, the half-way point of their trek.

Calabozo was a dusty cattle-trading station in the middle of nowhere and here, to the travellers' astonishment and delight, they came across a local inventor, a Señor del Pozo, who had never heard of Volta or Galvani but had read about electricity in Benjamin Franklin's *Memoirs* and on the strength of what he could glean from them had, with his own hands and against almost insuperable odds, built an electrical apparatus almost as good as the most advanced designs in the leading laboratories of Europe. Among his simple, cow-punching neighbours in this one-horse town he was regarded as the genius of the *llanos*.

But it was an electric apparatus of a totally different sort that most excited Humboldt's attention in Calabozo. Ever since his arrival in Venezuela he had been trying to procure an active and potent specimen of the notorious electric eel of South America, *Gymnotus electricus*[1], whose terrifying characteristics had first attracted his attention during his researches into animal electricity. This slimy, yellow-spotted freshwater fish (it looked like an eel but was actually related to the minnow and the carp) could deliver a paralysing shock of up to 650 volts DC from the electric organ occupying most of its three to nine foot long body, and from a distance kill a large animal or stun a man. So far Humboldt had been unsuccessful in obtaining a specimen, for the terror this undesirable creature evoked was so great that not even a handsome reward could induce the Indians to go and catch one. At Calabozo, however, he met with better luck. The swampy *caños* in the neighbourhood of the town were crowded with electric eels—so crowded, in fact, that at one of the fords several horses had already been killed by them. The Indians here, moreover, had a foolproof way of catching them—they would '*embarbascar con caballos*' (stupify [the fish] with horses).

From the surrounding plains they rounded up thirty horses and mules and these they drove into a marshy pool where the electric eels were thought to lurk. At the same time they formed a close circle round the pool and with wild cries and blows from their spears and sticks prevented the animals from escaping.

Almost immediately the electric eels, driven out of the mud by the terrific noise

[1]Now classified as *Electrophorus electricus*.

ABOVE *The electric eel of South America*; BELOW *Two species of freshwater dolphin from the Amazon and Orinoco*

OVERLEAF *Humboldt and Bonpland in their hut in the forests of the Orinoco. Painting by E. Ender*

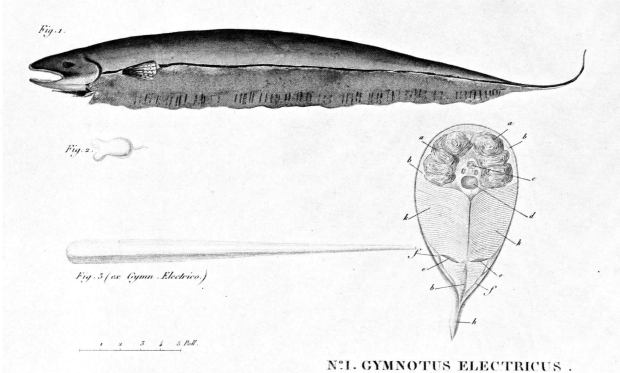

Nº II. GYMNOTUS ÆQUILABIATUS.

Fig. 1.

Fig. 2.

Fig. 3 (ex Gymn. Electrico.)

Nº I. GYMNOTUS ELECTRICUS.

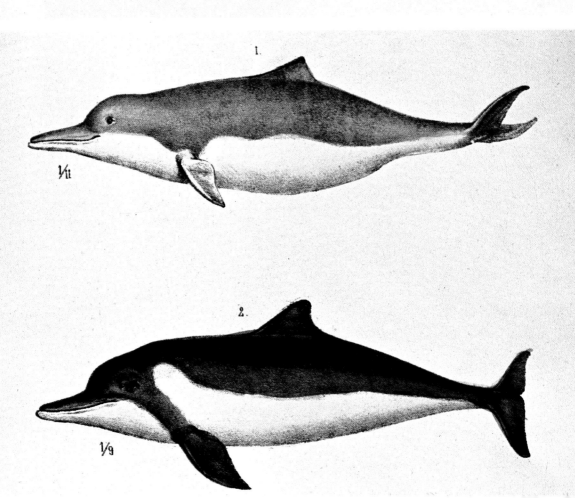

1.

1/11

2.

1/9

of the horses' hooves, appeared on the surface. One by one these livid, yellowish-green creatures, swimming like large water snakes, crowded along under the bellies of the horses and mules and repeatedly discharged their electric batteries, attacking simultaneously the heart, the intestines and the coeliac fold of the abdominal nerves. Several horses fell victim to these invisible shocks to their vital organs and collapsed into the water where they drowned. Other horses, foaming at the mouth, with manes standing on end and a wild and desperate terror in their eyes, reared up and tried to escape from the pool. Most of them were driven back by the Indians, and the few that did break through the ring of men were so exhausted and numb in the legs that they stumbled at every step and were forced to lie down on the sand until they had recovered.

Horrified by what was happening, Humboldt was convinced that this method of fishing could only end in the deaths, one after the other, of all of the animals involved. But the fish had only a limited amount of electrical energy in their batteries and soon they too were exhausted and swam off. The horses and mules calmed down and when the electric eels timidly approached the edge of the pool they were harpooned by the Indians and drawn ashore on long lines. In a few minutes five large eels had been captured and in the afternoon some more were caught in the same way. Most of them were only slightly injured.

With Bonpland's help Humboldt immediately began some simple experiments with the living eels on the bank and afterwards killed and dissected them. It was not long before some curious questions were raised. For one thing, why didn't the creature electrocute itself? For another, why wasn't it possible to observe the electrical discharge of this fish in the usual way? It didn't register on the electrometer, there was no magnetic effect, and no sparks were visible when the fish was irritated in total darkness. The only measure of electric discharge was the degree of pain the creature was capable of inflicting on the little frogs and turtles that, in all innocence, climbed on to its back in a tub of water, and on the long-suffering Bonpland and Humboldt themselves. This, Humboldt recalled, was unforgettable:

I do not remember having ever received from the discharge of a large Leyden jar a more dreadful shock than the one I experienced when I very stupidly placed both my feet on an electric eel that had just been taken out of the water. I was affected for the rest of the day with a violent pain in the knees and almost every joint . . .

Undeterred, Humboldt and Bonpland continued to prod and poke and provoke the eels, using their bare hands and every kind of implement. The Indians, unaccustomed to the antics of learned men, must have looked on with incredulous glee as Humboldt and Bonpland convulsed and anguished on the banks of that unprepossessing marsh. 'I can assert', wrote Humboldt, 'that after four successive hours of experiments with electric eels, M. Bonpland and myself felt a weakness in the muscles, a pain in the joints and a general malaise until the following day.'

The Maipures section of the Great Cataracts of the Orinoco. 'They had to steer through channels only five feet broad but twenty-five fathoms deep, where the water rushed with a frightening roar.'

Under such circumstances their persistence in continuing this first scientific examination of the dreaded electric eel was heroic indeed.

*   *   *

On 27 March 1800 the travellers completed their crossing of the *llanos* and arrived with their instruments and their collections at the Villa de San Fernando, the capital of the Missions of the Capuchins in the province of Varinas, Venezuela. It was a tiny place, founded little more than ten years previously at a strategic point on the Rio Apure, an important tributary of the Orinoco, and noted only for the excessive heat which prevailed there for most of the year. Here, by chance, they met the brother-in-law of the provincial governor, a cheerful and amiable character called Don Nicolas Sotto, who had recently arrived from Cadiz and who bravely agreed, at a moment's notice, to accompany them on their venture into the interior.

The travellers spent only three days in San Fernando. With the help of the local missionary they were able to obtain one of those very large canoes the Spanish called *lanchas*, together with four Indians to paddle it and a pilot who knew at least the first part of their route. Compared with what they had to put up with later, their accommodation on this *lancha* was almost luxurious. In the space of a few hours the Indian crew constructed a *tolda*, a kind of cabin at the stern roofed over with palm-leaf thatch and big enough for a table and some benches made of ox-hide stretched over frames of Brazil-wood. All the available space in the boat was taken up with Humboldt's instrument cases, Bonpland's plant presses, their little scientific library, firearms (almost useless in the damp climate of the river basin) and provisions for a month including live chickens, eggs, plantains, cassava, cocoa, and some casks of brandy for barter with the Indians along the Orinoco, besides sherry and some oranges and tamarinds which the Capuchin missionaries had given them to make soft drinks with. Since this voyage was going to last considerably longer than a month, however, they reckoned to eke out their larder with what they could forage—*pauxi* (wild turkey) and *guacharaca* (wild pheasant) from the banks, and fish, manatees, turtles and turtles' eggs, 'a foodstuff more nutritious than agreeable to the taste', from the rivers themselves. In an environment apparently so fertile and so abundant in game, they did not envisage that they would ever come near to starvation.

The first part of their journey—eastwards down the Rio Apure, then southwards along the Orinoco as far as the barrier of the Atures and Maipures rapids, known as the Great Cataracts—was relatively well-known to a small number of local missionaries, though no scientists had ever gone that way before. Beyond the Great Cataracts, however, lay *terra incognita*, a land reconnoitred at rare intervals in the past century by small bands of soldiers and conquering priests, and inhabited, then as now, by no more than a few scattered tribes of wild Indians and a handful

In March 1800 Humboldt and Bonpland set off down the Rio Apure for the unknown region of the Upper Orinoco. At night they camped on the banks of the river

of isolated missionaries. The discomfort and dangers of this region were not mere travellers' tales (or monks' tales, as they called them in those parts). Back in Cumaná, Humboldt and Bonpland had been very fully briefed by an errant young priest who had once been banished to the Upper Orinoco, and he had left them under no illusion as to what they could expect up there, and no illusion, either, about the existence of the mysterious Casiquiare canal, whose murky waters he had seen with his own eyes. Humboldt's journey to investigate this odd and disputed link between the two great river systems of the Amazon and the Orinoco was possibly the one journey of true geographical exploration, as opposed to what may be described as field research in out-of-the-way places, he made in his life, and as it turned out, he and his dogged companions were very fortunate to survive. For against some of the most inclement conditions to be found anywhere on earth they were armed with nothing but their sense of humour, their *joie de vivre*, and their unquenchable enthusiasm for scientific discovery.

Pauxi *or wild turkey. A sketch from Humboldt's journal*

CHAPTER 10

Beyond the Great Cataracts

A little before dawn, at 4 am on 30 March 1800, Humboldt's expedition to the Upper Orinoco and the unknown region of the Casiquiare canal set off from San Fernando de Apure. After the dry and dusty *llanos* the watery world of the river was a considerable change indeed: a less harsh world but a more confining one. Instead of the limitless views of the plains they were now shut in between a wall of forest along either bank, and instead of the physical freedom they had enjoyed on their mule trek they now had to sit motionless in the constricted space of a narrow dug-out canoe. Nevertheless, for Humboldt the scene had a peculiar attraction. In his time the wild life of these regions was very much more abundant than it is today and as his canoe glided along the banks of the river he was treated to a wonderfully close view of birds and animals of every conceivable variety. It was like being in a huge riverine zoo. Once they passed a low island inhabited by thousands of flamingoes, rose-coloured spoonbills and herons, all packed so closely together they seemed unable to stir. Another time he saw flocks of birds so dense they looked like dark clouds in the sky. Herds of fifty or sixty capybara, the largest rodent in the world, paddled round the boat like dogs, and freshwater dolphins played along-side it. Tapirs and peccaries trotted along the banks, unconcerned at the canoe that seemed to keep pace beside them, and there was hardly a moment when Humboldt couldn't see at a single glance half a dozen huge 20-foot alligators lying motionless on the sand with their jaws wide open. The water was infested with piranha or cannibal fish and stingrays. Even in the heat of noon, when the birds and animals took to the shade and nothing stirred, he was kept aware — by millions of tiny insect voices raised into one big buzz — of the myriad of creatures that filled the lower strata of the air.

At nights the expedition would land on the banks of the river and make camp in the open. Usually they slung their hammocks between the trees, but if there were no trees — on a sandbank, for instance — they slung them from canoe-paddles stuck in the sand, or, if the worst came to the worst, did without hammocks alto-gether and slept on ox-hides stretched out on the ground, a dangerous procedure on account of the snakes that snuggled up to them for warmth. Often their camp fires would attract the alligators, who would range themselves round and stare at it for hours. More bothersome were the jaguars, huge beasts which were unbelievably abundant by today's standards and much feared by the Indians— Humboldt once found two behind his hammock tree. These nights in the wild were seldom completely peaceful. Sometimes, at about eleven o'clock, a terrific noise would start up in the forest and put an end to sleep. There were the soft little cries of the sapajous, the moans of the howler monkeys, peccaries and sloths, and the shrieks of the parrots and curassows. Whenever a jaguar approached the edge of the forest, the expedition dog would stop barking and begin to howl, hiding itself under their hammocks for safety.

Even on the rare occasions when they stayed at an inhabited settlement the nights were no more comfortable. One of their stops along the Apure was at a small plantation

'There was hardly a moment when he couldn't see at a single glance half a dozen huge 20-foot alligators.'

belonging to a man who hunted jaguars for a living. This is how Humboldt describes this encounter in his *Personal Narrative*:

> He wore scarcely any clothing and was of a dark brown complexion like a zambo. This did not prevent his classing himself amongst the whites. He called his wife and daughter, who were as naked as he was, Dona Isabella and Dona Manuela. Without having ever left the banks of the Apure, he took a lively interest in the news of Madrid—enquiring eagerly about 'those never-ending wars'. I had brought with me a capybara, which I had intended to have roasted; but our host assured us, that such 'Indian game' was not food fit for 'white gentlemen like you and me'. Accordingly he offered us some venison, which he had killed the day before with an arrow, for he had neither powder nor fire-arms.

Humboldt and Bonpland's expedition camp by the Orinoco

We assumed that a small wood of plantain-trees concealed from us the hut of the farm; but this man, so proud of his nobility and the colour of his skin, had not taken the trouble of constructing even an *ajoupa*, or hut of palm-leaves. He invited us to have our hammocks hung near his own, between two trees; and he assured us, with an air of complacency, that, if we came up the river in the rainy season, we should find him beneath a roof. We soon had reason to complain of a system of philosophy which is indulgent to indolence, and renders a man indifferent to the conveniences of life. A furious wind arose after midnight, lightning flashed over the horizon, thunder rolled, and we were wet to the skin. While it rained in torrents on our hammocks and on our instruments which we had brought ashore, Don Ignacio congratulated us on our good fortune in not sleeping on the beach, but finding ourselves in his domain, among respectable white people.

Apart from Don Ignacio, the travellers had seen no other human being and met no other boat. It was a complete wilderness. On 5 April they reached the main

Humboldt's sketch of a black-headed cacajao (or uakari) of the Rio Negro from which the coloured engraving (right) was later made. He obtained this little monkey, with its characteristic short tail, from the Indians of the Casiquiare and kept it as a pet till it died of a stomach upset at Carichana on the Orinoco

river and the scale of the landscape increased. An immense plain of water stretched before them like a lake as far as the eye could see. A vast beach, constantly parched by the heat of the sun and as arid and bare as the shores of the sea, stretched away on either side. The river was so broad that the distant mountains seemed to rise out of the water as if above the horizon of an ocean—huge blocks of granite, cleft and piled on top of each other like ancient ruins.

The wind blew strongly from the north-north-east. This was the right quarter for a sail up the Orinoco, but the effect of wind over current produced white-topped waves several feet high and the *lancha* was tossed about so badly that some of the party were actually sea-sick. Thus incommoded, they set course to the southward and the long haul to the Great Cataracts.

Simia melanocephala.

et fils, d'après une esquisse de Mr de Humboldt.   De l'Imprimerie de Langlois.   Bouquet sculpsit.

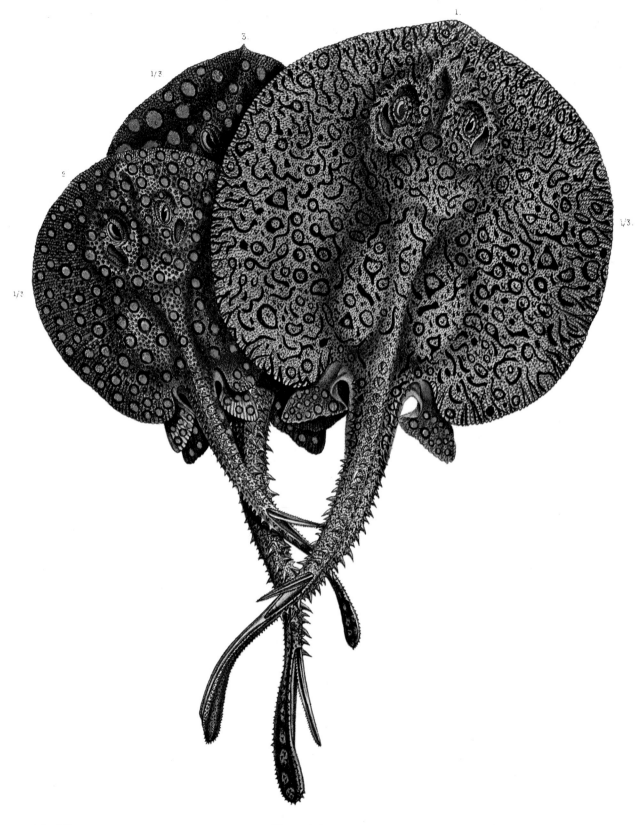

Oudart. Lith. P. Bertrand, éditeur. Lithographie Gény-Gros, Paris.

1. TÆNURA DUMERILII. Cast.   2. TÆNURA MULLERI. Cast.   3. TÆNURA HENLEI. Cast.

At eleven the next morning they came to an island famous throughout the Lower Orinoco for its annual harvest of turtle eggs. After the desolation they had grown used to since leaving San Fernando, the bustle of the crowds on the turtle island struck them as very curious. Three hundred Indians were encamped there, each tribal group distinguishable by the pigments with which their skins were painted, and among them were a number of white men—mostly small traders from the down-river town of Angostura. The arrival of Humboldt's expedition, with their foreign accents, strange clothes and peculiar equipment, caused understandable consternation among the tumultuous crowd of Spaniards and Indians there. A missionary pushed himself forward and asked them why they had come. 'How can anyone possibly believe', he said, 'that you've left your own country to come here and be eaten by mosquitoes and measure lands that don't belong to you?' And he proceeded to give them a highly exaggerated account of the sufferings they would have to endure on the Orinoco beyond the cataracts. Don Nicolas Sotto, the local governor's brother-in-law, soon allayed his suspicions, however, and during their short stay on the island Humboldt was able to learn something about the remarkable harvest of eggs.

Three feet below the sand lay a continuous stratum of turtles' eggs stretching as far as the eye could see along the shore. It was like a mining area, the claims staked out and the lots worked over with immense thoroughness. Every March, at the period of shallowest water on the Lower Orinoco, huge colonies of turtles arrived at three specific islands to lay their eggs in holes they scraped in the sand. Every April several hundred Indians of different tribes came from far and wide to set up their camps on the islands to collect the eggs and reduce them to oil. Formerly, the egg harvest was supervised by the Jesuit missionaries, who had been careful to ensure that a proportion of the eggs was left undisturbed and allowed to hatch. However, their successors, the Franciscans, took no such precautions. They allowed as many eggs as possible to be gathered and Humboldt noted that as a result the harvest of eggs was getting less each year. Nevertheless, the quantity of eggs was still prodigious. Humboldt was told that the three islands of the Lower Orinoco produced a total of 5,000 jars of turtle oil each year. He estimated that 33 million eggs were required to produce this amount, or 330,000 turtles laying an average of 100 eggs each. But the number of eggs collected was considerably less than the number of eggs laid. A lot of eggs were broken, some were eaten by the Indians straight away, others hatched out early—Humboldt himself had seen an entire beach swarming with baby turtles an inch in diameter trying to escape the pursuit of the Indian children. All told, he reckoned there were probably about a million turtles laying eggs each year along the Orinoco. Since then, however, even that huge population has been threatened by the mindless rapacity of man, and today the turtles of the Lower Orinoco are almost extinct.

The pilot of Humboldt's boat had found the stop at the turtle beach a good op-

Stingrays abounded in the sandy shallows of the Orinoco

Collecting turtle eggs in the Orinoco

portunity to restock their slender store of provisions and managed to obtain fresh meat, rice and biscuits for the white men, together with a boat-load of dried turtle eggs and live baby turtles for himself and the other Indians. He seems to have been a conceited kind of man because when they eventually set off again at four o'clock that afternoon he tried to show off his watermanship to all the Indians on the beach and nearly brought the whole expedition to a disastrous end as a result.

His aim had been to prove that by sailing close to the wind he could reach the middle of the river—which was over four miles wide at this point—on a single tack. The deeply laden canoe carried sail very badly, however, and the wind was blowing in dangerous squalls. At the very moment when he was boasting of his skill and boldness a squall caught the sail and threw the canoe on her beam ends. Humboldt was writing up his journal on a little table at the stern when the water suddenly washed over it and nearly carried the journal away. Bonpland was lying asleep in the middle of the canoe when he was rudely awakened by the rush of water and the shouts of the Indians. He was in time to see his dried plants and papers all afloat and the first volume of Schreber's *Genera Plantarum* sailing away on its long journey to the Caribbean Sea. Humboldt, who couldn't swim, was for one of the few occasions in his life helpless. It was Bonpland who became the hero of the moment. He remained completely cool and composed and offered to swim to the shore with Humboldt on his back if the worst came to the worst. But he saw that the lee-side was righting itself gradually during the squall and decided that all was not yet lost. The next few minutes proved him correct. The cordage of the sail suddenly gave way, the sail itself went about and the canoe came back on an even keel. The danger had passed. They baled out the flooded boat with calabashes, cursed the pilot roundly and in half an hour had restored everything to some kind of ship-shape condition. At nightfall they landed on a barren island in the middle of the river and by the clear light of the moon, seated on large turtle-shells they found scattered about the beach, they ate their supper with more than ordinary thankfulness. In spite of the intense heat of the night, the swarms of mosquitoes, the cries of the jaguars nearby and the absence of trees from which to sling their hammocks, their desert island seemed at that moment a perfect paradise.

On 7 April they found that the current was growing stronger as the river narrowed and the progress of their boat became much slower. They began to suffer from thirst as well, for the waters of this part of the Orinoco were hot and sandy and smelt and tasted very nasty because of the putrified caymans along the banks.

Humboldt and Bonpland in the Orinoco, surrounded by their botanical and zoological specimens

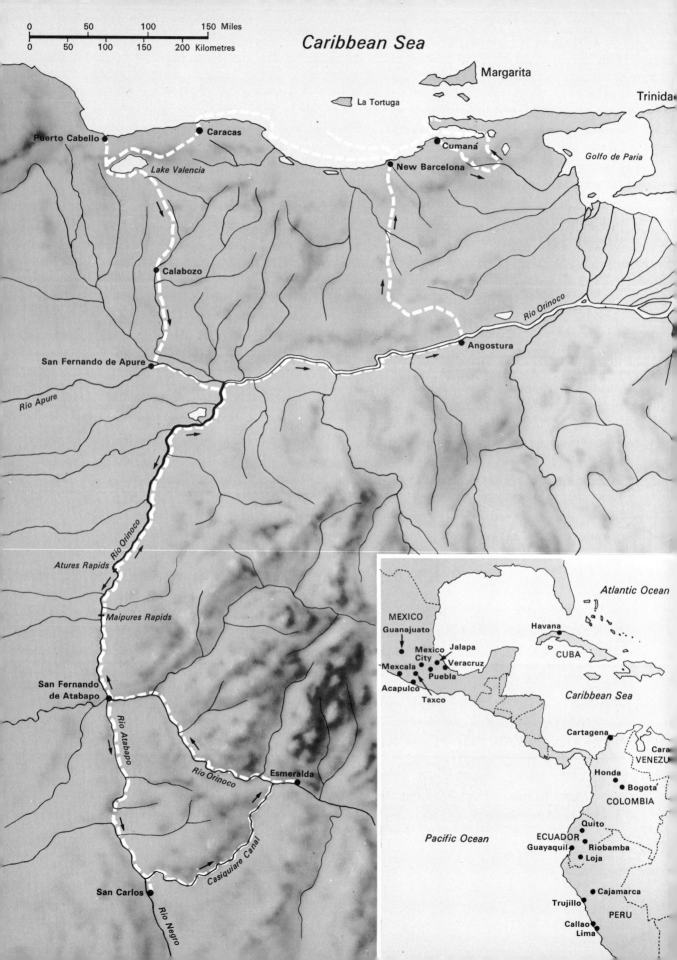

Scale
0 50 100 150 Miles
0 50 100 150 200 Kilometres

Caribbean Sea

Margarita

Trinida

La Tortuga

Puerto Cabello

Caracas

Cumana

New Barcelona

Golfo de Paria

Lake Valencia

Calabozo

Rio Orinoco

Angostura

San Fernando de Apure

Rio Apure

Rio Orinoco

Atures Rapids

Maipures Rapids

San Fernando de Atabapo

Rio Atabapo

Rio Orinoco

Esmeralda

Casiquiare Canal

San Carlos

Rio Negro

Inset map

Atlantic Ocean

MEXICO

Guanajuato

Mexico City

Jalapa

Veracruz

Mexcala

Puebla

Acapulco

Taxco

Havana

CUBA

Caribbean Sea

Cartagena

Cara

VENEZU

Honda

Bogota

COLOMBIA

Pacific Ocean

Quito

ECUADOR

Guayaquil

Riobamba

Loja

Cajamarca

Trujillo

Callao

Lima

PERU

Early the next morning they came to a place called Pararuma, where there was another encampment of turtle-egg harvesters, and here they found the missionary-monks of Carichana and the Great Cataracts seated on the ground, playing at cards and smoking long pipes. Their ample blue garments, their shaven heads, and their long beards made them look like natives of the Orient, but their pale and emaciated features—the result of malaria from which they had been suffering for several months—made it clear that they hailed from the unhealthy forests of the Orinoco.

This chance encounter was a fortunate one for Humboldt and Bonpland. One of the priests, Father Bernardo Zea, missionary of Atures and Maipures near the Great Cataracts, volunteered to guide them to the Rio Negro and back, and since the canoe that had brought them from San Fernando was too big and heavy to go through the rapids, another missionary agreed to sell them a smaller one at a moderate price.

This new canoe, which was to be their home for two months or more, had been hollowed out of a single enormous tree trunk. It was forty feet long but less than three feet wide, so that only two people could sit side by side in it. Moreover, it was so wobbly that if anyone stood up without warning it capsized. A lattice-work deck covered with a thatch roof—a sort of primitive poop of branches and leaves—had been built at the stern. It was meant to accommodate the four Europeans in the boat (Humboldt, Bonpland, Sotto and Zea) but it was so tiny that they either had to sit bent double or lie flat on their backs on painfully hard ox-hides or jaguar skins, in which position they were unable to see out and their protruding legs were soaked by the rain or broiled by the sun. It was stifling hot inside this uncomfortable structure during the day and full of mosquitoes during the night; they tried to escape their attention by hiding under a sheet or lighting a smoky greenwood fire, but it only made things more uncomfortable. One inconvenience was stowage space. The pilot stood in the stern and the four Indian canoemen occupied the bow portion of the boat, sitting naked two by two and keeping remarkably uniform time with their paddles by means of sad and monotonous songs. A mulatto servant from Cumaná took up the middle portion, along with his cooking utensils and boxes of provisions, while cages containing an ever-growing menagerie of birds and monkeys hung from any available niche. As a result there was nowhere to put the dried plants, sextant, dipping needle and meteorological instruments except in the space beneath the lattice desk, and every time they wanted to open a trunk or take out an instrument they had to paddle ashore and land. It required a good sense of humour and strong tenacity of purpose to put up with conditions like that for long. But Humboldt seemed made for the tropics.

At 10 am on 10 April they set off in their new craft—a departure marred by an unpleasant incident in the early hours of that morning. Only the local Indians knew the way through the labyrinth of the Great Cataracts. To make sure that there was a full crew for the canoe, therefore, the missionary had locked two of the Indians in a kind of stocks for the night and when one of them still refused to accompany the boat he was savagely beaten with a manatee-hide whip. In the early hours of the morning, Humboldt was woken up by his horrifying screams. 'Without these acts of severity,' the priest explained, 'you would want for everything. . . . The Missions would be totally deserted.' A point of view which Humboldt angrily refuted.

> These reasons appear to me more specious than sound. It is because the Indian of the forests is treated like a person in a state of villeinage in the greater part of the Missions, and because he does not enjoy the fruit of his labours, that the Christian establishments on the Orinoco remain deserts. To say that the savage, like the child, can be governed only by force, is merely to establish false analogies. The Indians of the Orinoco are not great children; they are as little so as the poor labourers in the east of Europe, whom the barbarism of our feudal institutions has held in the rudest state.

With the onset of the rains, the river was already rising. As they drew nearer to the rapids their course became more and more obstructed with immense blocks of granite. They had to steer through channels only five feet broad but more than

Indian hunters with a tapir

'The Upper Orinoco remained a land of fable, its source unknown, its numerous tributaries unexplored, its forests inhabited by scattered tribes of savage and mutually antagonistic Indians about whom little was known but their name.'

twenty-five fathoms deep, where the water rushed with a frightening roar and at times their canoes became tightly jammed between rocks. As the strength of the current increased they found it more difficult to make headway against it. On 12 April, the Indian canoemen had to paddle non-stop for twelve and a half hours with only a few plantains and a little cassava to sustain them—a feat of endurance which Humboldt, himself no loafer, found quite remarkable. Whenever progress became totally impossible, the canoemen would jump into the water, make a line fast round the point of a rock, and warp the boat along—a tedious business. It was on these rocks, of all shapes and sizes, rounded, jet black, glossy like lead and bare of vegetation, that they were forced to spend the occasional bleak night, their sleep disturbed by the howling of their dog, the booming of the rapids all around them and the rolling of the distant thunder. From these elevated mid-river perches they could look out over a wild and spectacular landscape: huge piles of granite blocks, vast sandy shores, forests and distant mountains.

Late on the night of 15 April the party reached the foot of the Atures and Maipures rapids, the Great Cataracts. These forty miles of shattered rocks and violent water—

one of the longest and most perilous sets of rapids in South America—marked the end of navigation for shipping along the Lower Orinoco. For centuries they had sealed off the unexplored interior of Venezuela from the populated coastlands to the north. Only light canoes in the hands of expert local Indian watermen could enter that treacherous labyrinth and hope to reach the calm waters at the other end.. Usually the canoes became waterlogged in the process, often they capsized and on occasions were smashed to pieces against the rocks so that the Indians, battered and bleeding, had to swim for their lives. If progress by water became impossible then the canoes had to be manhauled with immense difficulty over land.

Humboldt and Bonpland spent two days at Father Zea's humble house at Atures while the Indians struggled to haul the unladen canoe through the cataracts. They found the small mission, a mile or so from the river, in the most deplorable state. The Indian population was reduced to less than fifty—partly due to the 'guilty practice of preventing pregnancy by the use of deleterious herbs'—and they lived in wretched conditions and suffered continually from sickness. Father Zea himself had been ill with his *calenturita*, his 'little fever', for eight months and was often attacked with fits of malaria during the journey. Moreover, it was abominably hot and clouds of biting insects filled the air so thickly that Humboldt was unable to see the sky through his astronomical instruments.

From now on, in fact, the insects were to become the dominating factor in their lives. Father Zea, after observing that there were fewer insects above a height of fifteen feet, had built a kind of tree house where it was possible to breathe more freely, and every evening Humboldt and Bonpland used to climb up a ladder to this refuge in order to dry their plants and write up their journals. Even so, they were beginning to suffer visibly from the immense quantity of bites they had received at Atures, and their hands had swollen considerably.

People who have not navigated the great rivers of equinoctial America, can scarcely conceive how, at every instant, without intermission, you may be tormented by insects flying in the air; and how the multitude of these little animals may render vast regions almost uninhabitable. It is impossible not to be constantly disturbed by the mosquitoes, zancudos, jejenes, and tempraneros, that cover the face and hands, pierce the clothes with their long needle-formed suckers, and getting into the mouth and nostrils, cause coughing and sneezing whenever any attempt is made to speak in the open air. In the missions of the Orinoco, in the villages on the banks of the river, surrounded by immense forests, the plague of the mosquitoes affords an inexhaustible subject of conversation. When two persons meet in the morning, the first questions they address to each other are: 'How did you find the zancudos during the night? How are we today for the mosquitoes?'

In the Great Cataracts this suffering may be said to attain its maximum. I doubt whether there is a country on earth where man is exposed to more cruel torments in the rainy season. What appeared to us very remarkable is that at different hours of the day you are stung by distinct species. From half past six in the morning till five at night the air is filled with a tiny biting fly called jejen. An hour before sunset the tempraneros, a species of small gnat, take their place. Their presence scarcely lasts an hour and a half; they disappear between six and seven in the

'When the forest was flooded they shortcut the river bends by navigating through narrow channels between the trees.'

evening, or, as they say here, after the Angelus. After a few minutes' repose, you feel yourself stung by zancudos, another species of gnat with very long legs. The zancudos, the proboscis of which contains a sharp-pointed sucker, causes the most acute pain, and a swelling that remains several weeks. The Indians pretend to distinguish the zancudos and the tempraneros 'by their song'. At fixed and invariable hours, the air is peopled with new inhabitants, and we might guess blindfold the hour of the day or night by the hum of the insects, and by their stings.

It is neither the dangers of navigating in small boats, nor the savage Indians, nor the serpents, crocodiles, or jaguars, that make Spaniards dread a voyage on the Orinoco; it is as they say with simplicity, '*el sudar y las moscas*' (the sweat and the flies).

Some of the devices for escaping these insect hordes were as ingenious as Father Zea's tree house. Some Indian tribes slept in little clay ovens full of smoke from a wet brushwood fire—Bonpland used to creep into these suffocating places to dry his plants. Others buried themselves up to the neck in sand and covered the face with a cloth. Some daubed themselves with mud or turtle oil, others recommended the insect-repellant qualities of a putrescent crocodile or smouldering cow-dung. In the Great Cataracts the Indians took refuge at night on rocks in the middle of the river, and Humboldt himself suggested that Europeans might travel sealed inside linen bags stiffened with whalebone hoops. But for the most part the only effective thing a man could do during the tortured hours of daylight was wave his arms about and slap himself. 'The more you stir yourself,' the missionaries would say, 'the less you'll be stung.' The Indians, Humboldt noted, automatically slapped each other in their hammocks even in their sleep.

On the evening of the 16 April, the travellers heard that the canoe had been safely negotiated through the Atures rapids. The next morning they set out along the bank to rejoin it and after two arduous days on the river reached Father Zea's mission at Maipures—a solitary place, full of the distant roar of the cataracts but mercifully free of insects.

The rapids of Maipures were even grander and wilder than the Atures, and Humboldt and Bonpland never tired of gazing down on them from the top of a nearby hill. For several miles the broad bed of the river was filled with an archipelago of islands—massive iron-black rocks covered in luxuriant forest trees and joined together by granite dikes. Through the narrow channels between the islands and over the falls formed by the dikes the river roared and swirled in a series of torrential cataracts. The surface of the water was a sheet of foam, and a thick mist, a whitish fog, hung over it for as far as the eye could see. In the evening the refracted sunlight formed rainbows which appeared and disappeared among the falls like will-o'-the-wisps—an exquisite optical illusion. The noise of this enormous weight of falling water was deafening, especially at night.

Beyond the Great Cataracts an unknown land began. All that Humboldt knew about it was what he had learnt by hearsay, for nothing had ever been written about it by anyone who had ever been there. Even at the time of his visit, nearly 300 years after Diego de Ordaz first nosed his way into the Orinoco and Sir Walter Raleigh ventured along its lower reaches in search of El Dorado, there were only half a dozen white men living there in the space of 300 miles—simple missionaries who believed the stories the Indians told them about men with dogs' heads or mouths below their navels or eyes in the middle of the forehead, and propagated these stories in the civilized world—'The padres have seen them, but far far above the Great Cataracts!' The Upper Orinoco remained a land of fable, its source unknown, its numerous tributaries unexplored, its forests inhabited by scattered tribes of savage and mutually antagonistic Indians about whom little was known but their name. 'After leaving my Mission,' the monk at Uruana had told Humboldt, 'you will travel like mutes.' The variety of languages spoken on the banks of the Meta, the Orinoco, the Casiquiare and the Rio Negro was so prodigious that a traveller, no matter how great his talent for learning languages, could never learn enough to make himself understood. So Humboldt and Bonpland, the first trained observers ever to enter this unobserved world, had to pursue their enquiries by means of sign language and such information as a handful of credulous monks chose to give them.

They spent two and a half days at Maipures and finally departed on 21 April. By now some of the novelty seems to have warn off the Orinoco expedition as each dawn produced the same heat, the same flies, the same riverine landscape. Dourly, they settled down to endure the weeks of hardship that lay ahead—the acute discomfort of their crowded canoe, propelled with agonizing slowness, inch by inch, against the force of the current; the poor, monotonous diet; and the long, hot, equatorial nights on the uninhabited banks of the river, where they were exposed to rainstorms and wild animals alike. Perhaps their preoccupation with their work kept them happier than they might otherwise have been, for they were tirelessly busy—Bonpland with his plant collection, Humboldt with his endless measurements of river temperature, ground temperature, air temperature, barometric pressure, magnetic dip, longitude and latitude.

As the days passed they drew nearer and nearer to the watershed between the Amazon basin and the Orinoco. On the night of 24 April they left the Orinoco altogether and turned right into a tributary, the Rio Atabapo, a so-called 'black water' river. When dawn broke the next morning it seemed to Humboldt as if they had been transported to a totally different country.

Everything had changed—the constitution of the atmosphere, the colour of the water, the species of the trees that covered the banks. They no longer suffered the torments of the jejenes during the day and beyond the Mission of San Fernando de Atabapo the zancudos disappeared at night altogether. The water of the Orinoco, a so-called 'white-water' river, had been muddy and smelled faintly of musk— often Humboldt had had to strain it through a linen cloth before drinking it. By contrast, the 'black-water' of the Atabapo was pure, cool, odourless and delicious to drink. The smallest fish were visible at a depth of twenty or thirty feet and sometimes the travellers could see the bottom of the river too—a quartzose and granitic sand of dazzling whiteness. 'Nothing', Humboldt wrote, 'can be compared with the beauty of the Atabapo.'

From 26 to 30 April the expedition continued its course along this delightful river—accompanied on occasion by fourteen-foot-long anacondas swimming along-side—then turned off into the Rio Temi, a smaller black-water stream. The forest was flooded at this point and the Indian canoemen were able to shortcut the river bends by navigating through narrow channels between the trees, hacking their way forward with a machete whenever the channel was blocked by vegetation. Once, in the thickest part of the forest, they found themselves surrounded by a school of fresh-water dolphins blowing spouts of compressed air and water—a remarkable spectacle 1,200 miles from the mouths of the Orinoco and the Amazon.

Finally, on 30 April, they reached the junction of the Temi and a still-smaller black-water stream, the Tuamini. Heading south-west down the Tuamini in the direction of the headwaters of the Amazon's great tributary, the Rio Negro, they came at length to the Mission station of Javita. This was their last port of call in the Orinoco—at least on the outward part of the journey—for at this lonely mission they were able to obtain the Indian labour necessary to haul their canoe seven miles through the forest across an isthmus of land separating the Rio Tuamini in the Orinoco basin from the little Caño Pimichin in the Amazon basin. This portage was reckoned to take four days and during the enforced stop Humboldt took the opportunity to have some painful egg-sacs dug out of his feet—they had been laid there by a burrowing sandfly called a chegoe—and to explore the surrounding forest. Many of the trees were magnificent specimens more than a hundred feet high, but botany caused the explorers more frustration than satisfaction, for most of the leaves and flowers were up in the forest canopy far beyond their reach. The Indians didn't help much. 'All these great trees', they repeated endlessly, 'bear neither flowers nor fruits.' They were like the botanists of antiquity, Humboldt complained, who denied what they had not taken the trouble to observe. They were tired of his questions, and exhausted his patience in return. They did manage to produce some samples of native wild rubber for him, though, and showed him how to use it in place of cork stoppers for his specimen jars.

Every day they went to see how the canoe was getting on at the portage. Twenty-three Indians were employed in dragging it overland using branches of trees as rollers—the canoe was heavier than most and special care was needed not to damage the bottom. Humboldt spent some of the time composing a formal letter to King Carlos IV in Madrid. If the portage was replaced by a canal, he wrote, then com-munications between the Portuguese possessions on the Amazon and the Spanish ones on the Orinoco would be made very much easier. He even blazed the trees along the route the projected canal would take. The missionary at Javita meanwhile did the best he could to make his unexpected guests comfortable.

At last, on 5 May, their canoe reached the Pimichin and the next morning at sunrise

'They were accompanied by occasional fourteen-foot anacondas swimming alongside.'

the expedition re-embarked. According to Humboldt the Pimichin twisted and turned more than any other river in America except the Rio Chagres in Panama, and was said to have a total of eighty-five bends to it. Not surprisingly, therefore, it took them four and a half hours paddling, going *with* the current this time, before they finally entered the Rio Negro, one of the greatest and most beautiful of all the rivers of the Amazon.

It was a delicious moment. The morning was cool and lovely. After a voyage of thirty-six days in a narrow canoe, bitten by flies, soaked by storms, endangered by rapids and falls, they were now within reach of their goal.

But there was still another thousand miles of dangerous waters in front of them before they reached their journey's end.

'More bothersome were the jaguars, huge beasts which were much feared by the Indians.'

CHAPTER II

The Lost World of the Casiquiare

On 7 May the expedition reached San Carlos, a small military post at the Brazil-Venezuela frontier on the Rio Negro. They were now almost half way between the mouth of the Orinoco and the mouth of the Amazon, and for a moment Humboldt was tempted to go the whole hog and sail all the way down the Rio Negro and along the Amazon to the Atlantic seaboard of Brazil. It was just as well he eventually decided against this plan, however, for the Portuguese authorities in Brazil had somehow got wind of his expedition to the Rio Negro and had issued a warrant for his arrest as a spy and political undesirable—'a foreigner who might possibly conceal plans for the spread of new ideas and dangerous principles among the faithful subjects of this realm at a time when the temper of the nation is in a condition so dangerous and so difficult to deal with.' Following his arrest Humboldt was to have been deported to Lisbon, but fortunately this eventuality never arose, for after a stay of only three days the expedition left San Carlos at the start of its return journey to the Caribbean coast of Venezuela—this time by way of the enigmatic Casiquiare canal.

On 10 May, only eight miles above San Carlos, the expedition turned right into the Casiquiare and began its journey through a lost world that half the armchair geographers of Europe believed could not exist. In fact, there was no more tangible proof of the reality of this unique waterway than the sudden and almost overwhelming onslaught of the insects that greeted them as soon as they left the Negro, for the Casiquiare carried the so-called white-water of the Orinoco and as a result the air seethed with insects of every kind, especially the tiny, agonizing jejen.

Humboldt was anxious not to stray too far from the mouth of the Casiquiare before he had taken an astronomical sighting of its position and they therefore spent the first night at the small Mission of San Francisco Solano, a little way up-stream. Here he was able to purchase from the Indians two additions to his travelling menagerie—a very young, highly mischievous toucan and a glorious hyacinth macaw. Humboldt's floating zoo was by now very large. Apart from their dog and their new purchases, it included seven parrots, two brilliantly coloured manakins, another brilliant jay-like bird called a motmot, two wild jungle hens called guans, two civet-like little mammals called manaviris, and eight monkeys—two spider monkeys; two nocturnal monkeys; a black-headed, short-tailed cacajao; a viudita and two tiny squirrel monkeys or titis. Father Zea whispered some complaints at the almost daily increase in the animal population of their small canoe, especially as some of the creatures were free to run around as they pleased, but Humboldt and Bonpland gained hours of pleasure from their curious antics, which sometimes amused them so much that they forgot the torment of the mosquitoes.

The newly acquired toucan, for example, which Humboldt thought had the manners and intelligence of a raven, soon made itself thoroughly at home on board the boat, stealing anything it could lay its great beak on and teasing the melancholy and irritable nocturnal monkeys remorselessly. The most popular creatures on board, however, were the titis. These elegant, beautifully coloured little monkeys, with their golden yellow hair and large round eyes, had brains which were relatively larger than a man's and faces remarkably like a child's—there was the same expression of innocence, the same playful smile, the same rapid transition from joy to sorrow, the same tears when they were frightened. Whenever it looked like rain they took shelter in the wide sleeves of Father Zea's Franciscan habit, and they were extremely fond of insects, especially spiders. One of them was clever enough to be able to distinguish the various insects illustrated in Cuvier's *Tableau Elémentaire d'Histoire Naturelle*. When Humboldt showed it the eleventh plate in this learned tome, which contained black and white engravings of grasshoppers and wasps, the titi shot out its hand in the hope of catching one, but it remained totally indifferent when it was shown engravings of skeletons or animal heads.

These twenty-five birds and animals, in the company of their thirteen human companions, left Solano in their crowded little boat quite late the next morning, but as there was every indication of an improvement in the weather the party did not attempt to travel far and at five in the evening they stopped near a solitary granite rock called Culimacari. For the first time for many days the skies were clear and Humboldt was able to make a good observation of latitude by the Southern Cross and determine the longitude with his chronometer by taking the altitudes of the two beautiful stars that shine at the feet of Centaur. These observations established with sufficient precision for the purposes of geography the position of the rock of Culimacari and hence the junction of the Casiquiare with the Rio Negro. Humboldt had thus achieved the main purpose of his expedition in the Upper Orinoco and confirmed once and for all the existence of this phenomenon, the only natural waterway in the world connecting two gigantic river systems.

Humboldt himself had never doubted its existence, nor for the last fifty years or so had anyone in Venezuela. Only in Europe was it denied. In 1798 the French geographer Philippe Buache, the first one ever to make use of contour lines, had published a map of the area which deliberately omitted the canal, noting: 'The long supposed connection between the Orinoco and the Amazon is a monstrous error in geography. To rectify the ideas entertained on this point, it is only necessary to observe the direction of the great chain of mountains which separates the water.'

The junction of the Casiquiare canal and the Orinoco (foreground).
Humboldt turned left to reach Esmeralda

But there were no mountains and as long ago as 1744 a certain Father Manuel Roman, a Spanish Jesuit, had sailed from the Orinoco to the Negro and back via the Casiquiare, while two or three canoes each year for the last thirty years had been taking salt and soldiers' pay to the garrison at San Carlos by the same route. What Humboldt had done, at the expense of much hardship, was to obtain proof of the position of this inland delta in the form of astronomical fixes which he could take back to Europe. All that was left for him to do now was to reach the coast safely again—with the possibility, if circumstances permitted, of a diversion towards the source of the Orinoco.

At half past one in the morning of 12 May, therefore, the expedition left the rock of Culimacari with the object of traversing the two hundred miles of the unhealthy Casiquiare as quickly as possible. But there was an 8 mph current against them now and it took fourteen hours of non-stop paddling to reach their next port of call, the tiny mission of Mandavaca, only ten miles away.

The missionary at Mandavaca had spent twenty years in the Casiquiare—an unbelievable penance—and his legs were so spotted with insect bites, notably the dried pin-head scabs of the jejen, that the original colour of the skin was no longer discernable. He spoke to his visitors of his loneliness—there were only two hundred inhabitants along the entire length of the canal, all of them Indians—and of the barbarity of the local tribes, whose atrocious crimes he was often forced to leave unpunished. A few years previously, for example, a neighbouring chief had fattened one of his wives and then eaten her, and even the best and gentlest tribes in his Mission quite frequently lapsed into periods of indiscriminate slaughter and cannibalism. Humboldt was soon to discover for himself just how widespread the practice of cannibalism was in this region. He had recently taken into his service a fugitive Indian from the Rio Negro—a quiet, affectionate and intelligent young man who was very helpful in setting up the instruments used for the nightly astronomical observations. Humboldt was talking with this young man through an interpreter one day when the conversation came round to the subject of monkey meat. To Humboldt's consternation, the Indian declared: 'The meat of the marimonde monkey, though blacker, tastes very like human flesh.' As if that wasn't enough, the Indian with gestures of savage gratification, went on: 'The part of a man my tribe likes best is the inside of the hands.' Whether Humboldt retained the Indian's services after that he never made clear, but there is no further mention of him.

During the week following their departure from Mandavaca the conditions along the Casiquiare seem to have become too much even for Humboldt. Defeated by rain and insects he appears to have given up his diary and concentrated all his energies on simply enduring.

> From the 14th to the 21st of May we slept constantly in the open air; but I cannot indicate the spots where we halted. These regions are so wild, and so little frequented, that with the exception of a few rivers, the Indians were ignorant of the names of all the objects which I set by the compass.

'No outpost of Spain was remoter, more impoverished or more dreaded than Esmeralda. In Humboldt's day it marked the end of the known world and was regarded as a place of banishment.'

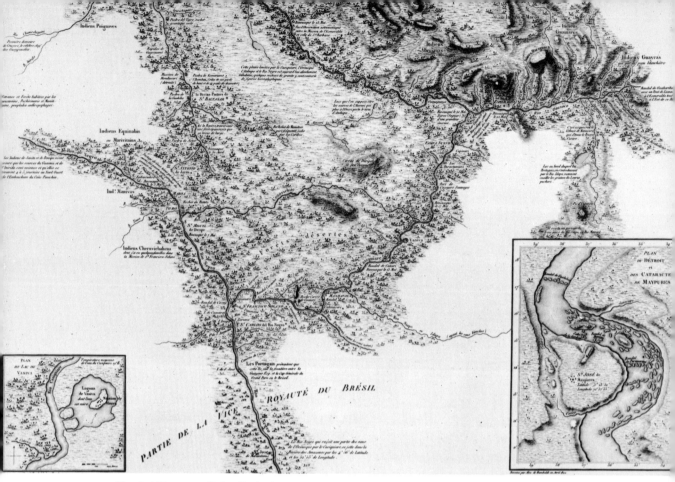

Humboldt's map of the Casiquiare canal. From his Atlas géographique et physique du Nouveau Continent

No observation of a star helped me to fix the latitude within the space of a degree. Our passage grew more troublesome the nearer we approached to the bifurcation of the Orinoco. The luxuriance of the vegetation increased in a way which even those who are familiar with tropical forests would find difficult to imagine. There was no longer a bank; a palisade of tufted trees formed the margin of the river. All you could see was a canal four hundred yards broad, bordered by two enormous walls clothed in lianas and foliage. We often tried to land, but without success. Towards sunset we would sail along for an hour seeking to discover, not an opening (since none exists), but a spot less wooded, where our Indians could clear space enough for a resting place for twelve or thirteen persons. It was impossible to pass the night in the canoe; the mosquitoes, which tormented us during the day, accumulated toward evening beneath the palm-leaf roof which served to shelter us from the rain. Our hands and faces had never been so swollen before. Father Zea, who had till then boasted of having in his missions at the cataracts the largest and fiercest mosquitoes, at length gradually acknowledged that the sting of the insects of the Casiquiare was the most painful he had ever felt. Though we were in the middle of a dense forest, we experienced great difficulty in finding wood to make a fire, as the branches of the trees in those equatorial regions were so full of sap that they would scarcely burn; and as there was no bare shore it was hardly possible to procure old wood. However, we only required fire as a defence against the beasts of the forest; for we had such a scarcity of provisions that we had little need for fuel on which to cook our food.

It is not generally realized that the primeval rain forests of South America, seemingly so fertile, are actually a kind of desert in which it is quite possible to starve to death. Humboldt's expedition, in fact, was in a fairly desperate position at this point, and they were reduced to eating ants and small portions of dry cacao, ground without sugar and washed down with a large quantity of river water, which deadened their appetites for several hours. But somehow they continued to remain cheerful and each day that passed brought them nearer to the Orinoco and the long run home. On 20 May they spent their last night on the Casiquiare—a night marred by a tragic accident to one of the most faithful members of their party.

The spot they had chosen for their camp was very near the bifurcation of the Orinoco. They had hoped at first to make an astronomical observation, as falling stars—the Indians called them the urine of the stars—could be seen through the vapours that veiled the sky. But before long the clouds thickened and they decided to turn in. At some time during the middle of the night Humboldt was woken by the Indians who warned him that they had heard very near by the cries of a jaguar. It had been attracted by the noise and smell of the dog which began at first to bark and then to howl and hid under the hammocks. As the camp fires were burning brightly Humboldt was not very concerned at the situation but the next morning he was grief-stricken when he learnt from the Indians that the dog had disappeared. They waited part of the morning in the hope that the animal had only strayed, but all their searching was in vain and it was clear that their constant companion had been carried off by the jaguar.

On 21 May the expedition rejoined the Orinoco. There were still 750 miles to go before they reached the town of Angostura, near the mouth of the river, but they would be going with the current now and this raised their spirits a little.

Grateful as he was to leave the Casiquiare behind him, Humboldt predicted a rosy future for this inhospitable waterway and saw a time when it would fix the

A sketch of a South American catfish, from Humboldt's journal

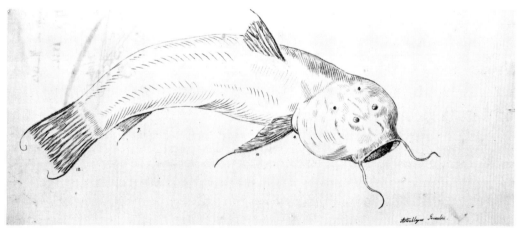

attention of the commercial world as one of the principal trade routes between Venezuela and Brazil, the Andes and the Caribbean Sea. His vision of the Casiquiare of the future, however, was never fulfilled. At the time of the rubber boom in the early 1900's it attracted a few score rubber tappers to its banks, and during World War II it was surveyed by the US Army Corps of Engineers as part of a possible inland route for wild Amazon rubber destined for US ordnance factories. But neither of these ventures ever came to anything and the Casiquiare remains as it has always been, a natural wilderness unchanged since the beginning of time. When the author travelled along it in 1968 it was if anything even more desolate than it had been when Humboldt was there. The jejenes were as maddening as ever, the jaguars as audacious, the forested banks as claustrophobic. But the missions had gone and so had the Indians, and along the 200 mile course of the Casiquiare there lived no more than two other human beings. It was still one of the loneliest and most inhospitable places in the world.

*   *   *

The Upper Orinoco is over a thousand miles from the sea at its junction with the Casiquiare, but it is still more than a quarter of a mile wide. A beautiful mountain range called Sierra Duida rises to a height of 8,500 feet on its right bank, and at the south-eastern foot of the mountain, twenty miles upstream from the Casiquiare, lies the tiny mission settlement of Esmeralda. This was Humboldt's next port of call.

There was no missionary at Esmeralda and the nearest one was over 150 miles away at Santa Barbara. An old officer was in charge of the place and he gave Humboldt and his party a hearty welcome, taking them for Catalonian shopkeepers who had arrived at his benighted domain for purposes of trade. When he saw their packages of paper intended for drying plants, he smiled at their simple ignorance. 'There's not much call for this kind of merchandise', he told them. 'We don't write much here. And when we want to wrap up our valuables—needles and fish hooks and things like that—we make do with leaves.' This old officer was in charge of both civil and ecclesiastical matters. He taught the children the Rosary, he rang the bells to amuse himself, and in his enthusiasm for the service of the church, he sometimes used his chorister's wand in a manner not very agreeable to the natives.

Esmeralda—so called because some veins of coloured quartzite in the foothills were once mistaken for precious stones—is a lovely place to look at. A wide and grassy plain, crossed by numerous streams of sweet, clear water, stretches from the river to the sheer blue flanks of the mountain, and wild plantains and pineapples of enormous size grow in abundance there. From the tops of the rocky outcrops and scattered hills the traveller can look across miles of open country and wander freely for hours; after the close confines of the forest, such physical freedom seems wonderful.

But, alas, it took Humboldt only a very short time to discover that Esmeralda was a terrible place to live in. In his day it marked the end of the known world of the Spaniards, and beyond this point there were no more white settlements and only the haziest notions of the lie of the land. No outpost of Spain was remoter, more impoverished or more dreaded than Esmeralda. Clouds of biting insects obscured the sky every day of the year, and in some seasons there was nothing to eat but howler monkey flesh and flour made from ground fish bones. Among the padres of the missions it was regarded as a place of banishment, a hell on earth, where a man was sent to be condemned to the mosquitoes.

But Esmeralda was also the most celebrated spot on the Orinoco for the manufacture of the famous poison—curare—which the Indians employed to kill or paralyse men and animals and to cure stomach ache. Though the existence of this product had been known since Raleigh's time, Humboldt was the first traveller to observe the precise method of preparation—it was normally kept a closely guarded secret—and to take samples of it back to Europe. Luckily, he had reached Esmeralda on the same day that most of the Indians returned from an up-river excursion to collect the liana from which the curare is made. Less luckily, all of these Indians were soon blind drunk and remained so for the next two days. All, that is, except one.

He was the chemist of the place, and known throughout the mission as the poison master. His hut was as neat and orderly as a chemistry laboratory and he seemed flattered by the interest the European scientists took in his chemical processes. 'I am well aware,' he told them, with a self-sufficient air and a tone of pedantry, 'that the whites have the secret of making soap and manufacturing that black powder which has the defect of making a noise when used for killing animals. But the curare which we prepare is superior to anything you can make on your side of the ocean. It is the juice of a herb which kills silently, without anyone knowing where the stroke comes from.'

Step by step the poison master of Esmeralda showed Humboldt and Bonpland his technique for converting a harmless liana called *bejuco de mavacure* (a plant of the *Strychnos* genus) into a black, sticky, tar-like venom. Then, with the selfless zeal of all true experimenters, Humboldt and Bonpland swallowed several small doses of this lethal substance and found the taste 'an agreeable bitter'. As the poison only takes effect when it enters the blood stream, they were careful to check that neither their gums nor their lips were bleeding, but in spite of all their precautions Humboldt nearly met with a fatal accident a few days later. A jar of curare which he had packed with his personal effects had spilt on to some clothing, and the toe of one of his stockings was saturated with the stuff. He realized this as he was about to put the stocking on and was thus able to save himself from what would probably have been certain death, for his feet were bleeding from wounds made by chegoes at the time.

The belligerency of the fierce Guaica and Guaharibo Indians up-stream from Esmeralda compelled Humboldt and Bonpland to abandon their half-formed plan to reach the source of the Orinoco and they got ready to leave on the long voyage down stream instead. They were now in poor physical shape. The insects, bad food, and cramped, damp conditions in their boat had taken their toll, and without being positively ill, they felt weak and lethargic. Their departure on 23 May was delayed until mid-afternoon while the crew tried to remove the innumerable swarms of ants that had infested the palm-thatch roof of their boat. Then, without any sighs of regret, they pushed off and entrusted themselves to the current of the great river as it swirled remorselessly down towards the sea.

As the Orinoco was free from shoals, the Indian pilot kept going all night, abandoning the boat to the stream. Apart from the time they spent on shore, preparing their

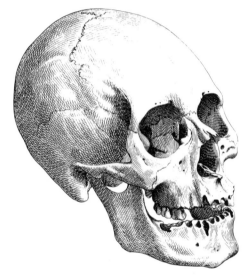

Skull of an extinct Atures Indian. Humboldt took the skull from the burial cave of Ataruipe and later J. F. Blumenbach made this engraving of it for his pioneer work on human physical types

food of plantains and rice, they took only thirty-five hours between Esmeralda and Santa Barbara, travelling at an average speed of nearly four miles an hour. During the last few days of May they again entered the roar and tumble of the Great Cataracts and before sunset on the 31st landed on the eastern bank of the Atures rapids in order to visit the sepulchre of the extinct Atures tribe—the cavern of Ataruipe.

The cave was located in a wild valley some distance from the river and Humboldt counted nearly six hundred well-preserved skeletons inside it. Each skeleton rested in a basket like a square bag, the size depending on the age of the dead, and all of them were so complete that not a rib or a tibia was missing. The Indians with Humboldt explained that the corpses had probably been buried in a damp ground to rot and after some months the bones taken out, scraped clean with sharp stones, and treated in one of three ways—either whitened in the sun, dyed red with *onoto*, or varnished like mummies with scented resins and wrapped in leaves.

None of the bones was of very great antiquity—probably no more than a hundred years old—and they belonged almost exclusively to the Atures, whose last few remaining families had still been living only thirty years before.

Humbolt took several skulls and the skeletons of a child of six and two full-grown men from the cavern of Ataruipe, and they caused him a lot of embarrassment on the return journey to Cumaná. Although he had disguised them in newly-woven matting and insisted that they were only manatee and crocodile bones, he was astonished to find that the Indians he met en route were able to smell the resin with which the bones had originally been coated and to recognize it as that of their old relations. It required the intervention of the local missionaries to overcome the

An Indian inhaling drugs through his nose (right foreground). The Ottomacs were addicted to a hallucigenic drug called niopo *which threw them into a state of madness*

Indians' aversion to handling such a macabre cargo.

The party stopped at Atures no longer than the time it took to pass their canoe through the Great Cataracts for the last time. The bottom of this frail vessel was now so thin that it required great care not to split it and obviously it would never go on another voyage again. Father Zea left the expedition here to rejoin his mission and though he still suffered from malaria it had become a habitual evil to which he paid little attention. Most of the Indians of his mission had gone down with some kind of dangerous contagion and were so ill they could not even leave their hammocks to obtain food. It seemed at first that the expedition might reach journey's end without any major illness but only a few days after leaving Atures it became obvious that Bonpland was sickening for something. He needed rest but instead he insisted on tramping about along the river bank on long plant-collecting trips and was wet to the skin several times a day.

On 5 June the party reached Uruana again and stayed at the mission inhabited by the Ottomac Indians. Humboldt found the Ottomacs a tribe in the rudest state and an ill-looking, savage, vindictive, restless, turbulent people, with unbridled passion, notoriously difficult to govern and addicted not only to drink but also to an hallucigenic drug called *niopo* which threw them into a state of madness. But what particularly distinguished these excessively unattractive folk from their neighbours was one of the most extraordinary physiological phenomena he had ever come across.

> They eat earth; that is, they swallow every day, for a period of several months, very considerable quantities to appease their hunger, and this practice does not appear to have any injurious effect on their health. They are omnivorous animals in the highest degree. While the waters of the Orinoco are low, they subsist on fish and turtles. When the river rises, however, fishing almost entirely ceases, and it is then very difficult to procure food. During this period, which lasts two or three months, the Ottomacs swallow a prodigious quantity of earth. We found heaps of earth-balls (five or six inches in diameter) in their huts, piled up in pyramids three or four feet high. This they called their principal food at the period when they can seldom procure a lizard, a root of fern, or a dead fish floating on the surface of the water.

On 7 June Humboldt, Bonpland and Don Nicolas de Sotto set out on the last 300 miles of their journey. Two days later Sotto left them to return home cross-country. The great river had altered course now; widening all the time, it passed between forests on the right bank and open *llanos* on the left, and the human population—mostly negroes and whites—greatly increased. Generally they slept on the boat as it drifted down on the current but at Boca del Infierno (Hell's Mouth) they landed to take a sight of the sun and spent the night on a vast beach of fine sand nearby. It was their last night in the open air on the banks of the Orinoco. On 13 June they reached journey's end, the town of Angostura, now called Ciudad Bolívar, in the river straits.

> It would be difficult for me to express the satisfaction we felt on landing. After the life we had led in the forests, our dress was not in the very best order, but nevertheless M. Bonpland and I hastened to present ourselves to the Governor of Guiana. Coming from an almost desert country, we were struck with the bustle of the town, though it contained only six thousand inhabitants. We admired the conveniences which industry and commerce furnish to civilized man. Humble dwellings appeared to us magnificent; and every person with whom we conversed seemed to be endowed with superior intelligence. Long privations give a value to the smallest enjoyments; and I cannot express the pleasure we felt, when we saw for the first time wheaten bread on the Governor's table.

Humboldt, Bonpland and Sotto (who now bows out of history for ever) had successfully completed the first scientific exploration of 1,500 miles of almost unknown territory between the headwater areas of the Amazon and Orinoco basins. They had measured the latitude and longitude of more than 50 places, including

The gas volcanoes of Turbaco in Colombia. From Vues des Cordillères

OVERLEAF *Humboldt and Bonpland set out for their famous climb of Chimborazo, 20,720 feet, then thought to be the highest mountain in the world. The man picking a flower is probably Humboldt. From* Vues des Cordillères

the Casiquiare canal, taken a series of important magnetic readings, and made a huge collection of plants, 12,000 specimens in all, many of them rare or new to science. In every respect the journey had been a remarkable success. Humboldt had been the driving force throughout but in his letters home he was quick to give due credit to the energy, tact and courage of his companion Bonpland. No explorer before Humboldt had ever been so aware of the value of publicity and in one of his letters to Willdenow he permitted himself one or two rather big fibs—well aware of their effect on the public once they were retailed to the newspapers. 'I have travelled 6,433 (sic) miles. We hardly ever entered a hut without encountering the horrible remains of repasts on human flesh!!'

There were setbacks, however, almost as soon as the travellers set foot in Angostura. When they opened their cases of plants to inspect their collection they almost wept. The extreme humidity of the climate had destroyed more than a third of the specimens and the remainder were in danger of suffering the same fate. 'We are daily discovering new insects, destructive to paper and plants. Camphor, turpentine, tar, pitched boards, and other preservatives prove quite unavailing here. Nor have we found any benefit from hanging the cases up in the open air. Our patience is almost exhausted.'

But worse was to come. Almost simultaneously, a few days after their arrival in Angostura, Humboldt, Bonpland and a mulatto servant from Cumaná were laid low by a severe sickness, probably typhoid fever picked up in the forest. The servant passed rapidly into a coma and as rapidly out of it. Humboldt, treating himself with a local remedy of honey and *cortex Angosturae*, the basic ingredient of Angostura Bitters, soon recovered. But poor Bonpland's fever was continual and aggravated by dysentery. For some days his condition was alarming in the extreme and he came near to death; even after the crisis had passed his recovery was extremely slow. 'I can't describe to you the anxiety I felt during his illness', Humboldt wrote to his brother Wilhelm. 'I could never have hoped to meet again with such a loyal and brave and hard-working friend.' It was a month before Bonpland was fit enough to endure the arduous trek across the *llanos* to Nuevo Barcelona. From there they caught a small coaster bound for Cumaná but they were waylaid by a privateer vessel from Halifax and would have been taken all the way to Nova Scotia if a ship of the British naval blockading force had not come up to rescue them. Ironically, the very people Humboldt and Bonpland had done their best to avoid for so long were in the end their means of salvation, and Humboldt was enchanted by the impeccable gentlemanliness of the British officers and their excellent education. It was the end of August 1800 before the two travellers finally reached Cumaná and by then they had been away for the best part of a year. The first phase of the South American expedition was over.

Hummingbirds, called Pichincha Hill Stars, on the slopes of Pichincha.
Painting by John Gould

CHAPTER 12

The Ascent
of Chimborazo

On 24 November 1800, Humboldt and Bonpland set sail for Cuba in a small cargo ship laden with meat. It was not an agreeable voyage. They were alternately delayed by calms and half-capsized by storms, and barely a week out from Venezuela the ship caught fire—an unpleasant event in a small sailing vessel built entirely of wood, though the flames were speedily brought under control. It was nearly Christmas, after a protracted voyage of twenty-five days, when they eventually docked in Havana—then one of the busiest ports in the world and the Spanish colonial navy's most important base.

At this stage Humboldt's expedition plans were to explore the west coast of America as far as the Canadian lakes, go south by way of the Ohio and the Mississippi, still a largely unexplored river in those days, then return to Europe via Mexico, the Philippines and the East Indies. He intended to stay in Cuba only long enough to have a look round the island and to arrange the shipment of his collections home.

The problem of communications with Europe was possibly Humboldt's biggest headache throughout the entire duration of his expedition. It was bad enough at the best of times—ships foundered, ran aground, caught fire, were captured by pirates or otherwise failed to reach their destination—but in this period of war at sea it became precarious in the extreme. The British naval blockade of the European and Caribbean coast was extraordinarily effective. Sailings by Spanish ships were now so infrequent that Humboldt's letters sometimes had to wait in port for many months before they were despatched, and even then he doubted whether more than one in four ever reached their addresses, since the captains of the mailboats were apt to throw the mailbags overboard at the mere mention of the Royal Navy. The return traffic fared no better, and in the space of three years Humboldt actually received from his brother a total of no more than half a dozen letters. 'One is completely cut off from the rest of the world here,' he complained, 'as if one was on the moon.'

Alexander had got into the habit of repeating the same news in several letters. In this way, he argued, *one* of them might get through. In the same way he and Bonpland now divided up their collections and manuscripts in Havana. They kept one small herbarium for their own use, sent a second to France and a third containing 1,600 species of cryptogams and grasses to London via Charleston, USA. Similarly they kept one manuscript description of 1,400 new or rare species of plants for themselves and sent the other through a French vice-consul to Bonpland's brother in La Rochelle. 'Nothing makes me more anxious than the safety of manuscripts and herbariums', Humboldt wrote to Willdenow from Havana. 'It is really quite uncertain, almost unlikely, that both of us, Bonpland and myself, will ever return home alive. How sad if by such misfortune the fruits of all our labours should be lost forever!' In fact, a great many *were* lost. One batch went down off the coast of Guinea. Another—a collection of geological specimens—fell into the hands of the Royal Navy and was acquired, many years later, by Sir Joseph Banks, who offered to return it to its rightful owner.

Humboldt's visit to Cuba was suddenly cut short by an American newspaper report that Captain Baudin had at last set sail from France on his round-the-world voyage and was on his way to Cape Horn and the coast of Peru. When he read this Humboldt immediately abandoned his North American plans and decided to try and join Baudin in Lima. So, on 8 March he and Bonpland set sail from Cuba in a tiny 40-ton coaster and after a tedious voyage of twenty-five days arrived off Cartagena on the mainland of South America. A gale force easterly wind was blowing at the time and this was nearly the end of them.

Trying to butt their way into harbour against the high wind and rough sea, they were suddenly thrown on their beam ends. A tremendous wave broke over the tiny ship and threatened to engulf it and at that moment the helmsman cried out: '*No gobierna el timón!*' (The rudder won't work!). Humboldt gave himself up for lost

Havana from the sea

Rio Magdalena along which Humboldt and Bonpland had to travel to reach the eastern Cordilleras

but the crew managed to cut away a sail and the ship suddenly righted herself on top of another wave and found refuge from the storm behind a promontory.

Clearly it was not Humboldt's night. In order to get a better observation of an eclipse of the moon, he put to shore in a boat, but he and his helpers had barely set foot on *terra firma* when they were startled by the clanking of chains and saw a party of hefty negroes, escaped convicts from Cartagena gaol, rushing down on them with daggers drawn to sieze their boat. Humboldt and the others fled to the water and only just had time to clamber on board and push off from the shore.

Humboldt's speediest route to Lima would have been by sea via the Isthmus of Panama. But at Cartagena he learnt that the trade winds of the Pacific were over for the season and that the voyage could take as long as three months. He therefore chose to reach Lima by way of the infinitely more arduous overland route along the Andes—an itinerary which had the advantages of enabling him to map the country north of the Amazon and compare his plant collections with those of the greatest living authority on South America flora, the botanist José Celestino Mutis, who lived in Bogotá.

The travellers spent three weeks in Cartagena. There they made arrangements to ship their heaviest equipment to Lima by sea and at nearby Turbaco studied a group of curious gas volcanoes, twenty to twenty-five feet high, that belched mud and water every fifteen seconds. Then, on 21 April, at the jetty of Barancas Nuevas, they embarked on the Rio Magdalena for the first leg of their great trek.

144

The difficult pass from Honda to Bogotá

Humboldt, dressed as ever in his tall, turned-over boots, baggy striped trousers and high black hat, and clutching the great barometer he never let far from his sight, with his loyal companion Bonpland at his side and his baggage train with essential instruments bringing up the rear, turned his steps once again towards the interior of South America. After his exploration of the great river system of Venezuela, he was now to direct his energies to the exploration of one of the highest volcanic ranges in the world, the Andes of Colombia, Ecuador and Peru—a two-year expedition that was to make his name famous, once and for all, throughout the world.

The route inland to the foot of the eastern Cordilleras lay almost due south up the Rio Magdalena—a journey of nearly 500 miles through uninhabited forests to the tiny river settlement of Honda. To Humboldt and Bonpland it must have seemed like old times. For more than six weeks they were confined to an Indian canoe, tormented by insects and rained upon incessantly. The river was in full spate and their progress against the strong current was wretchedly slow—on average they advanced little more than ten miles a day. Out of their crew of twenty Indians, eight had to be sent home in a state of exhaustion, while most of the others developed foul-smelling tropical ulcers. Humboldt and Bonpland somehow stayed fit in the midst of this dank equatorial purgatory and kept up with their scientific work, but they were glad to reach the port of Honda towards the middle of June and at last turn their backs on the river.

From Honda the travellers had to climb 9,000 feet to the great plateau on which lay the city of Santa Fé de Bogotá, now the capital of Colombia, where Humboldt hoped to meet Mutis. They were unprepared, however, for the nature of the road they had to travel along, which Humboldt reported as indescribably bad. Though it was one of the principal roads in the country, it had not been improved in three centuries and resembled nothing so much as a watercourse, a path so wretched that in some places it consisted only of steps, 18 to 20 inches wide and almost too narrow for a mule to push through, cut between two walls of rock. As they forced their way higher up this excruciating thoroughfare of the eastern Cordilleras, through woods of walnut, nutmeg and cinchona, poor Bonpland began to go down with malaria and to suffer badly from headache and nausea. It was with some relief that they finally reached the plateau of Bogotá, with its cooling winds and inhabited villages and fields of corn.

The arrival of the expedition had been expected and the day after their arrival on the great plain before the city a cavalcade of finely dressed horsemen rode out to greet them and lead them, as the distinguished visitors of the highly respected Mutis, in triumphal procession into the capital. Humboldt was invited to sit in the archbishop's six-horse, London-built carriage, and behind him came Bonpland in another carriage, while on either side of them trotted a large escort of sixty or more of the leading citizens of Bogotá—an escort which increased considerably in numbers as they drew near to the city. Few scientists can have been accorded such a popular civic reception and Humboldt found the whole thing almost comical. A great crowd of schoolboys and street urchins, running and shouting and pointing, stretched for a quarter of a mile behind the coaches, and every window of every house was crowded with spectators. 'There hadn't been such bustle and tumult in this dead town for years and years', Humboldt noted in his journal with some satisfaction. For few of the inhabitants of Bogotá had seen a foreigner before, still less a heretic who appeared to have come from the other side of the world simply to compare his 'hay' with old Mutis' 'hay'.

> Mutis had made his brother's widow move out so that we had our own house and courtyard, garden and kitchen. In front of the house Mutis himself and his old friends were standing waiting, all dressed up very finely. As I climbed out with my barometer, the instrument I trusted to no one, in my hand, he smiled. We were warmly embraced and Mutis seemed embarrassingly modest in his behaviour towards us. We started talking straightaway about scientific matters. I began to tell of the plants I had seen during the day but he very cleverly steered the conversation round to more general topics so that the others standing nearby could understand. A marvellous banquet had been laid on for us and I just couldn't believe my eyes when the famous Salvador Rizo, to whom Cavanilles had dedicated a plant, appeared as a waiter and served us at table.

Mutis was an old man in his seventieth year when Humboldt met him. Born in Cadiz in 1732, he had become one of the first Spanish disciples of Linnaeus before he emigrated to Colombia in 1760. There his study of quinine and malaria control and his exhaustive work on South American flora as leader of the Royal Botanical

Mutisia grandiflora from Plantes équinoxiales *by Humboldt and Bonpland, and Don José Celestino Mutis, for whom the genus was named*

Lake Guatavita, Colombia. The early Spaniards referred to the Indian chief of Guatavita as 'El Dorado'. Later the name was mistakenly transferred to the fabled gold region of the Orinoco for which Sir Walter Raleigh sought in vain. From Vues des Cordillères *by Humboldt and Bonpland*

Expedition of New Granada spread his reputation throughout both the New World and the Old. His botanical library, second only to that of Sir Joseph Banks in London, was placed at Humboldt's and Bonpland's disposal, and the visitors were shown part of his vast collection of 20,000 plants and some of the many thousands of exquisite botanical drawings, done like miniature paintings by a team of thirty artists over the last fifteen years, none of which was published until 1955. They were intended to illustrate Mutis' monumental but never completed *Flora de Bogotá ó de Nueva Granada*. In all, it was a stimulating and rewarding encounter.

Bonpland's illness forced Humboldt to remain two full months in Bogotá but he seems to have been in no particular hurry to move on and found plenty to occupy himself with. During this time he received his first letter from Europe for more than two years, lunched with the Viceroy at his country house (protocol prevented the Viceroy eating with lesser mortals in his official residence in town), discovered fossilized mastodon bones, coal fields and vast deposits of rock salt in the surrounding plains, visited Lake Guatavita, and measured the heights of the neighbouring mountains, some of which rose to 16,000 feet. Then, on 8 September, when Bonpland was fully recovered, the expedition bade farewell to Mutis and left Bogotá for Quito via the dangerous and arduous high-level route through the Quindiu Pass. For the whole of the year that followed they were to live entirely at altitude among the highlands of the Andes, and their exploration of the great volcanic peaks was to turn them into the finest mountaineers of their time and revolutionize the geological views of the age.

Their route first of all lay westward and downward across the Rio Magdalena, through Contreras to Ibagué, one of the oldest towns in the kingdom of New Granada, and then upward again over the eastern spur of the Cordilleras via the snow-covered Quindiu Pass itself.

This pass was one of the most difficult roads in the whole of the Andes. At its highest point it reached nearly 12,000 feet above sea level and in parts it was so swampy that the party had to take oxen instead of mules as pack animals. Long stretches of the road wound through a dense and totally uninhabited forest and since it was clearly impossible to procure either food or shelter along it, they were forced to carry enough provisions to last them a month. The track was very narrow and for the most part resembled an open gallery cut in the rock. It ran along the bottom of 20-foot-deep ravines where underfoot the ground was a morass and overhead the vegetation was so thick that it excluded the light. If ever they bumped into a string of oxen coming in the opposite direction they either had to beat a retreat the way they had come or climb up the steep sides of the ravine and hold on to the projecting roots of the trees above. To make matters worse it started to pour torrentially as they were descending the western slope of the pass and swamps covered in bamboo spikes destroyed their boots so effectively that when they reached Cartago their feet were bare and bleeding.

In spite of the condition of their feet Humboldt and Bonpland refused to allow themselves to be carried by the *cargueros*, the Indian man-carriers. It was customary for mining officials in these districts to saddle the Indians with a chair and ride on their human beasts of burden for three or four hours a day. It made Humboldt's blood boil to witness this degrading practice and to hear the qualities of a human being described in terms that would be employed in speaking of a horse or a mule. He preferred to suffer himself than cause others to suffer in this way.

From Cartago they travelled south along the magnificent Cuenca valley to Popayán, where they spent most of November in botanical and geological excursions, including a trip to the crater of the volcano of Puracé (16,110 feet) which emitted with a terrific noise jets of steam impregnated with sulphuretted hydrogen. And then they were on their way again.

The hardest part of the journey was now ahead. They had to cross the Páramos of Pasto, a high desert region where all vegetation ceased and the cold was so intense that it penetrated to the very marrow. It was a horrible road, paved with the bones of mules that had perished along it from cold or exhaustion, and interspersed with swamps where their baggage animals sank up to their girths.

The whole region of Pasto was a bleak and frozen mountain plateau; the sky remained cold and grey, damp mountain mists rolled over the bare, unlovely spaces, and the only plants were low myrtle-like shrubs and alpine herbs. Everywhere around them now there was evidence of volcanic activity, and smoke streamed continually from the active solfataras. At nights, whenever there was nowhere to stay, the travellers

huddled out of the rain under tents the Indians had made out of *Heliconia* leaves—these overlapped like tiles, kept most of the water out, and in the morning could be rolled up again like umbrellas. The expedition spent Christmas at the little town of Pasto and after many numbing privations eventually reached the civilized comforts of Quito in early January.

Humboldt described Quito as a handsome city but cold and overcast. The great earthquake of 1797, which had shaken the entire province and killed 40,000 of the inhabitants of the central town of Riobamba, had proved a disastrous event in every conceivable way. The mean temperature had dropped considerably and fresh tremors, some of them extremely violent, were now a frequent occurrence. For all that, Humboldt found the inhabitants of Quito gay, lively and amiable. 'The town,' he said, 'breathed an atmosphere of luxury and voluptuousness, and perhaps nowhere is there a population so entirely given up to the pursuit of pleasure. Thus can man accustom himself to sleep in peace on the brink of a precipice.'

Humboldt spent six months based in Quito, where he enjoyed the company of some of the grandest and oldest feudal families of Latin America—the Selvalegres, the Miraflores, the Villa-Orellanas, the Solandos, the Guerreros and others. It was with the family of the Marqués de Selvalegre, the Provincial Governor, that he formed his closest relationship, however. The Marqués himself, Juan Pio Aguirre y Montúfar, found a fine house for the travellers to lodge in on their arrival, and his young son Carlos Montúfar, 'an estimable youth', became Humboldt's inseparable companion for the remainder of his South American expedition. Many years later, Rosa Montúfar, Carlos' sister, a young woman then and a noted beauty, recalled the impression the Prussian scientist made on her during his stay.

> The baron was always amiable and polite. At table he never remained longer than was necessary to satisfy the claims of hunger and pay courteous attention to the ladies. He seemed always glad to be out of doors again, examining every stone and collecting plants. At night, long after we were all asleep, he would be gazing at the stars. To us young ladies, this mode of life was even more incomprehensible than to my father the marquis.

For many years the Montúfars kept at their country home at Chillo outside Quito a half-length, life-size portrait of Humboldt, painted by a native artist during his stay in the city in 1802. The young German scientist, then thirty-three years of age, was shown wearing the uniform of a Prussian mining inspector, a dark blue coat with yellow facings, white waistcoat and white breaches. His right hand rested on a book suitably entitled *Aphorism. ex Phys. Chim. Plant.*, and he looked lean, fit, alert, serious, commanding, handsome and almost sensual. This was Humboldt as he looked at the height of his physical powers, during the very months in which he secured world-wide fame for himself by one single outstanding physical act— the ascent of Chimborazo, the highest mountain, or so it was thought then, in the world.

During the half year Humboldt spent in Quito he devoted most of his time and energy to examining all the major volcanoes of the area in succession—Pichincha, Cotopaxi, Antisana, Tungurahua, Iliniza, Chimborazo—sometimes in the company of Bonpland, sometimes not. At that time mountaineering was a virtually unheard-of activity, the physiological effects of altitude were not fully understood, there was no repertoire of established techniques and no special equipment or clothing—you simply put a woollen poncho over your everyday dress and slogged straight up. Humboldt's achievements as a high-level mountaineer were the result of experience acquired by trial and error on the spot, a considerable degree of motivation, and a long period of acclimatization above 10,000 feet.

His very first climb, however, was a total failure. High up on Pichincha, the 15,672 foot volcano that looms over Quito, he suffered from attacks of giddiness and eventually passed out altogether. Undeterred, on 26 May he tried to reach the summit of the volcano a second time, with only an Indian called Aldas as a companion.

Street scene in Quito, Ecuador

All went well and they were working their way gingerly across the snow-covered slope of the cone when Aldas, with a loud cry of terror, sank up to his chest in a crevasse. Without realizing it, they had crossed a snow-bridge overhanging the crater, and a few steps away they could see daylight through the holes.

Humboldt pulled Aldas out of the crevasse and, frightened but undeterred, decided on a different approach. This time they managed to reach a narrow oblong rock, twelve feet long by six broad, which projected out over the abyss like a balcony. Every two or three minutes this precarious eyrie was shaken by violent earth tremors but Humboldt edged along it and was soon established above the mouth of the volcano.

It was a terrifying sight. The gorge of the volcano formed a circular hole about a mile in circumference and its dull black sides plunged down to an unfathomable depth. Humboldt picked out the peaks of several mountains sticking out of the gloom 2,000 feet below and saw bluish flames flicker far down in the depths—an unmistakable sign that Pichincha was on fire again.

By barometric measurement Humboldt calculated that he had reached a height just short of 15,000 feet on Pichincha and it was not until well past midnight on the 27th, after eighteen hours continuously on the trot that he got back to Quito. He was clearly in superb physical shape because on the very next day, he toiled up to his precarious perch over the lip of the crater again, this time with a full set of instruments with which to carry out geophysical observations and experiments. During this third ascent of Pichincha he was able to record fifteen quite pronounced shocks of earthquake in the space of thirty-six minutes—an observation which fascinated the intrepid Humboldt but mortified the citizens of Quito who spread rumours that the heretic German had deliberately caused the tremor by hurling gunpowder into the depths of the volcano.

Less than a fortnight later, on 9 June, Humboldt, Bonpland, and their young friend Carlos Montúfar left Quito for the lovely mountain of Chimborazo, whose rounded summit of gleaming snow reared to a height of 20,702 feet above sea-level. On 23 June 1802, they began their historic climb.

Fortunately, the attempt to reach the summit of Chimborazo had been reserved for our last enterprise among the mountains of South America, for we had gained some experience and knew how far we could rely on our own strength.

With great exertion and considerable patience we reached a greater height than we had dared to expect, for we were constantly climbing through clouds. In many places the ridge was no wider than eight to ten inches. To our left was a precipice of snow whose frozen crust glistened like glass. To our right lay a terrifying abyss, from 800 to 1,000 feet deep, with huge masses of naked rock sticking out from it. We chose to lean more to the right than the left . . .

The rock became more friable and the ascent increasingly difficult and dangerous. At certain spots where it was very steep, we had to use both our hands and our feet, and the edges of the rock were so sharp that we were painfully cut, especially on our hands. To make matters worse, I had for some time been suffering from a wound in my foot, caused by the repeated bites of the chegoes. . . .

We could no longer see the summit, even by glimpses, and were therefore doubly anxious to find out how much further we still had to climb to the top. We opened the tube barometer at a place where the ridge was wide enough to allow two persons to stand side by side in safety and found we were still only 17,300 feet up. . . .

After an hour's cautious climbing, the ridge of rock became less steep, but the mist unfortunately remained as thick as ever. One after another we all began to feel sick from nausea and giddiness, which was far more distressing than our difficulties in breathing. Blood exuded from the lips and gums, and the eyes became bloodshot. These symptoms were not particularly alarming, for we had grown familiar with them from our previous climbs. They vary greatly from individual to individual according to age, experience, constitution and tenderness of the skin. But in the same individual they constitute a kind of gauge for the amount of rarefaction in the atmosphere and the absolute height he has reached.

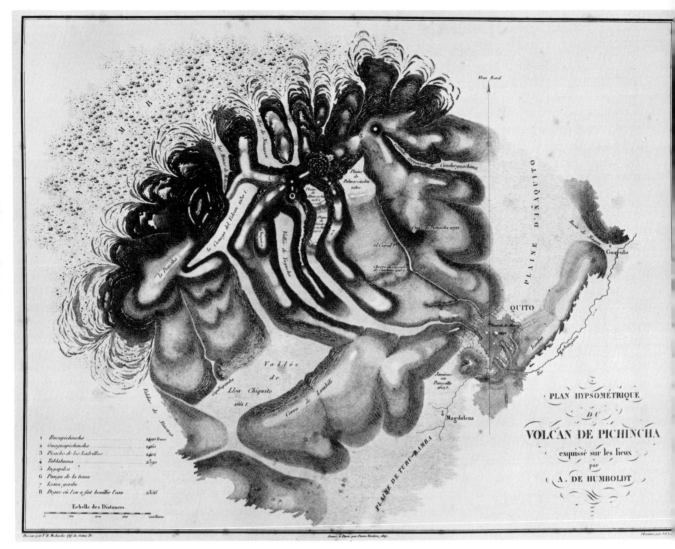

Humboldt's plan of Pichincha, 15,672 feet, shown with the improved style of shading he devised

Suddenly the stratum of mist which had hidden every distant object began to clear. Once more we recognized the dome-shaped summit of Chimborazo, now very close. What a grand and awe-inspiring spectacle! The hope of conquering it renewed our strength. The rocky ridge, which only had a thin sprinkling of snow here and there, became somewhat wider. With this surer surface underfoot we hurried on—only to be stopped dead in our tracks by a ravine some 400 feet deep and 60 feet wide. This was an insurmountable barrier. The softness of the snow and the steepness of the slopes made it impossible to scale the sides.

It was now 1 pm. We fixed up the barometer with great care and found it stood at 13 inches $11\frac{2}{10}$ lines. The air temperature was only 3°C below freezing but after our long stay in the tropics even this amount of cold was quite benumbing. Our boots were wet through with snow water. According to the barometric formula given by Laplace we had now reached an altitude of 19,286 feet.

We stayed only a short time in this dreary waste, for we were soon enveloped in mist again, which hung about us motionless. We saw no more of the summit of Chimborazo, nor of the neighbouring Sierra Nevada, still less the high plain of Quito. We felt as isolated as in a balloon.

As the weather was becoming increasingly threatening, we hurried down along the ridge of rock and found that even greater caution was necessary than during the ascent. We delayed no longer than sufficed to collect fragments of rocks as specimens of the mountain structure, as we foresaw that in Europe we should frequently be asked for a fragment from Chimborazo.

When we were at a height of about 17,400 feet we ran into a violent hailstorm and twenty minutes later into a snowstorm so heavy that the ridge was soon several inches deep. We saw a few rock lichens above the snow line, at a height of 16,920 feet. The last green moss we noticed was growing about 2,600 feet lower down. M. Bonpland captured a butterfly at a height of 15,000 feet and a fly was seen 1,600 feet higher. We did not see any condors, however, which had been so numerous on Pichincha. At a few minutes past two we reached the spot where we had left the mules.

Such is Humboldt's own spare account of the journey which took him to the highest altitude ever attained by any human being in history up to that time. It is devoid of heroics and indeed of any special sense of achievement—yet it was this solitary event of a single day in June 1802 that first established Humboldt's enormous popular reputation and maintained it for the next half-century or more. It was a record-breaking 'first' and when, many months later, the exploit was made known in the Paris journals, it captured the imagination of the public. And though Aimé Bonpland, Carlos Montúfar and a half-caste Indian from the neighbouring village of San Juan had climbed just as high up the mountain, it was Humboldt who was popularly proclaimed the hero and he alone who was accredited with a world climbing record that remained unbroken for more than thirty years. It was not entirely to Humboldt's credit that he never made any explicit effort to share this glory with his companions. Years later, when the British surveys of the Himalayas revealed peaks considerably higher than Chimborazo, Humboldt was quite upset. 'All my life I have imagined that of all mortals I was the one who had risen highest in the world— I mean on the slopes of Chimborazo!' Even in his extreme old age Chimborazo remained for him one of his most cherished memories—a symbol, perhaps, of that supreme moment when physically he came nearest to both heaven and earth, the twin components of the cosmos.

Humboldt's exhaustive investigation of the major volcanoes of Ecuador had more significant results than the achievement of a sporting record alone, however. He had made important observations in the fields of seismology and the geography of plants, and the weathered streams of lava and pumice revealed conclusively the volcanic origin of the great range of the Andes. The alignment of the volcanoes began to lead him towards the idea that mountain ranges had formed along geological faults, deep subterranean clefts where the earth's crust changed its formation. He had arrived in South America a convinced disciple of Werner, his former professor at Freiberg, then the leading exponent of Neptunism—the theory that all rocks had formed from liquid deposits. But having seen the the difference between eruptive and sedimentary rocks with his own eyes, and examined for himself the change that can take place in the structure of minerals in the neighbourhood of a volcanic explosion, Humboldt radically changed his opinion, and to the subsequent dismay of some of his associates, Goethe in particular, became a Volcanist, a confirmed adherent to Plutonism—the theory that mountains formed as a result of violent upheaval.

It was while he was in Quito that Humboldt finally received news that Baudin's expedition would definitely not be calling at Lima during the course of its voyage round the world. From now on, he decided, he would rely on his own resources—indeed, he had little option. Leaving Quito with Bonpland and Montúfar, he now turned his steps south towards Peru via the extreme upper reaches of the river Amazon.

Their route took them down by gradual stages into the gentler climate of the cinchona forests and the former land of the Incas. At Riobamba, where they stayed with Montúfar's brother, the local magistrate, Humboldt was given the opportunity to study unique sixteenth century manuscripts, belonging to a descendant of the Inca kings and written in an extinct dialect, with a later Spanish translation. These told of events before the conquest of the Incas and of the great eruption of the volcano of Nevado de Altar which blew away part of the summit and caused volcanic ash to rain down on the neighbouring towns for seven years. On the way from Riobamba to Cuenca across the lofty Páramo of Azuay he examined the remains of the great Inca road, constructed of specially hewn porphyry paving stones and as good and as straight as the best of the Romans roads of Europe, that once led all the way to the Inca capital at Cuzco; and nearby he visited the ruins of the palace of the Inca Tapayupangi with its so-called summer house cut out of solid rock, located in such a way as to look over an enchanting landscape view. 'Our "English" gardens contain nothing more elegant', he noted, full of admiration for the former public works of the destroyed Inca nation, whose vanished culture he was later to champion so stoutly in Europe.

After crossing Azuay and passing through Cuenca, where bullfights were held in their honour, the travellers took the road to Loja to complete their investigation of the cinchona tree (*Cinchona condaminea*) from whose bark was obtained quinine, the famous specific for malaria. They spent nearly three weeks exploring the headwaters of the Amazon in the region of Jaen in Peru, then turned their backs on the tropical forest again and recrossed the Andes near Cajamarca (where Pizarro ambushed and captured the Inca king, Atahualpa) at a point where the needle of the magnetic compass turned from the north to the south. They had crossed the magnetic equator, and Humboldt's measurement of the magnetic intensity of the earth at this spot served as a reference point for all geomagnetic measurements for the next half century. Not far from here, at a vantage point high up on the western slopes of the Andes along the road down to Trujillo, the world miraculously opened out before them and Humboldt saw far below, the ultimate goal of all his youthful dreams.

ABOVE *A suspension bridge over the Rio Chambo near Penipe, Peru;* BELOW *Raft near Guayaquil, after a sketch by Humboldt. Both are from* Vues des Cordillères *by Humboldt and Bonpland*

OVERLEAF *Humboldt and Bonpland high in the Andes of Ecuador. Painting by F. G. Weitsch*

The sky, which had been clouded over for so long, brightened suddenly. A fresh south-westerly breeze dispersed the mist, revealing a dark-blue heaven between narrow lines of high, feathery clouds. The entire western slope of the Cordillera, and the plains of Chala and Molinos as far as the coast near Trujillo, lay stretched out before our eyes. Now, for the first time, we had our view of the Pacific. We saw it distinctly in the glitter of a vast light, an immeasurable expanse of ocean.

For Humboldt, brought up since boyhood on the narratives of James Cook and Vasco Nuñez de Balboa, the first European to see the Pacific from the mainland of America, it was a moment of profound emotion—so profound, in fact, that in his excitement he forgot to take his usual barometric reading to determine the height of the pass.

In October 1802, after a year and a half of continuous travel in the highlands of the Andes, the expedition descended to sea-level again at Trujillo and after crossing the great desert plain of the Pacific coast of Peru reached the city of Lima on the 22nd.

They stayed a little over two months in Lima, arranging and packing their plant and rock collections for shipment to Mexico and Europe. Lima, the seat of the Viceroy of Peru, was then a small, run-down town and Humboldt was unsparing in his criticism of it. He hadn't seen any well-furnished homes or well-dressed women there, he said, and with the exception of the bullring there were no public amusements. At night he found it impossible to travel along the streets by carriage because of all the mongrel dogs and donkey carcasses that obstructed them. Gambling and family break-ups had disrupted all social life and in the whole of Lima there were no social gatherings of more than eight people at a time. He found a cold egotism there and a cruel indifference to suffering. It seemed to him that Lima was as remote from the rest of Peru as London was and he would be glad when they sailed for Acapulco in five or six weeks' time.

The time was not altogether wasted, however. He was able to make a successful observation of the transit of Mercury across the face of the sun and thus fix the longitude of the port of Callao accurately for the first time. And from the nesting grounds of the prodigious colonies of cormorants, pelicans and gannets along the coast and on the nearby islands, with some five million birds to the square mile, he obtained samples of the curious substance known as *guano*, a thick coagulation of bird droppings and other organic refuse, which he sent to Paris for chemical analysis. The rich fertilizing properties of *guano* had been known to Peruvian farmers for hundreds of years—it was over thirty times more effective than ordinary farmyard manure—but it was virtually unknown in Europe and North America until Humboldt first drew scientific attention to it.

On Christmas Eve the party embarked at Callao in a ship bound for Guayaquil and during the course of a slow voyage along the coast Humboldt, in accordance with his normal practice at sea, took regular readings of the flow and temperature of the cold ocean current that washed along the Peruvian coast. In no sense did he

Humboldt and Bonpland spent a year travelling in Mexico. ABOVE *Plaza Maior, Mexico City ;* BELOW *Mexican muleteers. Paintings by C. Nebel*

discover this current—it had been known to every fisherman between Chile and Payta for the last three hundred years—he was simply the first to make oceanographic measurements of it and examined its geographic properties. But if Chimborazo established his name with the public during his lifetime, it was that cold Peruvian current that kept it alive after his death. For in spite of all his protests, it came to be marked on all maps but his own as the Humboldt Current and so it has remained to the present day—ironically, the best known monument to his memory.

On 15 February 1803, Humboldt set sail from Guayaquil on a ship bound for Mexico and for the last time watched the shoreline of South America disappear over the horizon. Cotopaxi was in eruption then and two hundred miles out from land, above the slap of bow wave and creak of spar and timbers, he could still hear the muffled boom of its thunderous farewell.

A seal from the Pacific coast of Peru sketched in Humboldt's journal

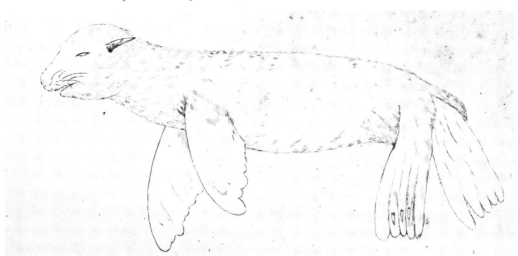

LEFT Cinchona condaminea. *Quinine is made from the bark of this tree. From* Plantes équinoxiales *by Humboldt and Bonpland*

CHAPTER 13

Friend of
Thomas Jefferson

In March 1803 Humboldt and his companions reached Acapulco and spent the whole of the following year travelling in Mexico, the richest and most developed of the Spanish American possessions. In many respects it was the most uneventful period of their expedition, for as much time was spent in offices and libraries as in the field. Humboldt's principal aim in Mexico was not so much exploration as intensive academic research into the geography, economics and politics of the entire country. This was to result in the first modern regional geographic essay ever produced, his *Political Essay on the Kingdom of New Spain*, a project made possible by the generosity of the Spanish Viceroy, who produced files and documents of all sorts and allowed him free access to the public archives for his statistical data.

Humboldt wrote only the most fragmentary description of his personal experiences in Mexico and any account of his travels must necessarily be spare—bones without flesh. Basing himself in Mexico City, he made several excursions into the countryside, climbing or measuring the volcanoes—Jorullo, Toluca, Popocatepetl, Cofre de Perote, Orizaba; descending into silver mines, notably Taxco, Real del Monte and the great mines of Guanajuato, where he stayed two months; fixing the latitudes and longitudes of many places, not least the port of Acapulco, which on some maps was out by as much as 4 minutes of longitude; and studying the remnants of Aztec art.

Then, on 7 March 1804, he sailed from Veracruz for Havana to pick up the scientific collections he had deposited there for safe-keeping more than three years previously.

*   *   *

When Humboldt set out on his abortive journey to join Baudin in Lima it seemed he had given up once and for all any notion of visiting the northern part of the American continent. At the end of November 1802 he wrote to the Institut National in Paris confirming that he hoped to return to Europe via Mexico and Cuba by the autumn of the following year. 'I think of nothing but of preserving and publishing my manuscripts', he wrote. 'How I long to be in Paris!' His decision to delay his departure for home and pay a visit to the United States instead seems to have been a last minute one, prompted doubtless by his enormous respect for the US President, Thomas Jefferson, whom he felt it his duty to salute before leaving the New World, and by his curiosity in Jefferson's plans for the exploration of the American Far

The volcano of Jorullo, in western Mexico, was created on the night of 29 September 1759. It was still on fire when Humboldt and Bonpland climbed into its crater in September 1803, and the cones all around it emitted a dense vapour which made the air unbearably hot. From Vues des Cordillères *by Humboldt and Bonpland*

Le Terrain soulevé vu de l'Ouest.

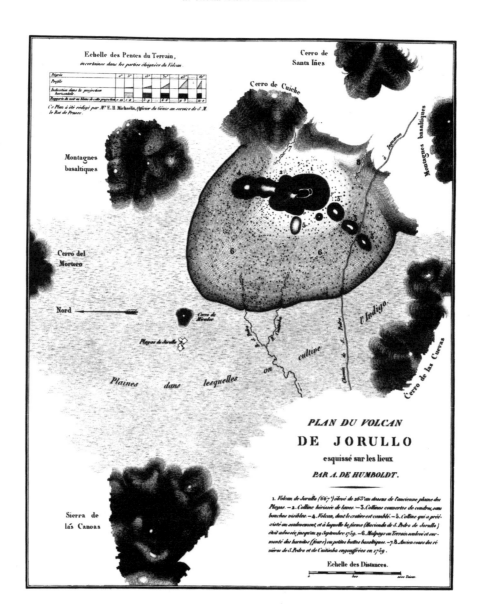

Echelle des Pentes du Terrain,
incertaines dans les parties éloignées du Volcan.

Ce Plan a été rédigé par Mr. E. H. Michaelis, Officier du Génie au service de S. M.
le Roi de Prusse.

Cerro de
Santa Iñes

Cerro de Cuiche

Montagnes
basaltiques

Montagnes basaltiques

Cerro del
Mortero

Nord

Cerro de Mirador

Playas de Jorullo

Plaines   dans   lesquelles   on   cultive   l'Indigo

Cerro de las Cuevas

Sierra de
las Canoas

PLAN DU VOLCAN
DE JORULLO
esquissé sur les lieux
PAR A. DE HUMBOLDT.

1. Volcan de Jorullo (66.7) élevé de 263 au dessus de l'ancienne plaine des
Playas. – 2. Colline hérissée de laves. – 3. Collines couvertes de cendres, sans
bouches visibles. – 4. Volcan, dont le cratère est comblé. – 5. Colline qui a préé-
xisté au soulèvement, et à laquelle la ferme (Hacienda de S. Pedro de Jorullo)
était adossée jusqu'au 29 Septembre 1759. – 6. Malpays ou Terrain soulevé et sur-
monté des hornitos (fours) ou petites buttes basaltiques. – 7. 8. Ancien cours des ri-
vières de S. Pedro et de Cuitimba engouffrées en 1759.

Echelle des Distances.

Etendue de la masse soulevée.   *(latitude 19°9'; Longitude 1°54' à l'Occid. de Mexico.)*

West, particularly the region between the Rockies and the ill-defined US-Mexican border, which Humboldt knew well—at least from the Mexican side.

On 29 April 1804, Humboldt and his companions Bonpland and Montúfar set sail from Havana on board the Spanish frigate *Concepcion* bound for Philadelphia, running into a terrible storm in the Bahama Straits that blew for a week and caused Humboldt to fear for the safety of the scientific collections he had with him. Twenty-four days later the ship arrived safely in the more tranquil waters of the Delaware and the travellers had their first view of the USA.

From a distance it was not an unpleasing view. The shores of the bay and the river Delaware were low and covered in forest except for occasional stretches of marshland, but as the ship approached the port of Philadelphia—until recently the capital of the country—the banks of the river became higher and the western side was dotted with numerous neat farm-houses built in clearings in the forest where the cultivated land extended down to the water's edge. As soon as they had weathered a well-timbered point of land the spires of Philadelphia itself came into view about three miles away up-stream. From a distance, especially after a long sea voyage, it looked a most attractive place, but closer at hand it presented a less prepossessing appearance, for nothing was visible from the water but jumbled piles of wooden warehouses and wharves littered with stinking refuse. Behind the waterfront, however, lay a clean, well laid-out city of 75,000 people. It was still the biggest town in the States and reminded Humboldt very much of Europe. The streets were paved with cobblestones and lined with poplars and at night the watchman went round calling out the hours. The red-brick houses were generally three storeys high, and many of them had marble steps up to the front door and were furnished inside with considerable elegance. The principal public building, apart from the State House, was Philosophic Hall, the headquarters of the American Philosophical Society— an institution which was to become the focal point of Humboldt's stay in the USA and whose learned members took it upon themselves to make the necessary arrangements for their distinguished guest's visit. For though Philadelphia was no longer the capital, now that Washington was in course of construction, it was still the cultural and scientific centre of the new republic.

Humboldt and his two companions found themselves accommodation at an inn on Market Street not far from the harbour and the local papers duly reported their arrival. 'Baron de Hombott arrived in this city on Wednesday night', wrote *Relf's Philadelphia Gazette and Daily Advertiser*, while the Baron himself meanwhile wasted no time in establishing contact with the President. On 24 May he wrote, in French, as follows:

> Mr President,
>   Arrived from Mexico on the blessed ground of this republic, the executive power of which has been placed in your hands, it is a pleasant duty for me to present my respects and express my high admiration for your writings, your actions and the liberalism of your ideas, which have

Three aspects of the Jorullo volcano. From Atlas géographique et physique du Royaume de la Nouvelle-Espagne *by Humboldt and Bonpland*

inspired me from my earliest years. I flatter myself in the hope of being able to express my sentiments to you in person, remitting at the same time the enclosed parcel which my friend the United States Consul in Havana asked me to send to you. . . .

For moral reasons I could not resist seeing the United States and enjoying the comforting sight of a people who understand the precious gift of liberty. I hope I will be permitted to present my respects to you personally. . . .

While he waited for the President's reply from Washington, Humboldt was taken up by the members of the American Philosophical Society, of which Jefferson was also President, who made him their guest of honour and elected him a member. The society had been founded in 1743 by Benjamin Franklin along the lines of the Royal Society in London, and in Humboldt's time it was located in Fifth Street, between Chestnut Street and Wall Street, south of the High Court. In this institution were centred all the scientific aspirations of the Republic. Here Joseph Priestley had related his celebrated discovery of oxygen and Benjamin Franklin had lectured on physics. Most of its present members lived locally and Humboldt spent a great deal of time in their company: men like Dr Caspar Wistar—noted for his attempts to make vaccination compulsory; Benjamin Smith Barton—botanist and expert on American Indian culture; and Dr Benjamin Rush—one of the signatories of the American Declaration of Independence who, as a medical man, was particularly interested in Humboldt's views on the curative properties of cinchona bark.

Charles Willson Peale, a painter, lay scientist and friend of Jefferson, became Humboldt's constant companion in the USA and showed him his famous museum— a museum, he said, that was unique in the New World. A sign above the entrance to the wooden building that housed his collections read: SCHOOL OF WISDOM, while below was another sign which read: THE BOOK OF NATURE OPEN—EXPLORE THE WONDROUS WORK AND INSTITUTE OF LAWS ETERNAL. Inside were rooms packed with specimens of birds, insects, stuffed alligators, mountain lions with glass eyes and real eye-lashes, a five-legged cow suckling a two-headed calf, pantaloons made from a whale's intestines, a mammoth and the shoes and socks of an Irish giant called Obrian, who was 8 feet $7\frac{1}{2}$ inches tall. Peale also had a collection of paintings of famous Americans for sale and an apparatus called a physiognotrace, a present from an inventor called Hawkins, which enabled anyone to trace his own or anybody else's silhouette. Peale, who seems to have had an outsize personality and an eye for the main chance, persuaded Humboldt to sit for his physiognotrace while he ran off a large stack of silhouettes of his profile.

It was while he was perusing the table of contents of a scientific journal in the library in Philadelphia that Humboldt came across an item of news that caused him to shout with joy: 'Arrival of M. de Humboldt's manuscripts at his brother's house in Paris, by way of Spain.' This incidental reference was the first intimation he had received of the fate of the collections and notes he and Bonpland had shipped from Cuba early in 1801—*over three years previously!*

On 26 May Humboldt, Bonpland and Montúfar, accompanied by Peale, who

City and port of Philadelphia. From an engraving by Thomas Birch

promised to introduce them to Jefferson, from whom Humboldt had not yet received any reply, and by Dr Thomas Fothergill of Bath, England, and the Reverend Nicholas Collin, left Philadelphia by coach for Baltimore and Washington. Humboldt's dynamic and friendly personality had left a great impression on the Philadelphians. By contrast, sadly, his companions Bonpland and Montúfar seemed to have left no impression at all—partly, one assumes, because they spoke not a word of English—and increasingly their rôle became that of mere appendages to Humboldt's brief but comet-like progress through America.

Peale kept a diary of the journey to Washington. The mail stage, for the record, cost them eight dollars a head and Humboldt never stopped talking, his repertoire of travel stories including several shocking anecdotes about life in the European courts. Their companion, the Reverend Collin, afforded some amusement, since he was both short-sighted and absent-minded: at the ferry on the splendidly named River Brandywine he misjudged the distance between bank and boat and stepped into the water, and after hanging up his money-sock (and his money) to dry at the next inn along the road he forgot it when they set off again in the morning. There were now eight more people in the coach but it is doubtful if this in any way inhibited the flow of Humboldt's conversation. Peale noted:

> The Baron spoke English very well, in the German dialect. Here I shall take notice that he possessed surprising fluency of Speach (sic), & it was amusing to hear him speak English, French and Spanish Languages, mixing them together in rapid Speach. He is very communicative and possesses a supprising (sic) fund of knowledge, in botany, mineralogy astronomy Philosophy and Natural History: with a liberal Education, he has been collecting information from learned men of allmost (sic) all quarters of the world; for he has been travelling ever since he was 11 years of age and never lived in any one place more than 6 months together, as he informed us.

Just *what*, one wonders, had Alexander been filling their heads with as they rattled through Pennsylvania on that summer rural ride?

On 1 June the party reached Washington and checked in at Stelle's Hotel and City Tavern, a large hotel with big stables for the horse teams, in time for a late evening meal. The *United States Gazette* duly reported their progress:

> Yesterday arrived from Philadelphia, the celebrated Dr. Fothergill, sen. Baron Humboldt, and Dr. Collin. These gentlemen are on a tour to the southward.

Of Bonpland and Montúfar, not a word.

In the meantime Humboldt had received his reply from the President, dated 28 June:

> A lively desire will be felt generally to receive the information you will be able to give. No one will feel it more strongly than myself, because no one perhaps views this New World with more partial hopes of its exhibiting an ameliorated state of the human condition. In the new position in which the seat of our government is fixed, we have nothing curious to attract the observations of a traveller, and can only substitute in its place the welcome with which we should receive your visit, should you find it convenient to add so much to your journey.

Thomas Jefferson, third President of the United States. Detail of a copy of a painting by Gilbert Stuart

At the time of Humboldt's visit Washington, which had been made the new capital of the United States in 1800, was still a frontier town—'the best city in the world for *future* residence.' It was only half built and contained less than 5,000 inhabitants and no more than 800 houses, mostly centred round the Capitol, the President's house and the Navy Yard on the Potomac river.

Humboldt was welcomed in the skeletal capital with characteristic American warmth and cordiality. He was invited everywhere for lunch, tea and dinner. He was driven in a coach to the top of Capitol Hill for the view, invited on board a US warship in the Navy Yard, taken to the temporary quarters of the House of Representatives. In the next two weeks he was driven to Mount Vernon and back again in half the time by a drunken driver, and wined and dined by the best of them—by James Madison, the Secretary of State and later fourth President and the so-called father of the constitution, Albert Gallatin, Secretary to the Treasury, by Gilbert Stuart, the famous painter, and Dr William Thornton, the naturalist. Wherever he went and whoever he met he impressed them all with his vivacity and breadth of knowledge. On 5 June Mrs Dolly Madison, the Secretary of State's wife, wrote to her sister:

> We have lately had a great treat in the company of a charming Prussian Baron von Humboldt. All the ladies say they are in love with him, notwithstanding his want of personal charms. He is the most polite, modest, well-informed and interesting traveller we have ever met, and is much pleased with America. He sails in a few days for France . . . He had with him a train of philosophers who, though clever and entertaining, did not compare with the Baron.

On his second day in Washington, a Saturday, Humboldt had received an invitation to lunch with the President at the Executive Mansion at 3.30 pm on the coming Monday. The President's official headquarters at this time were as unfinished as his capital. The house still needed a lot doing to it and the lawns looked like cow pasture. Jefferson's study was also the 'Cabinet', a spacious room full of a variety of official and private lumber including his books, charts, maps, gardening tools, household utensils, pots and roses and geraniums and a cage containing his favourite mocking bird. It was thought to be in this room that Jefferson had his detailed discussions with his Prussian visitor.

Jefferson was an unpretentious, devoted family man, then sixty-one years of age, and the lunch on Monday, a very select meal but quite devoid of ceremony, was a great success. Peale was there and noted in his diary that not a single toast was given or called for and that the subject of politics was not brought up at all, the company preferring to talk about natural history, the customs of different countries, and ways of raising living standards.

Jefferson and Humboldt evidently had a great deal of respect for each other and Jefferson considered Humboldt the most scientific man of his age he had ever met. They shared the same political convictions, the same hopes for the future of America and, of course, the same interest in science. Jefferson was no tyro in scientific matters.

Charles Willson Peale, painter and lay scientist, inside his famous museum in Philadelphia. Self portrait

As US Ambassador in Paris he had carried out meteorological observations, in Italy he had studied agricultural techniques and had even designed a plough. He knew all about the works of Buffon, Cuvier and Blumenbach and had a good working knowledge of astronomy and palaeontology. The two men got on so well that Jefferson placed his Washington residence at Humboldt's disposal and invited him to visit his beautiful Palladian home at Monticello in the Virginia countryside.

Sharing in Jefferson's domestic life in this way, Humboldt was afforded some fascinating glimpses of the third President of the United States in his few, unguarded off-duty moments. One morning he found Jefferson on the floor, surrounded by half a dozen of his little grandchildren playing a noisy game of romps. The President was so distracted that for a few moments he failed to notice Humboldt standing

James Madison, Secretary of State and later fourth President of the United States

there but when he did he stood up and shaking hands with him said, 'You've found me playing the fool, Baron, but I'm sure I don't need to make any apology to you.'

On another occasion, when Humboldt was breakfasting with the President's secretary, William A. Burwell, Jefferson suddenly stormed down the stairs with a newspaper clipping in his hand. It contained, he said, 'the grossest personal abuse of himself', and he was going to give it to Humboldt so that it could be placed in a European museum as 'evidence how little mischief flowed from the freedom of the Press, when notwithstanding innumerable pieces of similar nature issued daily from the Press, his administration had never been more popular.'

What Jefferson really wanted from Humboldt was accurate and detailed information about the vague and disputed frontier territory with Mexico. For as a result of the Louisiana Purchase Treaty the US Government had acquired from Napoleon, at a cost of $15 million, an additional million square miles of American territory. The nation had thus gained a frontier with New Spain, stretching along the Red River as far as the upper reaches of the Missouri basin, about which no American had any first-hand information at all. In effect, without a shot being fired, the USA had doubled its size overnight. Jefferson had great ambitions for the opening-up and development of the interior of his country and envisaged a vast empire stretching from the Atlantic to the Pacific. He had already despatched Lewis and Clarke on their historic exploratory first crossing of North America, and now he found on his doorstep an uninvited German explorer of the highest calibre who was ready to place at his disposal a wealth of maps and statistical data concerning the geographical resources of the very area he was most concerned with. On 9 June he sent Humboldt a memo on the subject:

> Jefferson asks leave to observe to Baron de Humboldt that the question of limits of Louisiana between Spain and the US is this, they claim to hold to the river Mexicana or Sabine and from the head of that Northwardly along the heads of the water of the Mississippi to the source either of its Eastern or Western branch, thence to the head of Red River & so on. Can the Baron inform me what population may be between those lines of white, red or black people? and whether any & what mines are within them? the information will be thankfully received. He tenders him his respectful salutations.

Humboldt was completely free with his information and lent Madison his maps and allowed Albert Gallatin, the Swiss-born Secretary of the Treasury, to transcribe his statistical data. After a session with Humboldt, Gallatin wrote to his wife, Hannah, in New York:

> We all consider him as a very extraordinary man, and his travels, which he intends publishing on his return to Europe, will I think, rank above any other production of the kind. I am not apt to be easily pleased, and he was not particularly prepossessing to my taste, for he speaks more than Lucas, Finley and myself put together, and twice as fast as anybody I know, German, French, Spanish and English, all together. But I was really delighted, and swallowed more information of various kinds in less than two hours than I had for two years past in all I had read or heard. He does not seem much above thirty, gives you no trouble in talking yourself, for he catches with perfect precision the idea you mean to convey before you have uttered the third word of your sentence, and, exclusively of his travelled acquirements, the extent of his reading and scientific knowledge is astonishing. I must acknowledge, in order to account for my enthusiasm, that he was surrounded with maps, statements, &c. all new to me and several of which he has liberally permitted us to transcribe.

And then as abruptly as he had arrived, Humboldt was gone. On 13 June he left Washington, spent a few days with the local intelligentsia of Lancaster, and by the 18th he was back in Philadelphia. The next week or so was spent in preparations for his return to Europe. From the British Consul he obtained a grudging laissez-passer intended to let him through the British naval blockade on both sides of the Atlantic, a major source of concern to Humboldt on this final stage of his great expedition, and from the US Secretary of State, James Madison, he obtained a similar document and, at the last minute, the return of his precious maps. To

Gallatin he sent $100 to pay for his hotel bills. To Jefferson and all his friends in Washington and Philadelphia he sent letters of thanks and farewell. He had fallen genuinely in love with America and his letters were full of praise of 'this beautiful country, 'a beautiful dream', 'the only corner of the earth where man possesses liberty and where the small evils are compensated by the great goods'. There was one small evil he could not overlook, however—the problem of slavery. 'Before being free,' he wrote to William Thornton, 'it is necessary to be just, and without justice there is not a durable prosperity.' Slavery or no—and he had the highest hopes of its eventual abolition—he hoped one day to return to America, and so, with some fervour, did the Americans, for without hesitation they now counted him as one of their number.

On 30 June 1804, Humboldt, Bonpland and Montúfar embarked with their forty cases of scientific specimens on board the French frigate *La Favorite* bound for Bordeaux. That same day the ship weighed anchor and nosed down the wooded banks of the Delaware and after weathering Cape May crowded on sail and set course to the eastward. Ahead lay Europe and old friends and new hopes and a different life. The expedition of Humboldt and Bonpland to the New World was at an end.

* * *

The private two-man expedition of Humboldt and Bonpland—which cost Humboldt over a third of his capital—was one of the most remarkable in the history of scientific exploration. In five years these two very brave and indefatigable men travelled 6,000 miles through the remotest rain forests and highest volcanic ranges in the world and took back to Europe with them forty-five cases of specimens which included no less than 60,000 plants and a wealth of geological, zoological and ethnographical collections. Humboldt had always said that his main aim had been to collect ideas rather than things and so his notebooks, with their measurements and statistics and sketch maps and profiles, contained material at least as important as the objects inside his packing cases. He had a mass of astronomical, geological, meteorological and oceanographical data, innumerable latitudes and longitudes, and 124 magnetic readings taken over $115°$ of longitude and from latitude $52°$ North to $12°$ South which clearly showed that magnetic intensity increased with latitude and later led Gauss to formulate his theory of magnetic fields. Humboldt's work in South America, in short, formed the basis for a new direction in the study of geography, and the starting point of modern geophysics. Above all he had come to see in the infinite variety of nature a general scheme, a kind of cosmic law. 'Whether in the Amazonian forests or on the ridge of the high Andes,' he wrote when he was safely home again, 'I was ever aware that *one* breath, from pole to pole, breathes *one* single life into rocks, plants and animals, and into the swelling breast of man.'

CHAPTER 14

Aftermath

On 1 August 1804, after an Atlantic crossing of only twenty-three days, *La Favorite* anchored in the Garonne off Bordeaux to await clearance through quarantine, and Humboldt and Bonpland—alive, well and still friends after their great adventure—looked again upon the vine-clad hills of France. After six years' absence it was like coming to an unknown land, and like all returning travellers they now had to adjust to their changed situation and pick up the threads of their old life.

Humboldt took the opportunity of the delay in quarantine to write a letter to the Institut National in Paris and its contents were instantly passed on to his sister-in-law, Caroline, who was in Paris at the time. The letter simply contained news of Humboldt's safe return to Europe but it caused a commotion because many people by now believed he was dead. The newspapers had reported his demise several times. In the summer of 1803 they said in Paris that he had 'perished among the savages in North America'; and the *Hamburger Correspondent* of 12 June 1804, announced: 'We regret to learn that the celebrated traveller, Herr von Humboldt, has been attacked with yellow fever, and has died at Acapulco.'

Nobody could have looked further from death than Humboldt when he eventually reached Paris on 27 August in the company of Carlos Montúfar—Bonpland had gone to stay with his brother at La Rochelle—and was reunited with his friends and his brother's wife and children. Caroline, seven months pregnant and waiting her confinement in Paris, wrote to her husband Wilhelm, then Prussian Envoy at the Vatican: 'Alexander has not aged in the least during his six years' absence. His face is decidedly fatter and his vivacity of speech and manner has increased—as far as that is possible.' He was maturer, manlier, and 'awfully busy'.

Humboldt was lionized in Paris. Wherever he went, whether at the public meetings of scientific institutions or the more intimate soirées of private salons, the handsome and even glamorous young German who had caught the fancy of the public imagination with his record ascent of Chimborazo was fêted like a returning hero. 'It has rarely fallen to the lot of any private individual,' wrote Caroline, 'to create so much excitement by his presence or give rise to such widespread interest.' And he loved it. 'Alexander lets himself be swept off his feet by French charm', the patriotic Caroline complained a little later, in some alarm. His flair for self-publicity—those carefully contrived letters from South America, with their intriguing blend of pioneer science

The Brazil nut, Bertholletia excelsa, *from* Plantes équinoxiales, *named by Humboldt for his friend Comte Claude Louis Berthollet (right), French chemist and salon host*

and personal adventure—had turned him into a popular celebrity before he had even set foot in Paris. To most Europeans of that time, their lives confined to a tiny area of familiar ground occupied by familiar forms of the animal and vegetable kingdoms, the unexplored continent of South America was as unfamiliar, as inaccessible and as beguiling as the moon. To the man who had climbed its mountains, penetrated its jungles and endured its terrors in the cause of human knowledge and endeavour, the Paris public accorded the kind of welcome we reserve for lunar explorers today. When he opened the first exhibition of his collections and drawings at the Jardin des Plantes in October—an event eagerly talked about for weeks beforehand—the crowd peered at his rocks from Chimborazo and his quinine bark from the Amazon as if they were moon dust. Six weeks after his return the Institut National organized a special meeting at which Humboldt outlined the scientific results of his expedition before an absorbed audience. The applause of that assembly was rapturous and afterwards one of its leading figures, the great French chemist Berthollet, in whose honour Humboldt named the Brazil nut tree *Bertholletia excelsa*, remarked: 'That man is a complete walking academy.' Nobody grudged him the acclaim he received—except one

178

It seems fairly clear that there was at this time in Europe only one man who enjoyed greater fame than Alexander von Humboldt and that was Napoleon Bonaparte himself. Predictably, the meeting of these two thirty-five-year-old men—the first and only time they ever came face to face—was not a success. 'The Emperor Napoleon', Humboldt wrote later, 'behaved with icy coldness to Bonpland and seemed full of hatred towards me.' All that Napoleon could find to say to Humboldt when he was presented at Court was: 'So you're interested in botany? So is my wife.' And with that insult he turned his back and never addressed another word to him. Napoleon was well aware of Humboldt's real achievements and was even prepared to grant his request for a 3,000 franc pension for Bonpland; but it seems he regarded Humboldt himself—a foreigner from an enemy nation—as both excessively popular and politically suspect, and some while later he tried to have him thrown out of the city on suspicion of espionage.

For all that, there was no more suitable place for Humboldt to base himself than Napoleon's Paris. It had changed a great deal in his absence and in some ways for the worse. When he left it in 1799 the ideals of the revolution were more or less intact and France was still a republic. When he returned he found the revolutionary movement distorted beyond recognition and an ambitious general occupying an imperial throne. But Humboldt, though he never once changed his political beliefs, was always very skilful at adapting to the government in power and surviving under an unsympathetic régime. He thus included himself among the guests who attended Napoleon's coronation in December—dressed in a new frock coat he had had specially embroidered for 800 francs—'one can't afford to look as though one has gone to the dogs'. And in the end he lasted longer in Paris than Napoleon and all his ministers.

Politics apart, the rule of Napoleon had distinct advantages. The imperial lavishness he bestowed on official buildings, art collections and court life he also extended to scientific institutions. Under his aegis Paris had become the science centre of the world, and in the fields of mathematics, physics and natural science in particular, men of outstanding ability, whose names are still remembered today, actively cooperated in scientific development. For Humboldt, who needed the stimulation of brilliant minds and first-class facilities with which to prepare his South American material and plan future travels, Paris was the only sensible place to live in the world. Here were the scientific collaborators, map engravers, illustrators and publishers whose assistance he needed in the preparation of the monumental work he proposed to publish about his expedition. Besides, all his friends were here, and the expansive and brilliant social life of the cafés and the salons suited his temperament. In vain his brother Wilhelm, an ardent Prussian nationalist, tried to persuade him to acknowledge his *Deutschheit*, his German-ness, and return to Berlin, where his duty and his true reward lay, or so he said. In vain Kunth explained to him how he could earn 2,000 to 3,000 thalers a year in Berlin 'without doing a hand's turn'. Berlin, Alexander told them, was in his view a sand desert. 'You can be sure,' he said, 'that I shall never find it necessary to set eyes on the spires of Berlin again.' And for the next quarter of a century, with the exception of a few short periods, he never did.

From the outset, Humboldt plunged himself into a frenzy of work in Paris. Caroline reported that he worked and talked all the time: his first appointments were as early as six in the morning and he did not breakfast with her before nine. 'His collections are immense', she wrote, 'and to work them over, to compare and develop his ideas, will require from five to six years.' A great deal of his time was taken up in arranging these collections and sharing them out among institutions and individuals who had a need or a right to them. There was not always enough to go round and few specimens remained in his own possession. Bonpland retained the most complete collection of plant specimens, while a duplicate set was presented to the Jardin des Plantes and others found their way to Berlin and Kew.

His labours with his collections, his publications, his never-ending experiments, and his half-formed plans for a future expedition to Northern Asia, left him precious few hours for anything else. 'I've had no time to enjoy myself', he wrote to a friend in Germany, 'In fact, I've really bitten off more than I can chew.' He saw a lot of Caroline—'He really does treat me with great affection'—and lunched with her in her apartment whenever he was free. Their close relationship was upset, however, when her new-born baby, Luise, died in October. In the violence of her grief Caroline, who had already lost her eldest boy not long before, accused Alexander of 'demonstrations of sentimentality rather than real feeling', and on Christmas Day returned home, bereft, to Italy.

Sometimes Alexander attended the famous parties that Berthollet threw in his country house in Arceuil, near Paris, where eminent people of various callings—scientists, artists, politicians—sharpened each other's wits and honed each other's ideas in many-sided conversations of forbidding brilliance and originality. On one of these heady occasions he met a twenty-seven-year-old physicist called Louis Joseph Gay-Lussac, then at the beginning of an outstanding career.

It had not been an auspicious encounter. Among the people assembled in the drawing-room at Arceuil, Humboldt's attention had been attracted to a tall young man 'of a modest but self-possessed demeanour'. This was Gay-Lussac, who only a few weeks previously had beaten Humboldt's world altitude record of 19,286 feet on Chimborazo by making an extraordinarily courageous solo balloon ascent to a height of over 23,000 feet to measure the oxygen content of air at different altitudes. This alone could not have immediately endeared Gay-Lussac to Humboldt, who had been very proud of his world record. But to make matters worse, Humboldt recalled that it was this same Gay-Lussac who had written such a blistering attack on one of his lectures on eudiometry at the Institut National back in 1799. Rancour and envy, however, were not in his nature. He went straight up to Gay-Lussac, congratulated him on his aeronautical ventures and shook his hand. It was the beginning of a lifelong friendship.

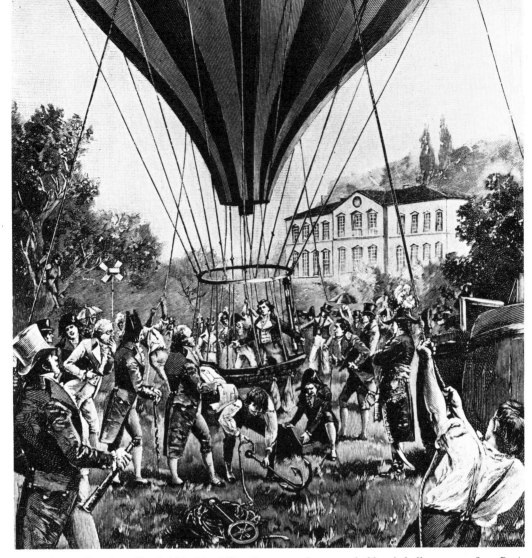

On 16 September 1804, Humboldt's friend Gay-Lussac made a remarkable solo balloon ascent from Paris in order to carry out scientific observations at high altitude. He reached a height of 23,000 feet, thus beating Humboldt's own world altitude record on Chimborazo

In the spring of 1805 Humboldt and his new friend made a journey to Italy together. Humboldt had two reasons for this. Firstly, after a separation of seven years, he wanted to see his brother in Rome. Secondly, he wanted to continue his measurements of the magnetic intensity of the earth at different latitudes and assist Gay-Lussac with his investigations into the composition of the air. On 11 March, armed with a declination magnetometer, gas analysis apparatus and a meteorological balloon, they crossed the Alps, on foot, over the St Bernard Pass.

In Bologna they stopped off to visit the extraordinary Count Zambeccari, sailor of fortune, martyr of science and boldest of the pioneer balloonists, who was engaged at the time in similar experiments to themselves. He was over fifty when they met him and had led an incredible life. He had served as a mercenary in the Spanish Navy and the Russian Navy, been chased out of Spain by the Inquisition and thrown into prison by the Turks. He had successfully flown the first experimental balloon in England in 1783 and recently invented a combination balloon, part hydrogen and part hot-air, with predictably catastrophic results. On his first flight he had vanished into the sky covered in flames and on the second flight he had dropped into the Adriatic covered in ice. As a result he had to have six frost-bitten fingers amputated and was still in bed recovering from this operation when Humboldt and Gay-Lussac called on him. 'Next time,' Humboldt remarked, without exercising any particular talent for clairvoyance, 'he will blow himself up.' And eventually he did.

In early May, after six weeks on the road, they reached Rome. There is no account of the meeting of the two Humboldt brothers, but after the lapse of so many years it was presumably a heartfelt occasion. Though they differed greatly in thought and temperament and pursued widely divergent ends—Alexander the exploration of the outer world, Wilhelm the development of the inner man—they nevertheless retained an indestructible affection for each other. If anything they were more serious than they used to be and it seemed that Wilhelm's personal sorrow—the sudden death from fever of his eldest son two years previously—had left an indelible mark on him. Otherwise they had changed little in the intervening years.

Wilhelm was at this time Prussian Envoy to the Vatican, a post to which as diplomat, man of letters and lover of the arts he was ideally suited by taste and inclination. It was not a very exacting job. According to Alexander it mainly consisted in obtaining divorces for the Roman Catholic members of the Prussian aristocracy. In his ample spare time Wilhelm devoted himself to his studies of languages, which were becoming the ruling interest of his life, and to keeping open house for foreign artists, some of whom were set to work at once to turn Alexander's South American sketches (including the views of Cayambe and the Icononzo bridge) into proper paintings and engravings for his books.

It was while he was in Rome that Humboldt met for the second time a small, twenty-one-year-old Venezuelan revolutionary with black hair, sombre black eyes and an alert but at the same time dreamy expression, called Simón Bolívar. They had already met in Paris the previous autumn. Bolívar, wandering through Europe in mourning for the sudden death of his young wife in Caracas, was by then moving towards the idea of Spanish American independence, and he had asked Humboldt, the established authority on Spanish America and its political climate, whether in his view the Spanish colonies would be able to govern themselves. The precise gist of Humboldt's reply is not known for sure. According to one of Bolívar's Boswells, the Creole-Irish aide-de-camp, General Daniel Florencio O'Leary, Humboldt was supposed to have given his opinion that the Spanish colonies had 'already reached maturity but that he knew no man who could lead them to freedom'. Humboldt, who had known Bolívar's relatives and friends in Caracas, listened attentively and admired Bolívar's passion for his cause. Bolívar, for his part, never ceased to have immense respect for Humboldt, whom he described as 'the discoverer

Humboldt commissioned this engraving of the natural bridge of Icononzo from one of the artists staying at his brother's house in Rome in 1805. It is based on his own sketch and appears in Vues des Cordillères

of the New World' and a man whose study of America 'had done more good than all the Conquistadors put together'. It has sometimes been assumed, not least in Spanish America itself, that Humboldt was the catalyst in the wars by which Bolívar, 'the Liberator', was destined to win the independence of Spanish America a few years later; as such he is still revered in those countries today. It is most unlikely that this was the case, however. As a liberal Humboldt would undoubtedly have shown sympathy for Bolívar's cause; but as an older and wiser man, far more aware of the immense complexities of the Spanish American problem, he would have counselled caution rather than immediate revolution; and in any case, as he admitted many years later, he considered Bolívar was just another youthful dreamer, highly unsuited to leading an American crusade. It was Bonpland who gave Bolívar the encouragement he wanted, not Humboldt; and no one was more taken aback than Humboldt when he learned that the impulsive youth he had known in Paris and Rome had become the head and hero of very nearly an entire continent.

On 15 July Humboldt, Gay-Lussac and their eccentric and brilliant friend Leopold von Buch set out post-haste to Naples, where Vesuvius was on the point of erupting.

Simón Bolívar, Liberator of Spanish America

There they tarried some weeks, measuring the volcano's violent convulsions, before retracing their steps in time to cross the Alps into Germany before winter.

On 16 November 1805, Humboldt returned to his native city of Berlin. He had been away for nearly nine years and, to all accounts, Berlin welcomed their hero as enthusiastically as Paris had done. A medal was struck in his honour and he was invited to give a special lecture at the Royal Academy of Sciences. He was inundated with fan mail from the public—often as many as forty letters a week—and showered with favours from the King. 'His attentions are almost oppressive', Humboldt told his friend, the Swiss physicist Pictet. 'They take up too much of my time.' On the one hand he was given an annual pension of 2,500 thalers with no strings attached, an award he found entirely acceptable; but he was also made a Royal Chamberlain, an appointment he found completely ridiculous. 'Please,' he begged Pictet, 'don't mention that on my return to my home country I was made—a Chamberlain!'

Humboldt hated Berlin. The state of social and official life had deteriorated even more in his absence, and after Paris he found the city dull and lifeless. Going from Paris to Berlin, he said was like passing from life to death. He complained of the cold climate and, after years of uninterrupted health in the dreaded tropics, promptly fell ill with—appropriately—German measles, besides suffering bouts of tooth-ache, tummy-ache, rheumatism and nervous depression. His letters were full of complaint. 'I am living, isolated and like a stranger, in a country that has become a foreign land to me.' He did see something of his old friends—Henriette Herz, Rahel Levin, Nathan Mendelssohn, and Willdenow—but politically he felt very estranged from the majority of Prussian conservatives around him. In some quarters he was attacked for his lack of *Deutschheit*, and rumours circulated to the effect that he was planning to write his works in French, a charge he wholly denied.

Why then, if life was so miserable in Berlin, did Alexander extend his stay so long beyond the requirements of a courtesy call? The northern winter had come and gone, Gay-Lussac had left for Paris, and still he dragged his feet in this hated city. Why?

Partly it was his own doing. Once he had arrived, there were many things to detain him. For example, he had found a young astronomer, Jabbo Oltmanns, to handle the reduction and publication of his South American astronomical observations, and this took time. He had also found a talented young architect, Friedrich Friesen, to do the maps of Mexico for his *Atlas*. The preparation of his South American works, some of them already printing in Stuttgart and Paris, involved him in voluminous correspondence with friends, publishers and scientific institutions that took up several hours a day. His work on the geography and economics of Mexico in particular occupied his attention at this time and he tried hard to interest an English mission—sent to Berlin to organize an alliance against Napoleon—in the value to English business circles of his prolific data on the Mexican silver mines.

I have become great friends with Lord Harrowby, Mr Hammond, Lord Gower, Mr Pierpoint and the whole diplomatic tribe. They had expected to see me completely frenchified and couldn't understand how I can speak English so fluently and hold the fork in my left hand. This connection has been very useful to me in the sale of my books.

The statistics [of Mexico] have turned the heads of these diplomats; Mr Hammond says they are worth a thousand pounds. Well, they shall have the statistics. I hope that every English soul will feel glad at the sight of so many piastres. . . .

In the midst of these protracted labours, which took up most of the day, Humboldt also found time to read numerous papers to the Academy, and to start a series of nocturnal observations of the earth's magnetism which took up most of the night. His instruments were housed in a wooden out-building erected in the garden of a wealthy brandy-distiller called Herr George, who also harboured a historian, Müller, and a philosopher, Fichte, in his grounds, and here Humboldt spent every night from May 1806 until June 1807 recording the magnetic declination, the deviation of the compass from true north, between midnight and morning. In all, he made 6,000 readings and once spent seven sleepless days and nights by his instruments taking a reading every half hour, an ordeal which left him 'somewhat exhausted'. Later he had the help of his astronomer friend, Oltmanns, with whom he alternated the regular nightly watch so that they could both get some sleep. In this way, they discovered that the magnetic needle, which had deviated to the east during the day, had deviated still more by midnight but returned to the west by dawn. In December, they had the good fortune to observe the violent fluctuations of the needle during a display of northern lights (aurora borealis) and later found the same effect sometimes occurred when there were no northern lights visible. Humboldt ascribed this effect to what he called a 'magnetic storm'—a technical term which has passed into international usage.

So far Humboldt had seen his extended stay in Berlin as a voluntary exile—necessary but finite. When the time came for him to leave, however, he found he could not do so. The gates of the city had clanged shut with him inside. The voluntary exile had become an involuntary prisoner.

The cause of this unfortunate turn of events was once again Napoleon. On 14 October he had decisively defeated a large but ill-led and antiquated Prussian army at Jena and on 25 October entered Berlin at the head of the French army of occupation. For the Prussian nation, brought up on the memory of Frederick the Great, it was a moment of profound trauma. The King and his court took refuge in flight. The army and the bureaucracy, the two pillars of the state, lay shattered. Politically, Prussia had ceased to exist.

The winter that followed was grim. The French military régime was a hard one. Heavy war reparations caused an enormous rise in prices and food became scarce. Schloss Tegel, like other fine houses, was looted by both French and Germans alike; the furniture was smashed, manuscripts scattered, and the entire winter stock of potatoes was stolen; only the glass and china and the Greek and Roman antiquities, which had been buried in the garden, were saved. Humboldt, who was personally

The coronation of Napoleon. Detail of a painting by David

186

acquainted with Maret, Napoleon's Secretary of State in Berlin, and Marshal Daru, the Comptroller of the Imperial Household, was asked by the Prussians to mediate with the French occupation authorities. When Napoleon ordered the dissolution of the University of Halle, an outspokenly patriotic institution, it was Humboldt who had to plead for its continuance, a thankless task in which ultimately he failed. Torn equally between conquered and conquerors and grieving at the misery he saw around him, Humboldt turned his back on public life and retired into his work, escaping from the depression of that dismal winter into his memories of his beloved American tropics.

· The result was *Aspects of Nature*. In this one-volume work—the most popular book he ever wrote—Humboldt attempted to raise the spirits of the German people with an evocation of the freedom of the natural world. The book consisted of a series of descriptions of the wonderful landscapes and natural phenomena he had seen on his travels—the *llanos*, the forests of the Orinoco, the solitudes of the mountains of Mexico and Peru, the hunt for electric eels, the spectacular meteorite shower—presented in an unusual way. It was not a travel book nor a scientific text-book but an 'aesthetic treatment of natural history'—in other words it was intended to appeal to the emotions and inform the mind at one and the same time. Humboldt hoped that the book would instil in the educated but unscientific public an interest in the discovery of scientific truth, and in this it probably succeeded. Certainly it was very well received when it came out in 1808. It was hailed as one of the best works of its kind in the German language, translated into half a dozen other languages and republished in several editions. It was the first time Humboldt had reached a large audience and as a result *Aspects of Nature* was always his favourite book.

By now he was determined to get away from Berlin as soon as he could. In a letter to his friend Gérard, the painter, he wrote: 'The hope of reducing the distance between us gives me some comfort. I shall carry out this plan as soon as delicacy and my duties permit. I feel more and more convinced every day that I only produce good work where there are other people producing even better.'

His chance came unexpectedly within the year. Much to his surprise and glee, he was invited by the King to serve as equerry to Prince Wilhelm, the King's brother, on an important political mission to Paris, the purpose of which was to persuade the French to reduce the size of the reparations they were demanding from the Prussians. In January 1808 Humboldt was back in his favourite city again. While the Prince conducted his negotiations with Napoleon, Humboldt busied himself wholeheartedly with his private work. When the Prince was forced to return home empty-handed in the autumn, Humboldt demanded and was granted permission to remain in Paris in order to complete his great South American work—an undertaking even the most patriotic Prussian had to admit was impossible in Berlin at that time.

And for the next fifteen years nobody—not his brother, not his King, not his critics—could drag Humboldt away again. He had come home.

Humboldt and Bonpland brought 60,000 plant specimens back to Paris from Spanish America, many of which were later illustrated in 17 lavish volumes. Inga excelsa *appeared in a volume devoted to Mimosas and other leguminous plants*

CHAPTER 15

Famous in Paris

The Emperor Napoleon now ruled the greater part of Europe, and Paris had become the dazzling metropolis of the civilized world. Magnificent buildings and public monuments rose one after another, and art treasures of all kinds, plundered with consummate tact and exquisite taste from conquered cities throughout the continent, poured into the new Imperial capital. But whereas the greatest man in Europe was establishing his lavish Court in the Tuileries, the 'second greatest' was settling into a bedsitting room he shared with his best friend, Gay-Lussac, in the Ecole Poly-technique. In these modest quarters Humboldt was forced to try and enjoy in-dependence on forty sous a day.

For the truth is he was virtually destitute. His arrival in Paris had coincided with the worst financial crisis in his life and the prospects looked bleak—not only for the publication of his South American works, which he had to pay for out of his own pocket, but for his personal future. For the last three years since the French invasion of Prussia neither he nor his brother had received any profits from their Polish properties—their only regular source of income. The brothers actually owned 95,000 thalers in mortgages on estates in the Grand Duchy of Warsaw alone, but by a French edict of January 1809 certain private properties held by Prussian subjects in Poland had been sequestrated and both Wilhelm and Alexander were prevented for an indefinite period from using either the capital or the interest on their pos-sessions. Caroline and Wilhelm, who had returned to Berlin in 1808 as head of the Department of Education[1], were reduced to living in two sparsely furnished rented rooms. 'The captain'—that shadowy figure of a wastrel half-brother[2]—was up to his eyes in debt. And Alexander himself owed his bankers 16,000 thalers at an interest rate of 12 per cent. In other words he was as good as bankrupt. 'Everyone avoids this house', he wrote to Pictet from Paris. 'If only you knew how unhappy I have been.' And Caroline noted: 'I'm afraid his so-called friends in Paris cost him an awful lot. He eats dry bread so that they can feed on roast.'

This acute financial embarrassment, however, in no way diminished Alexander's

---

[1] In 1810 he founded the University of Berlin now Humboldt University, East Berlin.
[2] Heinrich von Holwede (1763–1817) was Frau Humboldt's son by her previous marriage and almost totally disowned by the Humboldt family.

industry. Obstacles only seemed to increase his formidable capacity for work, and his literary activities, his experiments and his social life continued unabated. In the first few months after his arrival in Paris he divided his time between the Tuileries, where his chief, Prince Wilhelm, was then negotiating directly with Napoleon over Prussian reparations, and the Ecole Polytechnique where he spent the nights and mornings, and seems, under the circumstances, to have conducted his life with commendable chirpiness. 'I am living entirely between "soda" and "potash",' he wrote with undergraduate hilarity at this time, 'between Thénard and Gay-Lussac. "Ammonia", M. Berthollet, comes to see us sometimes and then we feel hydrogenated.'

The daily routine he established at the start changed little for the remainder of his long sojourn in the city. He slept for only three or four hours a night. He got up before six in the morning and took half a cup of black coffee—'concentrated sunbeam'—rarely more. About eight o'clock, 'before the enemy was up to sieze me', he left his room with Gay-Lussac and set off for his morning's work. In 1808 this was downstairs at the Ecole—a laboratory in a basement so damp that Gay-Lussac had to go around in clogs and Humboldt was forced to put on the tall boots with turned-over tops he had found so satisfactory in the swamps of the Orinoco. In laters years these early morning hours became his garret hours, spent in poking about the nooks and corners of Paris, climbing into all the attics of the Quartier Latin, and searching out half-starved students of science.

LEFT *The Café Procope in the Rue de la Comédie Française, unchanged since 1800. Humboldt regularly lunched at the left-hand corner table by the window;* RIGHT *The Ecole Polytechnique, Paris, where Humboldt shared digs and a laboratory with Gay-Lussac*

Between eleven and twelve he normally ate a light meal, which later on he habitually took at the Café Procope, near the Odéon, at the left-hand corner table by the window, surrounded by an admiring crowd.[1] Then he resumed work—until that first autumn in the Tuileries, afterwards in the library of the Institut National where he studied and wrote his books till seven in the evening, though he sometimes took time off in the afternoon to visit his publishers or engravers. At seven he took dinner, usually in the company of friends—the painter Gérard, the physicist Arago, the writer Chateaubriand—and hardly ever at a restaurant or hotel. He never sat more than half an hour after dinner, however, before he rose to leave, and the rest of the evening he passed in society, wandering from salon to salon. He visited at least five receptions every evening and related the same incidents, with variations, at each of them. After half an hour he would rise, bow, retire with someone into a recess for a few minutes' whispered conversation, then slip away quietly to the door. His carriage, when he could afford one, waited below.

Except in his extremely rare moments of personal crisis he was a very sociable man and these visits at the homes of the rich and famous were always very popular. He was a great conversationalist. He could tell a story well. He was often very funny, usually at his own expense or at other people's. He seemed to know everything, from the most esoteric science to the very latest gossip. Above all he had what in show business would be called star quality.

Socially, however, Humboldt had his debit side. For one thing, he could be very sarcastic. For another, he could be extremely noisy. One evening at a reception where he had had the company in fits with his sarcastic quips about the guests who had just left the room, an elegant young woman was seen to get up to leave, think twice about it and at length sit down again with obvious signs of impatience. When the hostess asked her why she seemed so put out, the young woman, with admirable bluntness, replied: 'Oh! I'll never leave so long as that gentleman is here'—indicating Humboldt. 'I just don't want to be discussed by him.' As for his noisiness, here is what Sir Charles Hallé, whose misfortune it was to be a musician—pianist, conductor and founder of the Hallé Orchestra—had to say about an encounter with Humboldt some years later:

> When the invitation bore the words 'To meet Humboldt', the rooms were naturally crowded and he was the cynosure of all eyes. Wherever he stood a crowd of eager listeners assembled around him, all mute and full of reverence. He never attempted to lead or originate a conversation in the true sense of the word; he always spoke alone, delivering a lecture on one subject or on another, and was never anxious to hear anyone else's opinion. I was once asked to play for him, and looked upon this invitation as an event in my life. There had been a momentary silence in the rooms, but the moment I began to play von Humboldt began to hold forth on a new and evidently more interesting topic, his voice rising with every one of my *crescendos*, dominating my most powerful *fortes*, and

---

[1] The Café Procope is still there, and so is the corner table by the window. Voltaire used to write some of his satires in this restaurant, the interior of which has not changed since 1800.

In the summer of 1805 Humboldt made his first visit to Vesuvius, then in eruption. Painting by Philip Hackert

resuming its normal level only with my most delicate phrases. It was a duet which I did not sustain long.

When Humboldt left the last salon of the night he would return for another two hours' work or more in his own quarters. His digs in Paris—even after 1810 when his assets in Poland were unfrozen and he was solvent enough to move out of the bed-sitter in the Ecole Polytechnique—were extremely modest places for a man in his position and it was some time before he kept a manservant or ran his own carriage. He moved house fairly frequently but never strayed far from the Institut National where he assiduously attended all the meetings. For a year or two he shared an apartment with Gay-Lussac in the Rue de l'Estrapade and his later letters bear addresses in or around the student quarter, where he lived very much like a student himself. His bedroom was tiny and his study was generally a very simple room containing hardly any books, a few wooden chairs with cane bottoms, and a large deal table which served as a blackboard. This was possibly his most important possession, for on it he did his calculations and worked at his books. When the wood was covered in calculations and there was no room for more he called in a carpenter to plane them all off.

It was at this table, too, that he wrote all his interminable correspondence. In a world without telephones letter-writing was necessarily commonplace, but even by the standards of his time his output was prodigious. He wrote between one and two thousand letters a year, often at great length and always in his own hand—he refused to dictate them to a secretary for fear of losing the personal touch. His task was not helped by the fact that his right arm was permanently crippled with rheumatism caused by his hardships on the Orinoco. As a result he had to lift up his right arm with his left hand whenever he wanted to shake hands or start writing and this, of course, contributed little to the legibility of his appalling scribble—'my hieroglyphs'. Only someone very familiar with his handwriting could readily decipher his correspondence with its tiny letters, tight spacing, crooked lines, and blots, and to make matters worse he was in the habit of cluttering up the margins with afterthoughts so that a reader had to scratch out the deciphered parts as he went along.

Though Humboldt's circle of acquaintances was wide, as a bachelor without the normal emotional ties, without even a home in the normal sense of the word, he became increasingly dependent upon intimate friendships with a few other men. It is quite clear that by now these friendships had no explicitly sexual undertones, but they were more or less intense for all that, and they had their tiffs and reconciliations like any love match. At first it was Gay-Lussac who filled the rôle as an emotional focus for Humboldt in Paris, but within a year or two he had been superseded by the person who was to remain, above all others, the central passion, the key nexus of Humboldt's life for the next half century.

François Arago was a young and talented physicist of twenty-six—fifteen years younger than Humboldt—when the two men first met in Paris in 1809. A French

View of Cayambe, Mexico. One of several pictures Humboldt commissioned from his brother's friends in Rome in the summer of 1805, to illustrate his Vues des Cordillères

The Institut National, Paris

Catalan, born near Perpignan, he was a self-taught prodigy in mathematics and at a very early age became the Director of the Paris Observatoire and later Permanent Secretary of the Institut National. In 1806 he assisted in the extension of the triangulation of France to Spain and the Balearic Isles, and when war broke out between France and Spain he was thrown into prison. For two years thereafter he starved in a Spanish dungeon before being transferred to a concentration camp in Algiers for another year. Throughout this grim time his only concern was to save his notes and measurements for posterity and France, and his papers never left their hiding place under his shirt until he was able to hand them over to the French authorities when he was finally repatriated to Marseille. The news of his courage and tenacity prompted Humboldt to send him a letter of congratulation at the quarantine hospital, the first letter he received in France, and when Arago finally arrived in Paris his first act was to visit Humboldt to thank him for his kindness. This was the beginning of their lifelong friendship, which only ended with Arago's death many years later.

From now on, Humboldt saw Arago at least once every day and took to working with him regularly on experiments in the Observatoire in the Rue St Jacques. In his view, Arago was a genius and he acknowledged his intellectual superiority without hesitation. Both men had a lot in common, especially their liberal political opinions, their compassion and their strong spirit of independence. But in a period of reaction in Europe Arago was the more outspoken and more courageous of the two in defence of his increasingly heretical opinions; he was less ready to compromise and always put his principles before his personal relations. Perhaps it was his strength, perhaps it was his gentleness, that drew Humboldt so much into his company for so long. Whatever it was, it seems to have cast Humboldt into a curiously submissive, almost female rôle, and he was always touchingly gratified whenever he received a brief letter from his friend or met him again after an absence. For Arago was a devoted family man; consequently his capacity to return Humboldt's affection was very much less than Humboldt's capacity to give it, and in the end Humboldt had to make do with crumbs—crumbs which, pathetically, in later years became the main sustenance of his personal life.

Humboldt's faithful devotion to his friend, however, did not preclude friendships with others. He was warm and impulsive in his relationships, especially with those who were young, good-looking and in need of help. Thus between 1812 and 1814 he formed a very close association with an impecunious twenty-three-year-old artist called Karl von Steuben, a man of a 'shy, delicate nature' and 'quiet, noble disposi-

François Arago—'the central passion, the key nexus of Humboldt's life for the next half century.'

tion', who lived in Gérard's studio and supported an aged mother in St Petersburg from what he could scrape together by painting. Humboldt, though he could hardly afford it, commissioned Steuben to paint a full-length, nine-foot-high, life-size portrait of him in a South American setting as a present for Caroline, and for the next year and a half met him almost every day and spent so much time with him drawing and painting that his friends in Paris society wondered where he had got to. 'This company', Alexander confessed to Caroline, 'is my only joy.' When Wilhelm visited Paris in 1814 he found Steuben 'really a very pretty and charming man—though he hardly speaks any German'. As for the portrait of Alexander—'I can't say I've been impressed by the likeness. It just isn't there when you look at it closely'. The truth is, Steuben was not a great artist, or a particularly successful one. In 1818 and even as late as 1837 we find Humboldt touting for commissions for Steuben and rueing the fact that other artists took a poor view of him. And thereafter Steuben vanishes into obscurity.

As for women, Humboldt knew an immense number during his time in Paris and their names read like a roll-call of the *haut monde* of the Empire: the Marquise de Prie, the daughter of Madame de Staël, the Comtesse de Broglie, the Comtesse von Goltz, the Comtesse de Duras, Madame Récamier, the Comtesse de Mouchy, the Marquise de Montcalm—the sister of Comte Richelieu, and so on. What is doubtful is whether he cared to know any of them particularly well. A man of his reputation and good-looks was clearly an outstanding catch but he managed to elude all the predators who stalked the fashionable salons in search of prey—like Lady Randall and the Duchess of Devonshire, those 'leopards from Albion'—and preserved his independence, and possibly his virginity, intact. In 1814 he made a crayon self-portrait of himself in front of the mirror in Gérard's studio. The portrait showed a fine-looking man in his prime (he was forty-five but he looked at least ten years younger, as he did in all his portraits), with casually tousled hair, a face full of vitality, a sensuous mouth and large, alert eyes. How could such an attractive example of mature manhood remain so totally uninvolved except by radiating sheer indifference? All the same he was very popular with the ladies, and even Caroline loved him. 'Impossible to describe him', she recounted after a brief meeting in 1811. 'He's such an incredible mixture of charm, vanity, softness, cold and warmth. I've never met anyone like him.' At the end of 1812 the rumour circulated that he had received a proposal of marriage from a certain Miss R. living in Germany—a proposal he turned down on the grounds that he was already wedded to science and believed that to bring children into the world was a sin. Otherwise there is no evidence that Humboldt ever considered marriage at any time in his life and only one piece of evidence that he ever had any kind of relationship with any kind of woman that was more than simply dutiful or polite. That woman was a certain Pauline Wiesel (née César) and the evidence is a single letter from which one can construe anything one likes.

Humboldt, painted in 1814 by his friend Karl von Steuben, against a Mexican background

I wrote to you once from Frankfurt and twice from Paris. In view of your silence, my dear Pauline, I'm afraid someone is stopping you getting my letters. You know my joys and sorrows. We were very happy here for two long weeks, but I could have guessed that it wouldn't last for very long and everything would be destroyed sooner or later. I embrace you intimately. Everything here is so empty and desolate. I'd walk for twelve hours just to see you. We will be close to each other for ever. You know me. Please write to me soon.

Just how sincere were the feelings that seemed to be explicit in this letter we shall never know. But Humboldt's fear that someone was intercepting his letters to Pauline was sincere enough, for from 1807 onwards he was under the constant surveillance of the French Secret Police—from whose files, indeed, the above letter was taken. For many years, in fact, Humboldt's mail—especially his mail to and from enemy or occupied cities like Berlin, Vienna and London—was regularly opened and copied, and his servant was bribed to act as a secret agent and asked to explain any puzzling bits in his employer's correspondence. Whenever Humboldt was out of town, the Secret Police broke into his flat, rifled his bureau and copied out his papers—in those pre-Minox days they had to use a clerk with a quill pen. Their reasons for doing this were twofold: firstly, they were suspicious of him because he was a German living in France; secondly, his letters reflected more or less exactly the current

LEFT Humboldt's self-portrait. Lithograph made from a drawing of his reflection in a mirror, Paris 1814. He was then forty-five; RIGHT The title page of the first of Humboldt's South American publications, a copy of which he sent to Napoleon

ESSAI

SUR LA

GÉOGRAPHIE DES PLANTES

ACCOMPAGNÉ

D'UN TABLEAU PHYSIQUE

DES RÉGIONS ÉQUINOXIALES,

Fondé sur des mesures exécutées, depuis le dixième degré de latitude boréale jusqu'au dixième degré de latitude australe, pendant les années 1799, 1800, 1801, 1802 et 1803.

PAR

AL. DE HUMBOLDT ET A. BONPLAND.

RÉDIGÉ PAR AL DE HUMBOLDT.

A PARIS,

CHEZ LEVRAULT, SCHOELL ET COMPAGNIE, LIBRAIRES.

XIII — 1805.

political views of the Paris salons and the various individuals who attended them. At some stage Humboldt seems to have realized this, because he began to write his local Paris mail in code. But it must have served as a forcible reminder to him that his position as an alien in this foreign capital was very insecure, particularly in view of Napoleon's implacable distrust of him.

Humboldt had done all he could to straighten things with Napoleon. As soon as he returned to Paris in 1808 he sent the Emperor a careful, diplomatically worded letter explaining what his scientific intentions in the city were, and enclosed a copy of his *Essai sur la géographie des plantes* and *Géographie des plantes équinoxiales*, at the same time hinting at further literary gifts to come. Neither his courtesy nor his flattery seems to have had much effect on Napoleon, however. The Emperor remained convinced that Humboldt was a spy—after all, he was still Chamberlain to the King of Prussia! In 1810, appraised presumably of the subversive contents of Humboldt's mail, Napoleon ordered his Chief of Police, Savary, to give Humboldt 24 hours in which to leave Paris. Humboldt actually received this order, and went at once to his friend Chaptal, the French chemist and Minister of State, pleading with him to intervene. That same evening Chaptal went to the Tuileries and convinced Napoleon of Humboldt's integrity and scientific importance. 'But doesn't he devote his time to politics?' Napoleon asked. 'No', replied Chaptal. 'I've never heard him talk about anything but science.' Which was an answer that was neither true nor false, but for the moment satisfied Napoleon.

Humboldt's position in Paris remained for ever an extraordinarily delicate one. On the one hand the French authorities distrusted him: on the other hand the German patriots resented him. Both applied pressures to force him to leave: to both he presented an increasing determination to stay. This required constant vigilance, an ever-watchful minding of step. The newspapers were a continuous threat to his security. Now that he was a famous public figure their gossip columns began to sharpen their pens on him and rumour was given the credentials of print. Sometimes it was the usual harmless untruth. 'It is reported from Frankfurt', wrote one hard-pressed journalist, 'that M. A. de Humboldt, the well-known traveller, intends to leave Prussia and settle in Bavaria. He has bought a monastery twelve miles from Munich.' At the other times, however, a newspaper report could directly threaten Humboldt's toe-hold in France. The press at one time stated that he was on his way to Weimar to meet Madame de Staël and Friedrich Schlegel—both of them out-and-out enemies of Napoleon. Humboldt was quick to scotch that one and had the *Journal de l'Empire* print a speedy denial.

It says a lot for Humboldt's sense of diplomatic atmosphere, his instinct for political survival, that he was able to last out nearly a quarter of a century in the French capital and at the end leave voluntarily. This was just long enough to see his American publications—his 'interminable voyage'—through the press. And by the end of it he was nearly sixty years of age.

CHAPTER 16

The South American Publications

Alexander von Humboldt's great South American work, *Voyage de Humboldt et Bonpland 1799–1804*[1], remains a monument to his energy, tenacity and breadth of vision. It comprises no less than 30 volumes published over a period of thirty years: the first volume, *Essai sur la géographie des plantes*, appeared in Paris in 1805, when Humboldt was thirty-six years of age. The last volume came out in 1834, when he was sixty-five and had already been back from South America for thirty years. It was the greatest project of its kind ever undertaken by a private individual, and since it was brought out largely at his own expense it finally caused his financial ruin.

As early as 1801, when he was in Cuba, Humboldt had worked out a scheme for publishing the results of his expedition, and shortly after his return to Europe he planned to produce eleven distinct works, all of them to be published under the joint names of Humboldt and Bonpland. At first he had not envisaged that this would be such a time-consuming operation as it turned out to be. In 1805 he wrote to Pictet: 'Considering the remarkable energy of my disposition, I expect to see the whole thing out of my hands in a couple of years, or at most in two and a half years, as I'm now impatient to discharge my cargo in order to embark on something new.' But he was to experience many frustrations and delays, and each time his plans for a second great expedition came to nothing he reverted to the South American work, modifying and extending it until it reached its final colossal proportions.

Roughly the work falls into three main categories. The first one consists of the scientific results—the botanical, zoological, geological, astronomical and meteorological data—and includes two atlases. The second consists of treatises on the geography and economy of Cuba and Mexico. The third—the part best known to the general public—consists of an incomplete narrative account of his travels (*Personal Narrative of Travels to the Equinoctial Regions of the New Continent during the years 1799–1801*), together with *Vues des Cordillères* which is an odd mixture of descriptions and illustrations of mountain views and Aztec art, and a five-volume history of the discovery of America (*Examen Critique*). The books in the last two categories were written, in French, entirely by Humboldt himself. Those in the first category were the result of

[1]The complete title is *Voyage aux régions équinoxiales du Nouveau Continent fait en 1799, 1800, 1801, 1802, 1803 et 1804, par A. de Humboldt et A. Bonpland. Rédigé par Alexander de Humboldt, 1805–34.*

Aztec paintings, depicting the coming of the Spanish Conquistadors. From Vues des Cordillères *by Humboldt and Bonpland*

Fig. 1.

Fig. 2.

Fig. 3.

Fig. 4.

Fig. 5.

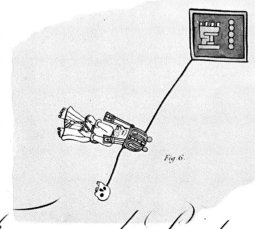

Fig. 6.

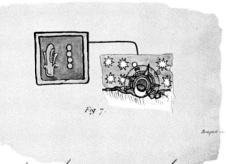

Fig. 7.

Fragmens de Peintures hiéroglyphiques Aztèques,

tirés du Cod. Telleriano-Remensis.

collaboration with a number of experts in the different subjects involved—Oltmanns did the astronomical and geographical calculations; Cuvier, Latreille and Valenciennes worked together on the zoology and comparative anatomy; and Carl Sigismund Kunth, a nephew of Humboldt's former tutor, wrote most of the botanical volumes in place of Aimé Bonpland, whose abilities in this direction soon proved highly unsatisfactory.

The story of Bonpland's contribution to the great work which bears his name is a sad one—indeed the story of the remainder of his very long life makes very distressing reading altogether. When he returned to Europe with Humboldt in 1804 he was at first entrusted with the classification and publication of all the plant material resulting from the expedition—altogether about 60,000 specimens representing about 6,000 species, of which more than 3,000 were new to science. But to Humboldt's consternation the man who had shown himself to be such a conscientious and indefatigable plant collector in the field turned out to be both incompetent and unco-operative when it came to desk work. Whether it was because the task did not suit his out-of-door temperament or because he felt it was beyond his capability or both, Bonpland consistently delayed or prevaricated, and in September 1810, Humboldt, who was at his wits' end, was compelled to send him a forthright letter of complaint.

> You haven't sent me a line on the subject of botany. I beg and beseech you to persevere until the work is completed, for since the departure of Madame Gauvin I have received only half a page of manuscript. I am quite determined that the results of our expedition are not going to be lost, and if in the space of eight months it is not possible to produce more than ten plates, which is only what any botanist in Europe would prepare in the space of a fortnight, there is no reason to expect the completion of the second volume of *Plantes équinoxiales* in under three years . . . I therefore beseech you again, my dear Bonpland, to persevere in this undertaking to the end. It's an object of the greatest importance, not only in the interests of science but for the sake of your own reputation and the fulfillment of the contract you entered into with me in 1798. So do pray send us some manuscript . . .

In the end, Bonpland managed to edit only four out of the seventeen volumes on South American botany which were finally published—and even these were severely criticized because of their many gross errors in classification. The remainder, including the great seven-volume *Nova genera et species plantarum*, with its 700 engravings and Latin classifications, were the work of Kunth. Humboldt, indeed, must have been greatly relieved when Bonpland returned to South America in 1816 and abandoned all further interest in the publications. And here we may digress for a moment to follow the unbelievably bizarre course this man's life subsequently followed.

Shortly after his return from South America, Bonpland had been appointed superintendent of the gardens at Empress Josephine's retreat at Malmaison outside Paris. There he spent probably the happiest years of his life in the creation of one of the most beautiful flower gardens in the world. After Napoleon's divorce of Josephine, Bonpland became the Empress's confidant, grew very attached to her

South American condor. From Recueil d'observations de zoologie
by Humboldt and Bonpland

and was beside her when she died in May 1814. After her death he lost all interest in his work at Malmaison, however, and became very restless; he made a disastrous marriage to a twenty-four-year-old French girl of dubious reputation and in 1816 was glad to turn his back on Europe and set sail for South America on a second plant-collecting expedition. In Argentina, now a newly independent Republic, he was appointed Professor of Natural History at Buenos Aires, and four years later he set out on an expedition bound for the Gran Chaco and Bolivia. He had got no further than the Paraguay river, however, before disaster overtook him. The area he had

Aimé Bonpland as an old man—'unmourned and unsung but loving life to the last.'

entered was the subject of a frontier dispute between Argentina and Paraguay, then ruled by a violent and paranoiac dictator, Dr Francia. On the night of 3 December 1821, at the orders of Francia, a troop of cavalry attacked Bonpland's camp, killed all his servants, slashed his head open with a sabre and put him in chains. In this condition he was carried off to a remote settlement in the interior of Paraguay, called Santa Maria, where he was kept under open arrest and put to work as the local garrison's doctor.

As soon as Humboldt heard of his friend's arrest he wrote directly to Francia and with the support of Canning, the British Prime Minister, and of Chateaubriand pleaded for Bonpland's release. His efforts were in vain, however, and it was nine years before Bonpland was finally set free in 1830. Loaded with medals, doctorates and honorary degrees from Europe, he settled down near the small town of Santa Borja in Uruguay, not far from the Brazilian border, where he spent the remaining years of his life in extraordinarily primitive circumstances surrounded by the half-caste offspring resulting from his liaison with a local Indian woman, his own wife having deserted him soon after his arrest. He lived in a remote mud hut on the pampas, slept on the ground and had abandoned the use of a knife and fork. Every year he sent Humboldt his pension certificate so that Humboldt could remit to him the annual 3000-franc pension the French Government had granted him in 1805, and from time to time, hankering for a more civilized life, he toyed with the idea of returning to Paris. But he was apprehensive of giving up his freedom and his plantations of oranges, peaches, figs and roses—'the society of my beloved plants'—in exchange for a city garret and a solitary rose in a window-box, and he never moved. In May 1858, at the age of eight-five, he died, unmourned and unsung, but loving life to the last. Even when he was dead, ill luck seemed to dog Bonpland, for a drunken peasant took offence at his embalmed corpse, which would not return his greeting, and angrily ran it through with a dagger.

Though his correspondence with Humboldt during his last years had remained as friendly and loyal as ever, Bonpland took with him to the grave a private envy of his friend's success, which he considered, not altogether unreasonably, had been achieved to some extent at the expense of his own. Such was the remarkable life of the man who made such an unremarkable contribution to the published works of Humboldt and Bonpland.

Among the various volumes in the purely scientific category of the South American work was one by Humboldt himself on the geology and climatology of South America. This was a quarto volume, the German edition of which he dedicated to his old friend Goethe. This important monograph contained a great many new ideas, not least the concept of the geography of plants itself, the change in the type and pattern of vegetation according to the climate in which it grows. This was very conveniently and dramatically demonstrated to Humboldt during his ascent of Chimborazo and Pichincha—high volcanoes which rose near the equator and contained within the

Profile of Chimborazo, showing the location of different plants at different altitudes—an ingenious graphic representation of Humboldt's treatise on the geography of plants

space of a few vertical miles virtually all the climates in the world and a correspond-ingly wide range of vegetation, from the tropical type on the plains, the temperate type half-way up, and the nearly Arctic type at the peak. Humboldt later graphically illustrated this distribution in his novel plant-profiles of Chimborazo—reproduced in his South American *Atlas*. Georg Forster's father was the first to recognize the rudiments of this subject during his voyage with Captain Cook many years previously. But it was Humboldt, with his systematic tabulation of botanical, meteorological and geographical data who laid the firm foundations of it—the bedrock, so to speak, of the modern study of ecology.

A lot of Humboldt's influence in science came from the novel graphic ways in which he presented his results. For example, by connecting all the points of equal mean temperature by lines on a chart—he called them 'isothermal lines'—he devised a method of comparing different climatic conditions throughout the world. He was a very good name-coiner and a number of technical terms which came into general usage were his invention, including 'isodynamics' (lines of equal magnetic intensity) and 'isoclines' (lines of equal magnetic dip), together with 'Jurassic' and 'magnetic storm'. With his researches in the mountains of tropical America and his subsequent systematic classification and comparative description of observed phenomena all over the earth, Humboldt laid the foundations of physical geography and geophysics. As time went by it became clear that he stood out like a colossus in the development of geographic thought, and along with his German contemporary, Carl Ritter, he came to be regarded as the father of modern geography and the leading exponent of its classical period.

The works in the second category—the exhaustive treatise on the geography and the economics of Cuba (*Political Essay on the Isle of Cuba*) and Mexico (*Political Essay on the Kingdom of New Spain*)—give a minutely detailed, highly statistical description

World chart showing isothermal lines, first devised by Humboldt in 1817

LEFT *Title page of Humboldt's* Atlas géographique et physique du Nouveau Continent *;* RIGHT *Mexican Indians in typical costume. From* Vues des Cordillères *by Humboldt and Bonpland*

of these two countries as they were in the last few years of the Spanish colonial era. The Cuba book caused some commotion with its exposé of the barbarity of slavery on that island, but it was the Mexico volume—the first modern regional economic geography—which had the biggest practical repercussions. Humboldt's main purpose in writing it was to draw the attention of European capitalists to the immense mineral resources of Mexico, especially the silver mines, which in his view could yield enormous profits if properly exploited. The book was immediately translated into English and was directly responsible for the Mexican mining industry coming under English control in the years after Mexican independence. Several companies were floated in London to purchase and develop the mines and Humboldt was even offered the chairmanship of one of them, along with £20,000 of shares—an offer he turned down on the grounds of his 'disinclination for public affairs'. Humboldt's highly optimistic opinion of the potential of the Mexican mines gave rise in London to the notion that easy money was to be made out of them, and speculators and unscrupulous operators, mindless of the fact that many of the mines since then had been flooded during the Mexican revolution and required huge injections of capital to get them working again, pushed share prices up to ridiculous heights. In 1830 the bubble burst, many shareholders were ruined, and 'the ingenious Humboldt', who had always acted in good faith, was publicly declared responsible in the English press on account of his 'exaggerated view' of the economic prospects of Mexico, an attack which he not unnaturally greatly resented.

Of all Humboldt's South American publications, however, none remained so long in the public eye as his narrative account of his travels, *Personal Narrative of Travels to the Equinoctial Regions*, first published in Paris in three quarto volumes between 1814 and 1819, and in London in a five-volume English translation in 1825. This book is still read today by the occasional enthusiast of exploration literature; and it is perhaps the only book he wrote which, as one of the few reliable descriptions of the unchanged regions of the Upper Orinoco, is still of some practical use to the traveller today. Alas, in spite of the many years Humboldt devoted to his South American works, the *Personal Narrative* remained incomplete, for it ends with his arrival in Cartagena, Colombia in March 1801. Humboldt had always intended to produce a fourth volume, with an account of the remaining three years of his expedition, particularly his year's march along the Cordilleras, and he had actually almost completed the manuscript when he suddenly decided to destroy it. To his and his biographers' everlasting disappointment, posterity has had to make do with what there is —a long and curious fragment of more than 1,200 pages.

The first thing to be said about the *Personal Narrative* is that it is neither strictly personal nor strictly narrative. From the start, Humboldt had been against a mere *conte de voyage* and in that respect he did his contemporary public a grave disservice. As early as 1805 he told Pictet that his inclination was towards doing a comprehensive view of nature rather than a 'narrative of personal adventure'. 'In this way', he added, 'the charlatanry of literature will be combined with utility.' What he eventually produced was, for the most part, a clinically objective description of the natural environment, people, and history of the tropical world of Venezuela, threaded on to a more or less chronological account of the expedition, the centrepiece of which was the venture to the Upper Orinoco. The book was the product of a sensitive and impressionable man who never forgot that his main concern was always with facts. As a writer Humboldt's main fault was his inability to leave anything out, and English reviewers, who were not terribly complimentary, were quick to seize on this. 'We may say of him in physics,' wrote one, 'what was said of Barrow in divinity, that he never quits a subject till he has exhausted it.' *Personal Narrative* was encyclopedic, disorderly, fascinating and boring by turns. As Arago remarked apropos his literary abilities: 'Humboldt, you don't really know how to write a book. You write endlessly but what comes out of it is not a book. It's a portrait without a frame.'

For all that, *Personal Narrative* has its merits, not least the personality and peculiar talents of its author which shine through many of the pages—his humanity, his humour, his extraordinary powers of observation, his passion for the natural world in all its forms. And during his lifetime it was an inspiration to a number of brilliant young naturalists, including Charles Darwin, Louis Agassiz and William James, who all carried Humboldt's book with them on their travels. Indeed, Darwin wrote from HMS *Beagle*: 'I formerly admired Humboldt, now I almost adore him'. And when he returned to England he asked Sir James Hooker to let Humboldt know

that 'my whole course of life is due to having read and re-read as a youth his *Personal Narrative*'. If only it could have been judiciously edited, shorn of its mass of extraneous matter, the work might have become a classic of its kind and a more lasting monument to the memory of a great man who in countries like England is today largely forgotten. As it is, Humboldt's *Personal Narrative* compares poorly for sheer readability with the works of other scientists who travelled in South America after him—Darwin, Wallace, Bates.

Looking at the South American publications as a whole, it is clear that Humboldt not only underestimated the length of time they would take but also the amount of money they would cost, for he was an indifferent businessman. The giddy reception he received when he returned to Europe may have given him an inflated idea of the extent of public interest in works of this kind, and he appears to have had only the haziest notion of the enormous expense his books would entail. There is no complete record of the final cost of the whole work but we have a few examples of the enormous bills Humboldt had to face. Thus, 1,200 pages of antique type on handmade paper cost 500,000 francs; engravings, 600,000 francs; printing and paper charges for 1,300 folio leaves of copper-plate illustrations, 240,000 francs—quite apart from the fees due to the artists and draughtsmen who so meticulously worked Humboldt's field sketches and plant specimens into a total of 1,425 finished black and white and colour plates. Humboldt was very demanding of his artists and often sent plates back to be done again, at great expense, if they did not meet with his approval.

Most of these crippling costs had to be borne by Humboldt himself, for the grant from the Prussian Government only amounted to 24,000 francs, and he even had to forgo his royalties to keep the printing in progress. Very few public institutions, let alone members of the public, could afford to buy a complete set, for in the bound version it cost 10,300 francs and unbound 9,574 francs—twice the price of the state-subsidized *Description de l'Egypte*, a lavish by-product of the Egyptian campaign for which Napoleon had granted 3 million francs towards the costs of production. Not even Humboldt could afford to possess a set of his own books. The Universities of Berlin, Breslau, Halle and Bonn each received a free de luxe set, by way of repayment of the Prussian loan, and the government of France, Austria and Russia purchased a number of copies for their universities and scientific academies. But in general it remained a scarce and costly work even in Humboldt's own lifetime and today this is even more the case.

Humboldt and Bonpland inspect basalt rock formations near the Real del Monte mine in north-east Mexico

CHAPTER 17

Farewell to Elysium

Even before he got back from South America, Humboldt had resolved to embark on another expedition—'the second great task of my life'—as soon as his current commitments were out of the way. He had set his heart on the great landmass of Asia, particularly the Himalayas, and in order to keep himself free for this venture he turned down several important jobs that were offered to him, including one as Minister of Education in Berlin and another as Prussian Ambassador in Paris. He prized his independence perhaps above all else in his life. 'Simple in my tastes,' he explained to his friend, Baron Rennenkampff, 'and preserving an intellectual independence in which I am sustained by a strong will, I prefer to follow my scientific career, relying on nothing but my own resources.'

It would have seemed that a traveller of his reputation would have found no difficulty in mounting a second expedition and that every door would be open to him, but the frustrations he was to face now were to be far greater than any that had confronted him before he set out to South America, and this time they were to defeat him almost entirely. At first, however, everything seemed full of promise. In 1811 the Russian Chancellor, Romanzov, invited him to join a mission that was being organized to Siberia, Kashgar and Tibet, and Humboldt, full of excitement, accepted. Even if he knew that out of nine men who set out only one would return, he said, he would still want to go. 'I don't know a single word of Russian, but I shall make myself a Russian in the same way I once made myself a Spaniard. Whatever I do, I do with enthusiasm . . . .' He had already said goodbye to his brother and met the Tsar Alexander in Pressburg, and was half-way through his preparations for this expedition which he envisaged lasting seven or eight years, when Napoleon once again thwarted all his plans by invading Russia. Disappointed but undefeated, Humboldt this time decided to make a private expedition to Persia and Afghanistan at his own expense, and began to take lessons in Persian. He reckoned that two-thirds of his South American work was now complete and that the rest of it would be finished by 1814, when he would at last be free to set out. But the defeat of the *Grande Armée* in Russia, the outbreak of organized resistance in Germany, the disintegration of Europe—in a word the mixture of war and politics as before—again prevented him from doing anything but sitting tight in Paris. And even that put him under greater moral pressure than ever before—a pressure that came not from the Parisians, who continued to treat him with every courtesy, but from his own people, and especially his own family.

In 1813, as the Russian army advanced across Poland, thousands of Prussians had risen up in arms against the French occupation forces in an upsurge of patriotic fervour such as the nation had not known for generations. Wilhelm had joined the patriots at allied headquarters. His son Theodor, only sixteen years of age, had volunteered for the partisan army, fighting alongside regular troops and Russian cossacks, Mongolian bowmen and the Austrian Imperial Guard in historic engagements against Napoleon's second army east of the Elbe. Among Alexander's friends in Berlin there was a universal jubilation he was unable to share. With the outbreak of the War of Liberation his sedentary life in a French library was becoming more and more anomalous. His absence from Germany in its hour of glory was now increasingly commented upon. 'And where is your brother?' the sixteen-year-old Prince Wilhelm, later to be Kaiser Wilhelm I, asked Wilhelm von Humboldt one day. 'In Paris', Wilhelm replied. 'My God!' retorted the Prince. 'Then he ought to kill Napoleon!' And Wilhelm wrote a note to Caroline the same day: 'Wouldn't that be a nice job for Alexander in Paris?'

In a later letter, Wilhelm wrote from his command post:

> I must confess quite candidly, that I cannot endorse Alexander's stay in Paris. It's true that he couldn't do anything for the war comparable in importance to what he did in Paris. It would have been an irreparable calamity if he had been killed in action. But the honourable thing is not to weigh profits. To value one's own person so highly is beyond all my estimation of a good character. Aeschylus would have considered it a very odd thing indeed if anyone had prevented his fighting at Marathon simply so that he could scribble a few more rhymes.

Not that Alexander, sitting in peace in Paris, was in any way oblivious of what was going on, of the momentous nature of the struggle that was convulsing Europe. War disgusted him and for the first time in his life he felt close to it and was agonized by it. He wrote to Caroline:

> My dearest Li,
>
> We are indeed living in wonderful times. Barely a week has passed since I wrote to you through a business firm and now we hear that the mail has probably been stopped and that my letters can't have reached you. Thus every avenue is closed and I shall live here as completely isolated as I was on the Orinoco. I don't want to grumble, though, and I'll get by joyfully if God in his over-ruling Providence should bring success to oppressed humanity. . . . Every battle fills me with anxiety about Theodore. For the first time I'm now experiencing what it is to be personally connected with the bloodshed of war. All one's hopes, plans, wishes are mixed up with a feeling of dread. I haven't had a line from Wilhelm since he went to Prague, though I've written to him there. Perhaps he's frightened of getting me into trouble. Although I've escaped myself, it's a fact that a lot of people have got into trouble on account of letters they've received from Germany. I am very well, except for fits of depression and annoying stomach-ache, and I'm working hard without feeling it to be an effort. Of my arm I can say nothing; at all events it's not worse. . . . God forbid that Theodore should ever be in a position to need my intervention— for his sake there's nothing I'd dread so much. Should Providence so ordain it, however, you

may depend, dear Li, upon my fondest love and sincerest affection. There is nothing I wouldn't then sacrifice to help him. Give him my love, and tell him how delighted I am to hear of his manly courage and praiseworthy conduct. . . . I'm not writing to Bill today; he will, I hope, see this letter, and he knows my inalienable affection for him. Kiss the dear children. Goodbye, my dear sister. These are wonderful times . . . With unchangeable love.

Ever yours
ALEXANDER.

Rarely, had Alexander been so moved by the events of the external world around him. Never had he had recourse to the words *God* and *Providence* before—certainly never with such apparent devoutness. And never had he displayed such a touching devotion to Caroline as in this confused and troubled letter, with its strange mixture of selfless anguish and petty complaint. Time, it seemed, was out of joint, the familiar world awry. For he saw only too clearly what few could yet see—'the waste of blood and treasure' the war involved, the crowned heads of the Holy Alliance waiting in the wings, a new oppression in an old form.

On 31 March 1814 the First Empire fell and the Russian army entered Paris, followed the next day by the crowned heads themselves, Tsar Alexander and King Frederick William III. It was the beginning of the restoration of the old order, the first gathering of the forces of reaction that were to suppress the old revolutionary ideals, and with them freedom of thought and action, all over Europe. Humboldt once again found himself called on to liaise between two sides for whom he felt an

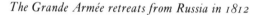

The Grande Armée retreats from Russia in 1812

equal sympathy. Once again he emerged from the seclusion of his study into the hurly-burly of an occupied capital and streets full of soldiers and guns.

His first act was to save the French scientific institutions from the blind resentment of foreign troops. When an infantry platoon was billeted in the Natural History Museum, the academicians became alarmed and Cuvier at once asked Alexander to intervene. By mid-morning he had received Alexander's reply.

Thursday, 11.30. In haste.

Five minutes after I received your letter my dear colleague, I went to the local Prussian Commandant, von Goltz (Quai Voltaire No. 3). He has just ordered the mayor to free your excellent institute from any military detachments. General Goltz has said he is willing to accede to any request the professors at the Jardin des Plantes may make. . . . I embrace you, my dear friend.

Humboldt was very good at arranging this sort of thing and later he managed to persuade the General to provide military transport to carry animal feed to the zoo.

That same day, 1 April, for the first time in seven years, he met his brother and his King again. All the acquaintances of his youth seemed to be there, but in strangely exalted positions—Metternich, a hereditary prince of the Austrian Empire and now Foreign Minister; Hardenberg, now Chancellor of Prussia; Friedrich von Gentz, now an influential conservative in the reactionary power-politics of Europe.

As for the King—a stupid but not unlikeable cuckold, with a stutter and a passion for winding clocks and designing new uniforms—he attached himself to Alexander like a leech. No Prussian knew Paris better than Alexander and few could beguile such ignorant ears with such bewitching chat. For the next few weeks Alexander had to spend every day showing him around art collections and historic monuments, and evening after evening accompany him to the theatre. When the King became indisposed Alexander had to read to him. He had become an indispensible companion. He turned this royal chore to his advantage, however. First, he persuaded the King and the Prime Minister to put up the money for his Asia expedition. Next, he obtained an advance of 24,000 francs towards the cost of the South American publications. And finally, he obtained a hand-out of 5,000 francs towards the cost of his house-keeping. Nor did he leave his friends out of it. For Gérard he obtained commissions for portraits from King Frederick William, Emperor Alexander, various princes and, later, the Duke of Wellington at 12,000 to 15,000 francs a time. He was a *very* persuasive man.

Only Arago (dear, uncompromising Arago) declined to share in the pickings. One day Humboldt informed him that the King would like to look over the Observatoire under Arago's guidance. Arago replied that he had no desire to see the King who had invaded France. Humboldt wrapped this abrasive reply into a suitable speech and delivered it to the King. The King replied that he would still like to look over the Observatoire. Humboldt went back to Arago and Arago still said no. Then one morning Humboldt, accompanied by a friend in travelling clothes, arrived at the

Observatoire to say goodbye. He was on his way to London, he said, and so was his friend. Their carriage was waiting at the door—could they have a look over the Observatoire? So Arago showed them over and when, somehow, the conversation turned to politics he became, as was his way, very forthright. He said he thought it was disgraceful the way these foreign kings came to France and started demanding reparations for the ambitious stupidities of Napoleon. Humboldt, looking very uncomfortable while all this was going on, drew his friend to one side. 'Would you mind moderating your language?' he said. 'You're speaking to the King.' He was unprepared for Arago's glee. 'I thought so', he said. 'That's why I've been so frank.'

Humboldt's visit to London in June 1814, after the Peace of Paris and the enthronement of Louis XVIII as King of France—his first visit to England since 1790—was in the rôle of the Prussian King's chum. With them went the Emperor, Metternich and brother Wilhelm. Though Alexander had no official part to play in this diplomatic visit, he soon attracted attention on account of his almost total lack of luggage and his extraordinary mental versatility. And though he did not care for England in summer-time and complained about the country incessantly, particularly about the weather, he turned this penance to his advantage, too. For he was able to sound out high-ranking officials in the British East India Company about his Asia expedition and obtain from the Prince of Wales, the future King George IV, an assurance of his support for all his plans. And with that assurance Humboldt returned to Paris and set to work, in this new era of peace in Europe, to hatch his next great enterprise.

His plans were ambitious. He intended to travel to Persia, then on to the Pamirs and the Kunlun Mountains of Tibet, cross the Karakoram Range and the Himalayas into the great plain of the Ganges and after traversing India from end to end sail from Ceylon to Malaya, Java and the Philippines, before returning to Europe via America. His main objects were to explore the prodigious and virtually unknown mountains between northern India and inner Asia in order to determine their altitudes and geological structure and to study the adaptation of plant, animal and human life in both high-altitude and desert environments. It was a project that was at once ambitious, dangerous and costly. This was absolutely pioneer exploration. For the roof of the world was also a blank on the map, its fabulous mountains little more than rumours, innocent of the tread of surveyor and scientist alike.

Humboldt's preparations for this venture were even more thorough than they had been before his South American expedition; his chosen companions were specialists of the highest qualifications; the King had underwritten the enterprise with a guarantee of 12,000 thalers in gold per annum towards the costs, together with the loan of all the necessary instruments. Only one thing was lacking—the authority of the British Government, or more precisely the all-powerful British East India Company, for the expedition to enter India. And this authority, despite every amount of string-pulling on Humboldt's part, was resolutely unforthcoming. Twice after Waterloo and the second Peace of Paris he went cap in hand to London—once

Wilhelm von Humboldt at sixty

in October 1817 with Arago, and again for a few days in September 1818 with the zoologist, Valenciennes. Twice he returned without an entry permit. In vain he made use of the good offices of Canning, the leading British statesman of the day. In vain he appealed to the Prince Regent for help. The British East India Company would not budge. They simply did not want Baron Humboldt on their domain.

Quite why the British regarded Humboldt as *persona non grata* has never been made clear. But it is not difficult to hazard a guess. The British East India Company was not exactly a progressive or liberal-minded organization and in its hold over Indian affairs it was both possessive and jealous of interference. Foreigners, broadly speaking, were not welcome within the borders of a nation of such inherent instability, particularly if their goal was the disputed northern frontier, and particularly if they were famous and nosey and sided with the natives—as Humboldt, in his public statements, had clearly done in South America. A man who had given offence to one colonial power could clearly give offence to another. To the British East India Company—or so one might surmise—Humboldt was both an embarrassment and a threat to security. They distrusted his investigations and feared his revelations. In a word, he was a hot potato. So they dropped him—as it turned out, for good.

And years were no longer on Alexander's side now. He was nearly fifty and time was slipping by. During his second visit to London in 1817 he had visited his brother Wilhelm, who had been 'exiled' there as Prussian Ambassador after falling out of favour with his government. Wilhelm reported to Caroline: 'Alexander is . . . more portly and greatly aged.' And he added: 'You know his passion always to cling to one person who temporarily strikes his fancy. Right now it's the astronomer Arago, from whom he cannot be separated.' Alexander, his brother continued, was more estranged from him than ever.

> You know him and his ideas well enough. They can't be ours, much as I love him. It's truly comical when we're together sometimes. I let him prattle on to his heart's content. What's the use of quarrelling when our basic principles are so different? Alexander is not only a unique and unusual academic with very broad views, he's such a good character as well, so soft, so helpful, so self-sacrificing. But he lacks inward peace and satisfaction. Because of that he doesn't understand people, though he lives with them so closely. . . . He really doesn't know much about art, though he understands all the technical side, and paints in a middling sort of way. . . . He talks to me for hours about people in Paris and what they are doing and I just sit there and think that I don't know any of them, they're not of any interest to me. . . . Latterly I've been thinking that my mother and father had two children and they had to have these two. No two people on earth could be further apart. And really Alexander hasn't become like that, living abroad hasn't changed him—he's chosen to live abroad because he couldn't live his kind of private life in Germany.

As for religion, Wilhelm noted, Alexander had none—'and doesn't even miss it'. And his finances were in a complete mess again. His bank account was always in the red. His assets in Germany amounted to 52,000 thalers, but his debts totalled nearly 40,000. Wilhelm tried to persuade him to invest the rest of his assets in a house or an estate, or even a library or a set of instruments, to give him a bit of security. But

Alexander said that as he might die any time he would like to enjoy the money now and that if the worst came to the worst '*someone* would look after him'. 'The money he spends is terrible', said Wilhelm.

As hopes of travelling to India faded Alexander toyed with other ideas. He formed the notion of setting up a research institute in Mexico City where he could surround himself with young enthusiastic scientists. 'I've got it in my head to end my life in the most agreeable and, for science, most useful manner', he told his brother. 'You may laugh to see me so passionately preoccupied with this American project, but when one doesn't have a family, or children, one's got to think of some way of embellishing one's old age.' But it came to nothing, and he went back to his books, and time passed.

He was by now a revered and venerable figure in the world of science, a living legend, and young men on the thresholds of their careers eagerly sought him out. He was already beyond the age of truly creative science himself but to the new generation of scientists he was tireless in his enthusiasm and support, both moral and, when he could afford it, pecuniary. Increasingly this became his major rôle—an inspirer, a father-figure, a fixer. Today perhaps he would have been the active head of an outstanding research team and certainly he had all the attributes of a great teacher. He was the first to recognize the mathematical genius of Gauss and the immense

LEFT *Justus Liebig, the founder of organic chemistry, in his laboratory*; RIGHT *Leopold von Buch, geologist —'as brilliant and dotty as ever'*

talents of men like eighteen-year-old Heinrich Berghaus, the geographer; twenty-year-old Justus Liebig, the future founder of organic chemistry; and twenty-five-year-old Charles Lyell, geologist. The twenty-year-old Jean-Baptiste Boussingault was a chemist who was planning to explore South America himself when he first met Humboldt in 1822.[1] This is his account of their meeting:

> Humboldt first of all wanted to get to know me, to weigh me up. He talked a great deal and very well. I listened to him as a pupil listens to a master; he was delighted that I appreciated the fine art of listening. Before very long he extended to me his very sincere friendship and continued to do so until the day he died. He gave me several instruments which he had used in America; a pocket barometer, an artificial horizon, a prismatic compass, a celestial hemisphere by Flamsteed, precious relics of which I made the greatest use and which I left to my companion, the unfortunate Colonel Hall.
>
> He did even more than that; he absolutely insisted on teaching me the use of his instruments: we fixed a day to meet for this purpose. He lived at that time on the Quai Napoleon, in rooms on the fourth floor with a view of the Seine, approximately opposite the Mint.
>
> Humboldt was then fifty-three years old, with a good figure, medium build, white hair, an indefinable look in his eyes, a spirited, mobile face with a few pockmarks he had acquired in Cartagena. His dress hadn't changed since the time of the Directory: blue coat, gilt buttons, yellow waistcoat, short trousers of striped material, high boots turned over at the tops—the last surviving pair in Paris in 1822—white cravat, and a black, battered, tired-looking hat. He dined at the Frères Provençaux; in the morning he always spent an hour or two at the Café de Foy, where he went to sleep after his lunch.
>
> Our exercises with the sextant began immediately after my arrival; we measured the angle between the spire of the Invalides and the lightning conductor on the Church of St Sulpice; we also took an altitude of the sun. He omitted nothing from my lessons; the means of verification, the determination of the error of collimation, all the calculations were made on the wood of the famous table. I soon became familiar with the use of the sextant and the artificial horizon.
>
> Humboldt was indefatigable. In order to help me, he produced a book of instructions which has been most useful to me. He insisted that I should take with me a small collection of trachytic rocks from Hungary. He went to Beudant, the curator of the collection of Count Bournon, removed some specimens, went to a joiner, had a box made on the spot to pack them in and at ten o'clock next morning he handed over the collection to me.
>
> We gave a farewell dinner for several scientists. It was interesting. We noticed that Humboldt was not wearing his boots. He was in silk stockings and had a new hat.

The company of young friends like these, however, could no longer dispel his increasing gloom. He found the atmosphere of Paris more and more oppressive, his own future more and more obscure and uncertain. Once he took a brief holiday in Britanny, but shut himself up in his room all day or tramped the countryside alone, looking at mines. He was restless and full of foreboding. Paris, the city that he had loved, was no longer what it used to be. There was censorship of the Press, books were banned, the old spirit of inquiry was dying. He shunned social life and pre-

[1] Humboldt was somewhat put out when in 1831 his protégé reached a height of 19,698 feet on Chimborazo, thus beating his own thirty-year-old world climbing record by more than 400 feet. Chimborazo was first conquered by the great English alpinist Sir Edward Whymper in 1880.

tended that he was indisposed. His favourite newspaper, the *Journal des Débats*, put out the story that he was sick. He was not sick but he was a lonely man beginning to face up to the prospect of an insecure old age. Those wonderful days in South America were very distant now and of the men who had climbed Chimborazo only he was still at large: Carlos Montúfar had been stood against a wall and shot for his part in the Spanish American revolution, and Aimé Bonpland had been dragged off in chains to the interior of Paraguay. Of his own family, Wilhelm, disillusioned with the re-actionary politics of Prussia, had already retired from public life into a philosophic solitude at Tegel, and Caroline, who had been seriously ill for some time, was slowly dying on her feet. Alexander, the professional survivor, teetered on the edge of limbo.

In the autumn of 1822 he was suddenly summoned to attend King Frederick William III at the Congress of Verona. After 'boring and monotonous Paris' he was enchanted at the sight of the lakes and glaciers and snow-capped mountains of the Alps and ecstatic when he overtook en route his old friend Leopold von Buch, who had been wandering for five months in the Tyrol, on foot and without a guide,

In the spring of 1827 Humboldt spent nearly an hour at the bottom of the Thames in the diving bell used by Brunel during the construction of the Thames Tunnel. He was forcibly reminded of his ascent of Chimborazo—blood vessels burst in his chest, he coughed blood and his nose bled until the next day

armed with an umbrella, an overcoat and a whole library in his pockets. For five refreshing days Humboldt tramped the countryside around Verona with Buch and found him as brilliant and as dotty as ever.

> The voluntary isolation in which he has always lived has increased his taste for independence and his irritability to the point where the mere idea of taking a guide makes him furious. I walk patiently with him for hours; he reads the map; we fail to find the village where we aim to spend the night; it pours with rain; we see a man in the vineyards; I would be totally despised if I dared to ask the way. . . . He is fifty years old and walks for fourteen hours a day—what he finds tiring, he says, is to have to talk to people all the time. When he is by himself he talks at the top of his voice. Quite alone, he argues with his opponents in mineralogy (he has the insanity to believe that nobody appreciates his talents) and finds it exhausting. From time to time he stands still, rubs his hands with increasing rapidity, lifts them up to the sky, and with his mouth half open, pince-nez on his nose, his head thrown back, he enjoys the Italian sunshine. However, side by side with his interest in granite and eupholite he loves to repeat everything his brother tells him of the adventures of the ladies of the Court of the late Queen. . . .

The assembly of the monarchs of Europe at the Congress of Verona was intended— at a time of liberal uprisings in Spain and Greece—to reaffirm the status quo and the principles of absolutism and reactionary conservatism throughout the continent. For Humboldt, a convinced liberal and republican and a known supporter of the rebel cause in Greece (like Byron, who died there), it was as if he had put his head into a wasps' nest. In his fundamental principles he was utterly opposed to every single member of the Congress, not least his King, and he only survived this precarious situation by artful compromise—a performance which caused Prince Metternich, who underestimated his potential influence, to dub him a political schizophrenic. It was like being in a cage all day, Alexander wrote to 'Bill', his brother. Even the mosquitoes of the Casiquiare had left him more in peace. The only useful thing he had learnt was how to make macaroni.

The King continued to favour him, however, and was always eager to hear what he had to say on any subject and was never far from his side. For the first time, the reactionary monarch and the liberal scholar began to recognize their mutual dependence on one another. For the King wanted Humboldt's brains just as much as Humboldt wanted the King's money. Together they visited Venice and Naples and attended by a retinue 300 strong, an extraordinary procession, climbed to the summit of Vesuvius. Together in January 1823 they returned to Berlin. It was the first time Humboldt had set eyes on his native city for fifteen years. In a sense, it was the beginning of the end.

Curiously enough, he seems to have enjoyed himself. For virtually the first time since his youth he stayed at Schloss Tegel, now much altered and improved by Wilhelm, and surrounded by his brother's family and the familiar landscape of his boyhood he seems to have found a temporary peace, a momentary rest from his endless motion. His brief stay made a tremendous impression on him; it was as if he had been a stranger to human love for years. From a stagecoach stop in Strasbourg on

In the spring of 1814 the Allies occupied Paris. Humboldt's first act was to save the French scientific institutions from the blind fury of foreign troops. A contemporary cartoonist depicts the invaders: ABOVE *The Cossack and Mongolian hordes of the Russian army with their plunder;* BELOW *English visitors in the Palais Royal*

his way to Paris 'stoned on warm beer and mulled wine', he scribbled a thank-you note to Wilhelm: 'The memory of this happy time will never fade . . . Never in my life have I been so loved.' And again from Paris: 'I'm always on the verge of tears whenever I write to you and when I think of you and dear Li and all the loving kindness you gave me when I stayed with you . . . Why aren't I with you now?' And again in April: 'I live in the past rather than the present and find it difficult to get used to a life without love and attention.' At heart he was a very lonely man.

Three more years passed. Alexander, as heedlessly generous and impoverished as ever, was now virtually dependent for his livelihood on the wages he received as Chamberlain to the King of Prussia. In the light of this, his continued stay in Paris seemed odder than ever. At last, in 1826, the King allegedly wrote him a letter.

My dear Herr von Humboldt!

You must by now have finished the publication of the works you considered could only be finished in Paris. I therefore cannot allow you to extend your stay any further in a country which every true Prussian should hate. I accordingly await your speedy return to the Fatherland.

Yours affectionately,
FREDERICK WILLIAM.

That same month, November, Humboldt hurried to Berlin. If he had intended to change the King's mind he clearly failed. He was offered a salary rise to 5,000 thalers per annum and four months' holiday every year to spend in Paris. Otherwise the King was adamant that he should go back to Berlin. It was with feelings of foreboding for the future that Humboldt returned to Paris to pack his pathetically few possessions and take leave of his friends.

In February 1827 Humboldt at last turned his back on his old familiar world, on the Institut National and the Observatoire, on Arago, on Gérard's Wednesday-night salon, on the nooks and crannies of the Quartier Latin he knew so well, on the intellectual cut and thrust and the social rough and tumble, on his friends, his young men, his twenty years of memories—and left Paris. Of his state of mind at that moment there is no record, but it would not be too difficult to imagine. 'I don't regret my decision for a single moment', he lied to Gauss, putting a brave face on it. It was, really, the end of an era.

He travelled to Berlin circuitously by way of London, where his brother's son-in-law, Baron von Bülow, had recently been appointed Ambassador, and in London that early springtime he seems to have found timely distractions. He rushed about all over the place. He visited Parliament, was a guest at Holland House and dined with the Lord Chancellor and the Foreign Secretary, Canning. He spent his mornings at Kew or Greenwich, or went on disastrous shopping excursions and spent all his money. 'I'm a fool', he said. 'I buy anything I set eyes on.' The climax of his visit was a descent, at the end of April, to the bottom of the Thames. Isambard Kingdom Brunel, the British civil engineer, who built the Great Western Railway and the

View of the Strand at about the time of Humboldt's visit to London in 1827. Painting by C. R. Stanley

Great Eastern steamship, was at that time twenty-one years old and engaged, with his father, on boring the first tunnel under the Thames, between Wapping and Rotherhithe. In order to be able to inspect a part of the workings he had devised a special diving bell and in this he accompanied his distinguished German visitor on a journey to the bed of the river.

They went down at high tide to a depth of 36 feet, both of them so well wrapped up that they looked like eskimoes. Going down Humboldt suffered a lot from ear-ache due to the increase in pressure but after a few minutes he got used to it and altogether they remained at the bottom of the Thames for forty minutes. In those days, before the London sewers were constructed, the river was an open drain and the water indescribably black and filthy; though they lit a lantern in the diving bell, therefore, they were unable to see anything of the bed more than a few feet away. When he went up again—the water boiling under his boots—Humboldt suffered even more from the change in pressure and was forcibly reminded of his ascent of Chimborazo many years ago; small blood vessels burst in his nose and chest, he coughed blood and his nose bled until the next day. Young Brunel, however, was quite unaffected. 'It's a Prussian privilege', Humboldt explained.

The diving bell preoccupied Humboldt more than anything else in London. Several accidents had occurred but Humboldt was shown an emergency device and found this very reassuring. As it happened, disaster struck the workings a fortnight later when the river burst into the excavations at high water—the first of many accidents that delayed the completion of the tunnel. But by that time Humboldt was already many miles away, safely ensconced in Berlin, his home for the rest of his life.

The Observatory at Greenwich

CHAPTER 18

Return to Berlin

At first Humboldt lived in rooms in a house belonging to the King's master carpenter in the centre of Berlin, not far from the Unter den Linden, but later the block was torn down to make room for some new museum buildings, and he was forced to move. His new quarters—a first-floor apartment in a small house at 67 Orianen-burger Strasse behind the new No. 4 Customs shed in the unfashionable 'Siberian' district of north Berlin—remained his home for the rest of his days. For the first time in his life he now had a permanent place of abode and a domestic staff—a young, good-looking ex-soldier called Johann Seifert and his wife—to look after him. It was from this modest and untidy base that Humboldt sallied forth to attend to his duties as Chamberlain at the court of the King at Potsdam and to which he returned as often as possible to resume his scientific labours.

If Berlin had seemed a desert when he last lived there twenty years previously, it was by now a veritable Sahara—'a little, illiterate and very spiteful town', is how he described it. Though it had grown a lot in size it was still a mean place. Houses like those of the Mendelssohn and Beer families stood in almost solitary grandeur, and when a small pane of glass was inserted into a window at the Royal Palace it was talked about for weeks afterwards. Society seemed to concern itself only with trifles, and philosophy and the arts (apart from the Opera, which was flourishing as never before) maintained an abysmal level. Only in science was there any real achievement, though many of the most distinguished scientists, like Gauss, Ritter, Buch, Bessel and Berghaus, lived in widely scattered places outside Berlin, working solitarily and never meeting together to discuss views and compare results. It was this lack of cross-pollinating personal contact that Humboldt found one of the most trying aspects of his new life in Berlin, though even this was bearable compared with the prevailing political situation.

For Prussia was now a repressive and oligarchical police state. Following the recommendations of Metternich at the signing of the Carlsbad Decrees in 1820, a rigorous censorship of the press and of public speech had been instituted. Many writers and university teachers were under arrest for their subversive views. Student bodies had been dissolved and all public meetings, even in learned societies, were regarded with grave suspicion. The Secret Police were everywhere active, and in-formers reported all private conversations that could be considered in any way

The savants of Berlin in the 1820's. 1. Wilhelm von Humboldt, 3. Alexander von Humboldt, 4. Carl Ritter and 7. Georg Wilhelm Friedrich Hegel

seditious. Even schoolteachers were denounced by their pupils. Political opposition and intellectual life were alike stifled by the heavy hand of the reactionary government in power. The hopes that had been raised for a democratic constitution and parliamentary government after the liberation of Prussia in 1813 were by now almost abandoned; the aristocracy were demanding a restoration of their former privileges and the few reforms that *had* been won from the régime—the liberation of the peasants, the emancipation of the Jews—were under constant threat of revision.

Under such circumstances it is not surprising that Alexander von Humboldt's arrival in Berlin was greeted in some quarters with rage or derision. Some of the smaller fry among the academics were simply jealous of him—like the pedantic Ancillon, the Crown Prince's private tutor, and later Prussian Foreign Secretary, who habitually referred to Humboldt as 'the encyclopedic cat'. Others, especially the *ultras*—the ultra-conservative members of the aristocracy and professional

Prince Metternich who called Humboldt a 'political schizophrenic'. Painting by Sir Thomas Lawrence

classes—hated him because of his liberal views and feared his political influence as a 'revolutionary' power behind the throne. Countess Goltz was heard on one occasion to damn the entire Humboldt family as a 'set of upstarts . . . a race of plebeians trying to force themselves into the ranks of high-born people', and in this vindictive view she was not alone. For some months after his return to Berlin the *ultras* consoled themselves with rumours that Humboldt had fallen out of favour with the royal family because he was never seen at the palace. Their hopes were dashed, however, when it was discovered that he had simply not bothered to turn up.

The truth is that though Humboldt's relationship with King Frederick William III was very close—more that of a friend than a court lackey—he never used this intimacy to exert any direct influence over political affairs, and in any case the King left the actual government of the country to his Cabinet. His precise rôle as Chamberlain, in fact, was tailored to suit his particular qualifications as cultural adviser—

he was required to make reports on artistic and scientific affairs and used these occasions to advance the interests of unknown scientists rather than political parties. For now that he was dependent on his Chamberlain's salary for his livelihood he was extremely careful not to put a foot wrong, and though he often complained about the stultifying atmosphere of the court—which he described as the most ignorant and uneducated place in Europe—he never said as much to the poor King, for whom indeed he seems to have retained some feelings of charity.

Humboldt may have had a number of enemies at court but he had plenty of friends outside it and seems to have been a frequent visitor to a wide variety of houses, from Field Marshal Gneisenau's on the one hand to Rahel Levin's and Dr Ephraim Beer's on the other. The reception he received at these gatherings was quite astonishing.

Humboldt's talent for holding the floor and ad-libbing on any subject for as long as an hour at a time was given a more formal outlet during that first winter when he exercised his right as a member of the Berlin Academy to lecture at the University. Between November 1827 and the April of 1828 he delivered a course of lectures on the subject of Physical Geography to a packed audience of students and professors drawn from all the faculties, and public interest became so great that Humboldt was persuaded to repeat the introductory lectures to a huge audience of Berliners in a local concert hall. They were an outstanding success—the talk of the season. They also marked the beginning of the opus which was to occupy most of the remaining years of his life—an opus to which he ultimately gave the name *Cosmos*.

Humboldt's main purpose in giving the lectures was to attempt to correct the baleful influence of the so-called nature philosophers of that time, who had gained a considerable degree of popularity. The principal exponents of this singularly cracked school of thought were Hegel and Schelling. They were part of the romantic movement in Germany and their aim was to comprehend nature *a priori* by means of intuitive processes—in other words to arrive at specific conclusions about natural phenomena without using scientific methodology. They viewed experiments as an unwarranted interference with nature, deplored the mathematical formulation of natural laws, which they said destroyed man's feelings of wonder and awe in the face of natural phenomena, and objected to the split between the emotions and the intellect which they claimed science brought about. In place of Newton's 'groundless hypothesis' they substituted oracular utterances of their own invention—masterpieces of wishful inspiration, such as:

> Diamond is flint arrived at consciousness
> Granite is ether
> Forests, as everybody knows, are the hair of the animal Earth. The bulge in the equatorial region is the belly of nature.
> America is a female figure, long, slender, watery and icy cold at the 48th parallel.
> (Degrees of latitude are years—a woman becomes old at 48.)
> The East is oxygen, the West hydrogen.
> It rains when clouds from the East mix with clouds from the West.

University of Berlin, founded by Wilhelm von Humboldt in 1810 and now known as Humboldt University

The main perpetrator of this pretentious nonsense was Schelling, who was then established as Professor of Philosophy at Berlin University. But in his attack on the nature philosophers Humboldt mentioned no specific names and was content to show that there could be no knowledge without verifiable experience and that real science—actual proven facts—could appeal to both mind and imagination. His aim, in short, was to introduce the world of science to a public that was almost totally ignorant of it, and in this he was triumphantly successful.

Altogether he gave 61 lectures before the University, at first two a week and later one a day. They were all delivered without any notes beyond a bare outline and covered in exhaustive detail a vast area, from the motions of the planets to the structure of the earth's crust and the distribution of plants and animals across it. His sixteen weekly lectures to the general public were necessarily simpler and more popular but they nevertheless embraced an extraordinary sweep of heaven and earth. From a brief outline discovered after his death it appears he lectured about volcanoes on the moon, sun spots, meteorites, the stars and the southern constellations, optics

Prince and Princess Frederick William at the Royal Palace, Berlin

and interference phenomena (at that time the very latest subject), as well as the history of physical science and the observation of nature by poets and painters. Behind it all lay his concept of harmony in nature, of the interrelatedness of phenomena, the unity of volcano, sea, star, plant and mineral within a cosmic whole. As a Berlin newspaper wrote at the time: 'By the lucid manner in which he grasps the facts discovered by himself and others in various branches of science and arranges them in one comprehensive view, he throws so clear a light upon the boundless region of the study of nature that he has introduced a new method of treating the history of science.'

To everyone's surprise Humboldt spoke fluent German and Berliners flocked in their thousands to hear his lectures. The concert hall was packed to capacity each week. There had never been such a socially mixed audience in the city's history. The King, the Crown Prince and Princess and other members of the royal family occupied the boxes. Officers of state, army generals, society ladies and literary men filled the stalls. Ordinary citizens, teachers and students sat in the orchestra pit. More sensational still was the presence of so many women, for they had hitherto been considered too stupid and ignorant for this sort of thing. According to one newspaper-man they still were. 'The hall could not cope with the audience,' he wrote, 'and the ladies in the audience could not cope with the lectures.' And when Humboldt was asked by one of the royal princes whether he thought the ladies could follow his lectures, he replied: 'It isn't necessary for them to. So long as they *come*, that's all one can expect of them.' As if to prove the point, one of his female audience was later reported to have ordered a new dress with a request that the upper sleeve should be equal to two diameters of the star Sirius!

Humboldt's pioneer effort in popular education succeeded in making an essential branch of knowledge acceptable to the intelligent general public in Berlin and aroused the enthusiasm of everyone except the most orthodox die-hards. Schoolgirls wrote doggerel verse in his praise. A special medal was struck to commemorate the lectures. 'You will be amazed', his brother Wilhelm reported, 'Alexander is really a *puissance*.' And even the usually matter-of-fact Zelter, the musician, felt strongly enough to write in a letter to Goethe: 'I felt that here was a man after my own heart, who gives everything he has, without stint. He makes no money from it, and has no preamble, no humbug, no artifice. Even when he is wrong one is happy to believe him.'

Humboldt's German publisher, Baron von Cotta, planned to turn these popular lectures to commercial account and offered Humboldt 5,000 thalers and a shorthand secretary to take the lectures down in writing as he delivered them. Humboldt refused. The spoken word, he said, was not fit for publication until it had been 'revised, refined, and sifted'—a process which was to engage his attention for very many years and result in the five volumes of his monumental account of the physical world, *Cosmos*.

Having overcome the public's prejudice against science, Humboldt next over-came the government's prejudice against scientific conferences. The very first meeting of the German Association of Naturalists and Physicians (*Versammlung deutscher Naturforscher und Ärzte*)—held in a Leipzig beer cellar in 1822—had been most unpopular with the political police. But in the summer following Humboldt's public lectures, the King agreed to Humboldt's suggestion that a meeting of the Scientific Association should be held in Berlin. Humboldt was appointed President of the meeting and spent a greater part of that summer organizing it. One of the biggest headaches was finding accommodation for the enormous influx of savants that was expected. Many of them wrote to Humboldt with a particular request for rooms free from bed bugs, as the Berlin variety was believed to be exceptionally voracious. Humboldt himself was most anxious that Gauss, the mathematical genius of the age, should attend and offered to put him up in his own flat. On 14 August he wrote from the palace at Sans Souci:

> The hotels here are very bad and easily get full up. True, I can only offer you one room, but it is a very spacious room, with a view over a nice garden, and you are welcome to have visitors and make use of the adjoining rooms. You can have breakfast, lunch and dinner with me or

without me at any time you want. If you bring a friend with you I can easily put him up in a house nearby. You will have a carriage at your disposal. All this can be left to me . . . You will find a hearty welcome at my house, though on account of my bachelor loneliness it has few charms to offer you.

In the end a total of 600 scientists arrived from all over Germany (Gauss among them) and representatives came from as far afield as Denmark and Sweden (Berzelius and Oersted) and even England (Babbage) as well. Such a huge turn-out of 'great men and little doctors' was regarded as a triumph not only for science in Germany but for the growing movement towards German unity. At the opening session of the Association in the concert hall, attended by the King of Prussia and the Duke of Cumberland, Humboldt delivered his presidential address on the social values of science—'a masterpiece' according to one who was present—and from 6 pm to 9 pm that evening entertained '600 of my friends' to tea in the theatre. It seemed that half the town was there. The King looked on from the royal box, while the Crown Prince and all the other princes mixed with the company down below. The fête was of great magnificence, the hospitality profuse, and at intervals the conversation was broken by music and singing. Humboldt was everywhere—welcoming, introducing, conversing, joking, and proferring tea and cake.

Carl Friedrich Gauss—'the mathematical genius of the age' on the terrace of the Göttingen Observatory

The Berlin conference served as an inspiration and model for similar associations that were subsequently formed in Britain, Italy, the United States and France. But Humboldt himself soon grew weary of them. It seemed to him that in the end such meetings provided nothing but an opportunity for all those 'nomadic philosophers' to indulge their 'roving propensities and love of music and feasting'. A few years later he wrote to Gauss: 'I value a few hours with you to all the meetings of the so-called scientists, who move about in such enormous numbers and in such a gastronomic way that as far as I am concerned there is never enough scientific contact. At the end of a session I often ask myself the question the mathematician put at the end of the opera: now tell me frankly, what does that prove?'

What the 1828 congress did do for Humboldt as a result of his contact with Gauss was re-stimulate his old interest in magnetic observations. In the autumn he had a special magnetic hut, which contained no metal but copper and was completely draught-proof, erected in the garden of his friend Abraham Mendelssohn-Bartholdy, the eldest son of Moses Mendelssohn and father of the famous composer, Felix, then twenty years old and already well known. Humboldt's magnetic hut was not far from the summer house where Felix and his sister, also an accomplished musician, practised for a forthcoming performance of Bach's newly discovered *St Matthew Passion*. While the sounds of their music drifted across the garden, Humboldt and a team of assistants peered through a microscope at a black line on an ivory scale illuminated by candlelight. Every hour, night and day, they recorded the fluctuations in the magnetic declination. Humboldt was particularly interested in obtaining simultaneous observations at different places in order to determine whether the variations were terrestrial in origin or depended on the position of the sun. To this end simultaneous readings were made in Paris and 216 feet down at the bottom of a mine in Freiberg, and later were extended, at Humboldt's instigation, right the way round the world.

This periodic measurement of the variation of the magnetic declination were carried on in the hut in the Mendelssohn garden until Abraham's death, when the house was sold. But before then a great event had occurred in Humboldt's life. For in the spring of 1829, in his sixtieth year, he was suddenly given the opportunity to realize the second great dream of his life and embark on his long-cherished expedition through Asia.

CHAPTER 19

Expedition to Siberia

Humboldt's sudden opportunity to travel to Russia arose in a very roundabout way. In the autumn of 1827 the Russian finance minister, Count Cancrin, had sought his advice about the issue of coins specially minted from platinum—a new metal which had recently been discovered in considerable quantities in the Ural mountains. In his letter Cancrin casually mentioned that the Urals would well repay a visit from a man of scientific eminence. Humboldt was quick to seize this chance. He wrote back to Cancrin to say that he didn't think much of the platinum idea (unlike gold and silver its world market value was unstable) but he thought a lot about the Urals and Lake Baikal. Hint taken, Cancrin replied in December and on behalf of the Tsar invited Humboldt to undertake a six-month summer expedition to study mining and geology in the Urals at the Tsar's expense.

Humboldt accepted the Tsar's kind offer, and the Tsar's kind money too, but asked if he could extend his itinerary as far as western Siberia. 'I implore his Imperial Majesty for permission to let me go at least as far as the Irtysh river. Tobolsk is a dream of my youth. I have a childish aversion to cold but I know how to live for higher purposes.' He would like to delay his departure, however, till he had finished writing up his previous expedition of twenty-five years ago and delivered his public lectures in Berlin.

On the subject of money he was more specific later. He was quite happy to pay for the journey from Berlin to St Petersburg and back out of his own pocket, he said, but any expenses above that he was anxious for the Imperial Treasury to pay. 'I have no intention of making a financial profit out of this trip,' he told Cancrin, 'but I would prefer not to make a personal loss as a result of it.' He would provide his own French-built carriage, and travel with a single German servant and a professor of chemistry and mineralogy, Gustav Rose, a very unassuming but well-informed young man. Humboldt had no wish for preferential treatment, but he was always very grateful for kindness. And he added: 'I still get about very nimbly on foot, nine to ten hours a day without resting, despite my age and white hair.'

The Russian Government would not hear of Humboldt spending a single penny of his own on this expedition—as far as they were concerned it was primarily intended to benefit the Urals mining industry—and advanced him about 7,000 thalers to defray all expenses. They also agreed to provide a mining official and a courier to accompany the expedition and allowed Humboldt to add a young zoologist, C. G. Ehrenberg, to his party. Humboldt was left to choose his own scientific programme and itinerary and in the end he decided to extend his objective as far south as the borders of Chinese Turkestan. In return for these almost unlimited facilities, Humboldt agreed to maintain a tactful silence in matters concerning the social and political conditions of the Tsar's Russian Empire to which, idealogically, he was diametrically opposed. He was no longer in a position to comment on the suppression of the peasants, or on serfdom, slave labour and all the cruelties and injustices of a despotic régime, in the way that he had once been able to comment publicly on the slavery of the negroes of South America.

By the beginning of March 1829 all was ready for the long haul by horse and carriage from Berlin to the very edge of China, but a sad event caused Humboldt to delay his departure. For a year his sister-in-law Caroline had been suffering from an incurable cancer and by the end of the winter her condition had worsened considerably and it was clear she could not last much longer. Through March she lingered on but she was fading fast and on the 26th, mercifully, she died. Alexander was with the King at Potsdam when the news was brought to him by special courier and he hurried to Tegel at once. He found his brother Wilhelm greatly aged and all but finished by his much-loved wife's death. According to her wish, they buried her in the park at Tegel in the shade of some lovely oaks, and the flowers on her grave were still fresh when Alexander gave Seifert orders to pack the coaches in readiness for his expedition's imminent departure.

On 12 April 1829, Humboldt's expedition set out from Berlin for St Petersburg. In the first coach—Humboldt's own, as it happened—sat the three scientists, Humboldt, Rose and Ehrenberg, engulfed in warm winter coats and wrapped in blankets. Behind them, in the second carriage, rode Humboldt's valet, Seifert, whose job was to look after the voluminous heap of trunks and boxes of instruments that filled the compartment and roof-rack.

It was a bad time of the year to set out to the east. All the way across the flat grey northern plain to the Vistula they drove into the teeth of howling blizzards of snow and sleet. It was the butt-end of winter and the ice on the rivers was breaking up; the carriages had to be ferried across on rafts which were bumped and pounded by the floating ice and the swirling current. At Königsberg, in East Prussia, they stopped for two days to visit the great astronomer Bessel, but beyond Königsberg the road conditions became even worse.

They were surrounded by all the horrors of winter and saw nothing but snow and ice as far as the eye could reach. They were considerably delayed by the rivers, which were either blocked with ice or could only be approached by roads so washed away that the front wheels became buried in the mud and the carriages had to be pulled out by extra horse teams and groups of peasants. 'These are some of the ordinary occurrences of returning spring', Humboldt noted.

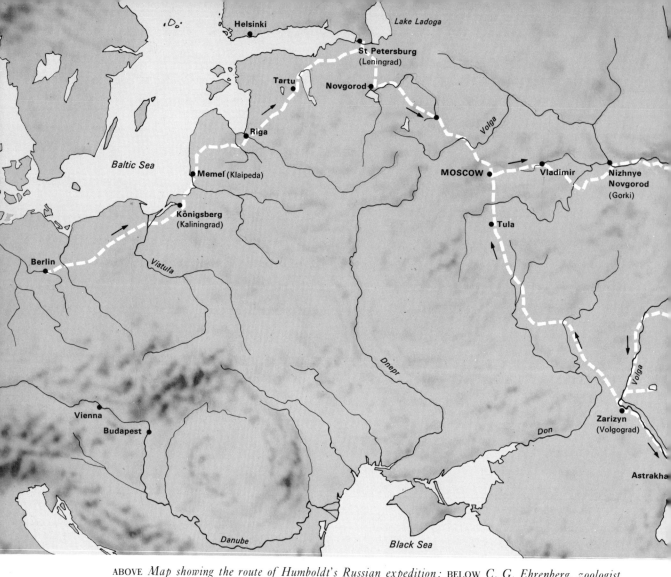

ABOVE *Map showing the route of Humboldt's Russian expedition;* BELOW *C. G. Ehrenberg, zoologist (left), and Gustav Rose, mineralogist (right)—Humboldt's companions in Russia;* CENTRE *Post-chaise station—'They were surrounded by all the horrors of winter and saw nothing but snow and ice as far as the eye could reach.'*

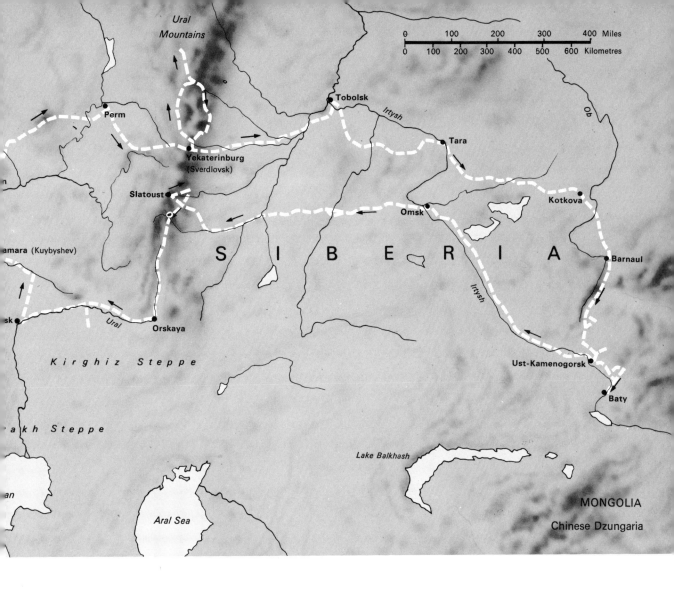

Ural
Mountains

Perm

Tobolsk

Irtysh

Ob

Yekaterinburg
(Sverdlovsk)

Tara

Slatoust

Omsk

Kotkova

S I B E R I A

Barnaul

amara (Kuybyshev)

Irtysh

sk

Ural

Orskaya

Kirghiz Steppe

Ust-Kamenogorsk

Baty

akh Steppe

Lake Balkhash

MONGOLIA

Aral Sea

Chinese Dzungaria

an

0   100   200   300   400 Miles

0   100 200 300 400 500 600 Kilometres

The road, if it could be called a road, ran along the Kurish Nehrung, a sandy spit of land between the Baltic Sea and an inner lagoon, where only a double line of trees showed the drivers which way to go. A strong wind had blocked the narrow opening between the sea and the lagoon with ice floes so that the crossing to Memel (Klaipeda) was impossible and the travellers had to put up in a small country inn till conditions had improved.

> The scenery consists of a ploughed field, three birches, and two pines; it sweeps along towards the north-east with a charming uniformity for two hundred and twenty miles ... The most characteristic feature of this unnatural nature is the Nehrung, where we stayed for four or five days and which yielded five shells and three lichens.

Soon it became plain that Humboldt's Russian enterprise had little in common with his South American one. Thirty years had elapsed between the two and Humboldt was now venerable, famous and official. As a European celebrity and a guest of the Tsar he was not allowed to travel incognito or in peace. At Riga, in Latvia, his party was met by a mail courier who rode out in front and gave them such a preposterous air that they had to pay 15 to 18 silver roubles for one night. The nearer they got to the Russian capital the more vociferous became their reception—a taste, but no more than a taste, of things to come.

> It would be wearying to speak of Tartu (in Estonia) and the celebrations there: a university coach and four, professional visits from 8 o'clock in the morning to 9 o'clock at night, a magnificent banquet given by the whole university with obliggato toasts, side by side with interesting people and interesting sights (above all Struve with his 2,000 double stars and the wonderful telescope). A blizzard, which has plagued us for three days, has made any observation of the sky impossible but by repeated experiments I have convinced myself that I can read the micrometer with an error of less than $\frac{1}{30}$ second.

Before they had reached St Petersburg they had been ferried over rivers no less than seventeen times and Humboldt was getting worried about the costs of the expedition.

> On these bottomless roads we need 12 horses (for both carriages) as against 6 to 8 before. The whole journey to St Petersburg will easily cost 900 thalers (still below the 3,927 thalers I have been given). The courier says a journey with 400 horses costs 370 to 400 thalers here.

At last, on 1 May, after a journey of three weeks, they reached St Petersburg, clattering past the Hermitage, the Winter Palace and the Admiralty before drawing up outside the Prussian Embassy in a cloud of horse steam and a hubbub of welcome. Humboldt reported with satisfaction that his health after the rigours of the wintry journey was excellent—he never once had to resort to Ehrenberg's four cubic feet of medicaments—and that his carriage had stood up to it all, without a nail missing, though one of the horses had smashed a shaft with a kick of its hoof. As for Ehrenberg and Rose, he found their company agreeable, and Seifert helpful and energetic. All augured well.

A street scene in Berlin. Detail of a painting by Wilhelm Brücke

The reception Humboldt was given in St Petersburg was overwhelming—more appropriate to a monarch on a state visit than a scientist on an expedition. 'I seem to be surrounded with excitement wherever I go', he wrote to his brother, 'and it would be impossible to be treated with greater distinction.' The Tsar, Nicholas I, treated him as a personal guest; every day he was invited to dine with the Imperial family in the strictest privacy—'covers being laid for four'—and spent the evenings with the Tsarina, a daughter of the King of Prussia, in a completely informal atmosphere which he found 'delightful'. Even the Tsarevitch, the heir to the throne, asked him to dinner 'so that he may remember me in time to come'. The War Minister gave him a collection of government maps and departmental heads were put at his disposal. Two beautiful new Russian carriages costing 200 thalers each (a lot, evidently) were provided for the journey into Siberia, and a third was laid on for the courier and the cook. 'Everywhere I go they offer me money like hay and anticipate every wish.'

On 20 May they left St Petersburg for a fortnight's stay in Moscow. Soon the extravagance of the Russian hospitality wore thin.

> We are continually the objects of attention of the police, government officials, cossacks and guards of honour. Unfortunately we are hardly left alone for a minute; we can't take a step without being led by the arm like invalids. I should like to see Leopold von Buch in such a position.

Oppressed like all celebrities by the tediousness of public adulation and the ceaseless receptions with their endless rounds of speeches and toasts—he could have remained drunk through the entire expedition if he had responded to all of them—Humboldt longed to set off for the quiet and solitude, or so he thought, of the Siberian wilderness. When they did at last head out of town, however, it was only too evident that the expedition had now taken the form of a travelling circus. High-ranking mining officials escorted them and the bureaucratic worthies of the local administrations preceded them; the whole cumbersome and exalted procession was driven at a breakneck gallop and at every stage-post they had to change as many as forty horses at a time. Their route took them due east across the monotonous Russian plains through Vladimir and beyond. The countryside was bathed in Russian spring weather. They passed through villages of little log houses, and rattled and juddered over main streets paved with wooden blocks. At night they put up at the mail stations or were billeted by the chiefs of police in the houses of the local well-to-do. At length they reached the ancient walled town of Nizhnye Novgorod (Gorki) and there they loaded their carriages on to a big Volga sailing barge for the river journey down to Kazan. Compared with the Orinoco the accommodation was de luxe. A canvas awning had been rigged up amidships and a table and benches placed beneath it. There was a brick stove for the expedition cook to prepare his simple meals on and the contents of his pantry were towed behind in a small boat. The wind was against them and the four Volga boatmen on board had to row the whole way, chanting melancholy Russian songs for hour after hour. The river was in full flood after the spring thaw

The mixed architecture of a Moscow street—wooden shacks, oriental church domes and fine, French-designed buildings. Detail of an engraving by Johannes Richter

and often the lush green banks, with their poplars and oaks and linden trees, were more than a mile apart. They were three days on the river and on 4 June they reached Kazan, a Moslem city of 50,000 people, once the ancient stronghold of Tamberlane's Golden Horde and now the centre of a lively regional university. Kazan was at the western limits of the vague frontier of Asia and it gave Humboldt his first whiff of the east—all Tartars and turbans and ruined oriental palaces.

In the bright warm weather of early June the coaches rolled on along good gravelled roads towards Perm and the Ural mountains, everywhere escorted by men with swords. 'A Siberian journey is not so pleasant as a South American one', Humboldt wrote home. 'Since Kazan we haven't come across a single inn. One sleeps on benches

Nicholas I, Tsar of all the Russias, treated Humboldt as a personal guest. 'Wherever you go you spread a life-giving influence', he told him

or in the carriage. But life is bearable and I mustn't complain.'

Humboldt, for all his years, was immune to the wear and tear of travel. One of the Russians in the party, an engineer called Helmersen who later became a general, described how Humboldt—dressed in a frock coat of dark brown, with a white scarf round his neck and a round hat on his head—*walked* in the Urals, with his head bent forward, whenever the opportunity arose.

> On excursions he never rode on horseback. When the carriage was unable to proceed he would set off on foot, climbing high mountains without any signs of fatigue, clambering over rough terrain like one accustomed to field work. His meals were always moderate, even after the most tiring march, when the Russians would oblige him to accept their lavish hospitality with mountains of food and an unending choice of drinks.

Night scene inside a Siberian peasant's dwelling where travellers were sometimes forced to seek rest

From the summit of Belaya Gora, Humboldt and Rose strained their eyes to the east and saw the vast steppes of Siberia stretching monotonously to the horizon. They were in Asia now and on the 15 June they reached Yekaterinburg (Sverdlovsk), their base for the excursions into the surrounding Urals which were the real object of their journey. For a month Humboldt and his companions tramped through the mountains studying the mines and the fabulously rich mineral deposits—iron, copper, malachite, beryl, topaz and especially gold and platinum—with which the Urals seemed stuffed full. Sometimes Humboldt spent the entire time on foot, as surefooted over boulders and scree as he had been on the slopes of Chimborazo. Often he didn't get to the pits until evening and insisted on being taken down them as late as nine o'clock at night. His observations were methodical and exact but the real excitement was the discovery of the first diamond ever found in the Urals— indeed the first diamond ever discovered outside of the tropics—an event in which Humboldt played a crucial part.

Before leaving St Petersburg he had told the Tsar he would not leave Russia until he had found diamonds in the Urals. This was no idle boast. Humboldt, in his geognostic work on the stratification of rocks, had noticed that in Brazil diamonds were often found in the same localities as platinum beds and gold sands. Hitherto diamonds had been thought to be confined exclusively to the tropics but Humboldt had very great hopes that they might now be discovered in the gold and platinum deposits in the Urals. He confided these hopes to Count Polier, who had joined the expedition at Gorki and who happened to own gold fields on the eastern slopes of the Urals. At every gold mine they came to Humboldt and Rose examined the gold-bearing sand under the microscope in order to examine the various mineral particles that composed it but though they had every indication that they were on the right track, they nowhere came across a glimmer of diamonds. On 2 July, after more than a fortnight of futile search, Count Polier left the expedition and returned to his own estates. Four days later, with his German overseer, Schmidt, he arrived at one of his gold placer works. That very day the first diamond ever found in the Urals was brought to him by a fourteen-year-old boy, Pavel Popov, who worked at the establishment. Its transparency was perfect and its lustre and crystallization left no doubt that Humboldt's prophecy had come true. Three days afterwards, another boy found a second stone, and not much later a third one was sent to Polier which was bigger than the other two put together.

Humboldt did not learn of this discovery until he returned to St Petersburg later in the year and found a parcel waiting for him with a diamond inside—a present from the Count to the man he regarded responsible for the discovery of the first diamond deposit in Russia.

On 18 July the expedition left Sverdlovsk and galloped night and day through Siberia to Tobolsk on the River Irtysh—in view of the huge distances between one place and another in Russia and the endless sameness of the landscape this headlong

'I implore his Imperial Majesty', Humboldt wrote, 'for permission to go at least as far as the Irtysh river. Tobolsk is a dream of my youth.'

dash was probably the most sensible way to cover the necessary ground and get back before the onset of the Russian winter. At Tobolsk, where Humboldt met of all people the son of Lotte Werther, immortalized in Goethe's first novel, the Governor was so concerned about his distinguished visitor's safe conduct that he appointed a special escort, consisting of a doctor, some cossacks, and the Governor's adjutant to attend him twenty-four hours a day. Henceforth they were to travel to Central Asia like tinned sardines.

The long road led south-eastwards through half the breadth of the Siberian steppes to Barnaul, the Altai and the border of Chinese Dzungaria. They travelled in Siberian long-carriages in which they had to lie stretched out on their backs, and on their heads they wore hot, suffocating leather masks with vizors made of horse-hair netting to keep out the voracious Siberian mosquitoes. Typhus, was raging in the scattered villages through which they had to pass and, in order to minimize contact with the inhabitants, they once again travelled night and day.

They suffered a great deal from the heat, dust and plagues of yellow midges but they travelled so swiftly over those monotonous grasslands that in nine days they covered a thousand miles and on the morning of 1 August arrived on the banks of the Ob opposite the mountain town of Barnaul in the Altai. A south-south-west gale was blowing from the Kirghiz steppe at the time and raged for seventeen hours. The Ob had waves like the sea and as it was quite impossible to cross they had to camp for the night on the bank. The light of the camp fires, rising high in the forest, reminded Humboldt vividly of his days on the Orinoco. It rained and it blew alternately, but it did at least mean they were rid of the mosquitoes and could take off their suffocating masks. Finally, at two in the morning, the gale died down and they were able to cross the Ob into Barnaul.

Now that they had penetrated 2,300 miles into Asia, Humboldt noted that the landscape had at last become Siberian. They had travelled so quickly that they had had seen little wild life on the way, but Humboldt was intrigued to learn that the big Siberian tiger inhabited these northerly latitudes and he actually saw the pelts of two of them, which he intended to purchase for the zoological collection in Berlin.

As for Barnaul, he found it a pleasant enough town, and greatly admired its splendid collection of old Chinese, Mongolian and Tibetan manuscripts. But the benevolence of the Government unfortunately led to a daily increase in the number of the party and before they left they were joined by the Commander-in-Chief of Tomsk and

Kirghiz encampment on the Siberian steppes. Typhus was raging when Humboldt passed through so he was forced to cover a thousand miles in nine days

his entire staff who announced their intention of accompanying Humboldt along the border as far as Omsk.

On 4 August the expedition left Barnaul and travelling in light native carriages via Ust Kamenogorsk reached the border of China. It was one o'clock on 29 August 1829, and they had come to the end of the road. Two wretched encampments manned by tattered Mongol soldiers, under the command of an impeccable young Chinaman in a blue silk gown and a conical hat with a peacock feather stuck in it, guarded both banks of the Irtysh to the north of what is now part of Russian Kazakhstan but was then Chinese Dzungaria. It wasn't much of a place. On top of an arid hill stood a little Chinese temple. In a valley a few camels grazed. On the left lay Mongolia, on the right China. To the south lay the steppes of Chinese Turkestan and the distant snow-capped ranges of the ramparts of Asia. From a small eminence the sixty-year-old explorer squinted into the hazy distance to catch a glimpse of the world that had been the goal of his ambition for more than a quarter of a century. Then he turned back.

They returned by boat along the Irtysh to Omsk and then skirted across the northern edge of the arid and desolate Kazakh steppes, where the only life they saw were scattered deer on the horizon and the occasional scorpion underfoot. From Astrakhan on the Caspian Sea they cruised about in wood-fuelled steam-launches

Ferrying travellers' carriages across the Irtysh in Siberia. Humboldt had to make 53 such river crossings on his journey to Central Asia

for a few days while Rose and Ehrenberg collected water samples for chemical and microbiological analysis and Humboldt took a series of barometric readings.

Towards the end of October 1829 they started homewards and on 3 November, safe and sound, and with a commendable wealth of data and specimens, reached Moscow. None of the carriages had broken down and nobody had fallen ill. The foolhardy cossack postillions had occasionally tumbled off the coaches during those long breakneck gallops, but they had always managed to roll out between the rear wheels, laughing. The statistics of their journey were intriguing. In slightly less than six months they had travelled 9,700 miles, including 460 miles by river. They had passed through 658 post-stations and used 12,244 post-horses. They had made 53 ferry crossings of rivers, including ten over the Volga and eight over the Irtysh. Out of the 20,000 roubles Cancrin had advanced him at the start of the journey Humboldt had spent 12,950, and eventually, somewhat to Cancrin's surprise, he handed the balance back.

The arrival of the expedition back in Moscow sparked off another round of exhausting receptions. The Moscow Academy of Science held a special meeting at which they invited Humboldt and his companions to discuss the scientific results of the expedition.

The affair was treated very seriously and was not without its comic aspects. The Governor-General and all the military and civil dignitaries turned up in gala uniforms with ribbons and decorations, while the professors strode about trailing their swords in military fashion, with their tricorn hats tucked under their arms. Humboldt, who had not been expecting anything like this, arrived in a simple blue coat and was very taken aback. He was forced to reply to a number of tedious speeches of welcome in the freezing corridor, and when at last he entered the hall the whole audience stood up. Humboldt had actually intended to put the geomagnetic and meteorological data he had collected in the Urals before the Moscow academicians. Instead he had to listen to a poem which began 'Humboldt, Prometheus of our days!' and peer with devout admiration at a plait made from the hair of Peter the Great.

In St Petersburg Humboldt was again overwhelmed with hospitality and oppressive Russian kindness, and again the Tsar and the Tsarina demanded his company almost daily. 'Your sojourn in Russia has been the cause of immense progress in my country', said Tsar Nicholas, who was ill in bed. 'Wherever you go you spread a life-giving influence.' And he gave Humboldt a sable cloak worth 5,000 roubles and a magnificent seven-foot-high malachite vase worth 40,000 roubles as parting gifts.

And so Humboldt turned his back on a nation whose habits he could not abide and a monarch whose politics he secretly despised and set course along the frozen trail back to Berlin again. Shortly after Christmas he arrived home. He had travelled 11,500 miles—nearly half the circumference of the earth—and after his brief taste of Russia he was almost glad to be back.

Cosmos

Humboldt never travelled on an expedition of discovery again. He had now achieved the second great ambition of his life and this time he was content to leave the publication of the scientific results of his Russian journey to his two capable young subordinates, Ehrenberg and Rose. His own work—a three-volume descriptive geography entitled *Asie Centrale*—did not appear till many years later, and by comparison with the South American publications it was a very modest and unelaborate affair. It steered well clear of all political and social controversy and confined itself solely to the facts and figures of Central Asian geography, including the exposition of Humboldt's ideas concerning the relative contribution of mountains and plateaux to the mean height of continents and some important observations on the climatology of this great northern land mass, along with data to complete the isothermal world map.

The practical achievement of the Russian expedition was the stimulus it gave to Humboldt's very ambitious and important plans for a chain of geomagnetic observation stations stretching right the way round the world—a major event in the history of geomagnetism and the development of international scientific collaboration, in which he played a leading rôle. In St Petersburg in 1829 he had already recommended to the Russian authorities the practical and scientific advantages to be gained from setting up a series of magnetic and meteorological stations all the way across European and Asiatic Russia—an area, he had pointed out, that was bigger than the visible part of the moon—and within six years a number of such stations were in operation all the way from St Petersburg to Peking and Alaska. In accordance with Humboldt's advice they made regular observations on identical instruments of the magnetic dip and declination, the barometric pressure, the temperature and humidity of the air, the direction of the winds and the amount of snow and rainfall. The USA already had a network of similar stations, and Gauss had arranged another network of observatories, called the Göttingen Association, across Europe from Ireland to Germany. Humboldt realized that to complete the round-the-world circle he needed to persuade the British Government to establish stations in their territories overseas and in April 1836 he wrote a letter to the Duke of Sussex—a student friend from his Göttingen days, and now President of the Royal Society—in which he proposed that permanent stations should be set up in Canada, St Helena, Cape of Good Hope, Jamaica, Ceylon and Australia.

The British response was as swift and whole-hearted as the Russian one had been. In 1839, at the instigation of the Royal Society and the British Association under the leadership of Sir John Herschel, Sir Edward Sabine, Sir George Airy and Humphrey Lloyd, the British Government ordered the establishment of fixed stations in most of the territories Humboldt had recommended and even went one better by equipping a special naval expedition under Sir James Ross for the purpose of making magnetic observations in the Antarctic. Ross's ships carried all the instruments necessary for his own work as well as the instruments for the St Helena, South Africa, Australia and New Zealand stations it passed en route, plus the men to run them—officers and NCO's from the Royal Artillery, equipped with detailed instructions drawn up by Humboldt and the Royal Society.

On the whole the British Empire stations, widely scattered across the globe, worked extremely well. Ross was able to locate the magnetic south pole at 76°S and 154°E. Sir Edward Sabine, the astronomer and geophysicist in overall charge of the British network, was ultimately able to find the cause of magnetic storms (Humboldt's pet obsession) in the periodic variation of sun spots. Only once did the gentlemen of the Royal Artillery fail in their duty when the detachment in Tasmania, much to Humboldt's dismay, abandoned their observations of a magnetic storm at midnight one Saturday in order to observe the Sabbath instead.

The international geomagnetic collaboration which Humboldt helped to organize after his return from Russia was the direct antecedent of the great International Polar projects of 1882–83 and 1932–33, as well as the International Geophysical Year of 1957–58. But as ever, his life had been running on several parallel courses during that time, and the intensity of the magnetic field of the earth was by no means his only preoccupation.

In the seventh decade of his life Humboldt was as active as he had ever been. Physically he was amazingly well preserved—his bright blue eyes sparkled as brilliantly as they had done in his youth, and his speech gushed from him in an unending torrent. Though he was now the grand old man of science, universally respected for his achievements and everywhere acclaimed as the father of modern physical geography, he showed no signs of resting on his laurels and of settling down. He interested himself in everything of concern to science, and busied himself with his books and with his endless correspondence. His time was now divided almost equally between his private studies and his duties as Chamberlain to King Frederick William III, and in the service of the King he continued to travel all over Europe, commuting regularly between Potsdam and Berlin, and accompanying the King on his visits to the Czech spas. After the July Revolution in Paris in 1830 he was sent on several diplomatic missions to the court of Louis-Philippe in Paris, the new constitutional monarch of the House of Orléans. He had originally done these journeys by stage-coach and on horse-back; before long he was doing them in trains and steamboats. Times were changing.

His numerous official sojourns in Paris during the 30's and early 40's were important to him because they enabled him to maintain that tenuous link with his beloved city and his beloved Arago, now Permanent Secretary at the Institut National and an active liberal politician in the Chamber of Deputies. Their visits also enabled him to endure his rôle as Court lackey in Berlin. So as not to be disturbed he adopted the plan of having two residences in Paris, sleeping in one and running off to the other—an inaccessible writing room belonging to Arago in the entresol of the Institut National—before eight o'clock in the morning. But he was by no means a recluse, and was readily available to help talented but struggling young scientists who tracked him down. One such was Louis Agassiz, the son of an impoverished Swiss clergy-

Louis Agassiz—'One of the ablest naturalists of the nineteenth century. ... For three hours he had Humboldt to himself and the time passed like a dream.'

man, and later one of the ablest naturalists of the nineteenth century. In 1832, when he was twenty-four, Agassiz had arrived in Paris to look through the collections of the Natural History Museum for his book on fossil fish. He had no money and no resources and when he first met Humboldt in his laboratory he had to confess that he found it so difficult to make ends meet that he was on the point of giving up his scientific work altogether. Humboldt encouraged him to persevere and took him out to an expensive restaurant to cheer him up. For three hours Agassiz had Humboldt to himself and the time passed like a dream.

> How he examined me, and how much I learned in that short time! How to work, what to do, and what to avoid; how to live; how to distribute my time; what methods of study to pursue; these were the things of which he talked to me on that delightful evening.

Humboldt was an infallible judge of scientific talent and there were few scientists of distinction in mid-nineteenth century Europe who did not owe something to him in their early careers. Agassiz' encounter was typical of many. When Humboldt failed to interest his own publisher in Agassiz' book he sent him a 'small credit' to keep him going. 'Consider it an advance which need not be paid for years,' he wrote, 'and which I will gladly increase when I go away.' The 'small credit' was a draft for a thousand francs—two-thirds of Humboldt's monthly income.

It was not always scientists that Humboldt helped out in this way with what little money he had at his disposal. One day a strikingly beautiful, raven-haired young girl entered a Paris hairdresser's and offered to sell her hair for 60 francs in order to support her sick mother. The hairdresser told her that he could buy black hair anywhere and offered her 20 francs. At this point an old, silver-haired gentleman, who was being attended to by the hairdresser, got up, took the hairdresser's scissors, carefully selected a single hair, snipped it off, gave the girl two banknotes, which she was too taken aback to look at, and walked out of the shop. Only then did she realize she was holding two 100-franc notes. She rushed out after the old man, followed him into his hotel and asked the porter his name. The porter replied: 'Alexander von Humboldt'.

In the spring of 1835 Alexander's brother Wilhelm died. Since the death of his wife Caroline a few years previously Wilhelm had lived in grief-stricken solitude at Schloss Tegel, toiling away at the philological researches that were now his only consolation. He had begun to suffer from an uncontrollable trembling of his arms and legs (probably Parkinson's disease) and at the end of March Alexander was informed that his brother's illness had taken a grave turn for the worse. For days Wilhelm hovered on the point of death. His intellect was unimpaired and he retained complete consciousness, but his voice was very weak, hoarse and high-pitched like that of a child and the doctors had to apply leeches to his throat. Most of the time Alexander was at his brother's bedside. 'I am quite bereft of hope,' he wrote to his friend Varnhagen von Ense. 'I didn't think my old eyes could have shed so many tears. This has gone on for eight days.' Towards the end pneumonia set in and on 8 April, at six in the evening, as the last ray of the sun faded from the room, Wilhelm von Humboldt—poet, translator, philologist, and dear brother—died. 'I am very much alone', Alexander wrote to Arago. 'I hope I shall be lucky enough to be with you this year.'

There were few men left in Berlin with whom he had anything much in common now. 'All around me is like a desert—so completely desert that there is absolutely no one about me to understand why I grieve.' His duties at the Court at Potsdam, where he was envied and distrusted by all but the King, were becoming increasingly wearisome. He had to attend the breakfast of the royal children and lunch with the royal family at two, an engagement that always irked him because it broke up the working day. For a man of his calibre it was an exceptionally prosaic job among exceptionally prosaic people. The King was as bad as the rest of them. He was so shy and inarticulate that he was unable to finish a sentence whenever he opened his mouth to speak, though for the most part he had nothing of interest to say. With the inauguration of the railway between Berlin and Potsdam in 1839, Humboldt found his attendance at court was demanded even more frequently, and complained that the rapid oscillation between the two royal residences caused him to live a very unliterary and bat-like existence. He did not dislike the King, but only with the Crown Prince did he find it possible to communicate intelligently.

Humboldt's only close friends in Berlin now were the surviving members of the Mendelssohn family, the banker Beer and his wife (the parents of the composer Meyerbeer), and Varnhagen von Ense, the husband of Humboldt's boyhood friend Rahel Levin (a very bright and personable salon hostess who had died in 1833). Varnhagen, an intelligent, highly literate man with liberal views and a strong dislike of the current reactionary government, worked in the Ministry for Foreign Affairs and had established a reputation for himself as a modern historian. For almost thirty years he maintained a close relationship with Humboldt, who treated him rather like a confidant, writing many sarcastic letters to him about the affairs of the day which revealed his true feelings about the court and Berlin society and caused a scandal when they were published soon after Humboldt's death. It was to Varnhagen, as it happened, that Humboldt first mentioned his long-contemplated plans for the masterwork of his old age, in a letter written towards the end of 1834:

> I have the crazy notion to depict in a single work the entire material universe, all that we know of the phenomena of heaven and earth, from the nebulae of stars to the geography of mosses and granite rocks—and in a vivid style that will stimulate and elicit feeling. Every great and important idea in my writing should here be registered side by side with facts. It should portray an epoch in the spiritual genesis of mankind—in the knowledge of nature. But it is not to be taken as a physical description of the earth: it comprises heaven and earth, the whole of creation. Fifteen years ago I started writing it in French, and called it *Essai sur la physique du monde*. In Germany I had originally thought of calling it *The Book of Nature*, after the one that Albertus Magnus wrote in the Middle Ages. But all this is uncertain. Now my title is *Cosmos, Sketch of a Physical Description of the Universe* . . .

Two watercolour portraits by Franz Krüger—Humboldt (left) and his confidential friend and literary adviser Varnhagen von Ense (right)

Humboldt had spent the previous half century contemplating *Cosmos*, and he was to spend the next quarter century writing it. It was truly a life's work, and only death put an end to it. As long ago as 1796, Humboldt had written: 'I have conceived the idea of a physical description of the world. As I feel the increasing need for it, so also I see how few foundations exist for such an edifice.' He was twenty-seven then, and under the influence of his friend Goethe, a universalist who believed in the essential unity of all phenomena of nature. It was not until 1828, however, that he finally gave expression to his concept in his Berlin lectures, and thereafter he laboured to produce his physical description of the universe in book form. It was quite literally a race against death. The first volume of *Cosmos* was published in 1845 when he was seventy-six, the second volume when he was seventy-eight, the third when he was eighty-one, and the fourth when he was eighty-nine, but the fifth volume was only half done when he died and had to be completed from his notes and provided with an index over a thousand pages long. On the whole the final work followed the scheme of the Berlin lectures reasonably faithfully.

Humboldt's aim in *Cosmos* was to provide an accurate scientific picture of the physical structure of the universe in such a way as to interest the general educated public and stimulate interest in scientific discovery among intelligent laymen. Conceived in the late eighteenth century, the work outlined all that the mid-nineteenth century knew of the physical world and enlisted the help of the most eminent scholars and the very latest research to explain this world to the ordinary man. It was the major product of a universalist in an age of specialists and though by our standards it can hardly be called popular science (its sheer bulk alone—nearly 2,000 pages in the contemporary English edition—is daunting enough) it was in its day spectacularly received: the first volume sold out in two months, the work was translated into most European languages, and Humboldt noted with satisfaction that 80,000 copies had been sold by 1851, no mean sale by any reckoning.

Humboldt saw nature as a whole and man as part of that whole. All branches of science were involved in his exposition, therefore, and in his section on the history of scientific discovery he also linked the sciences to the arts and the humanities. From the distant vastnesses of the Milky Way to the minutest animal organisms detectable under the miscroscope, from the nature of the interior of the earth to the migrations of the human race across its surface, Humboldt's quite phenomenal learning and sustained powers of minutely detailed, factual description ranged far and wide. It is impossible, in the space available, to give any adequate list of the host of subjects discussed in these extraordinary volumes, nor perhaps is it any longer necessary, for the information they contain has long been superseded or passed into the common pool of scientific knowledge. Many of the subjects, particularly those relating to the physical description of the earth itself, brought in Humboldt's own favourite fields of exploration. The geographical distribution of plants, the magnetic field of the earth, isothermal lines, ocean currents, the alignment of volcanoes, the evolution of mountain ranges—all were based on his own researches in the forests of the Orinoco, the slopes of Chimborazo and the steppes of Siberia, researches which he had been constantly updating through the years. His account in *Cosmos* of the propagation of seismic waves became the basis of modern seismology.

Humboldt never forgot that the main purpose of *Cosmos* was not to compile an encyclopedia but to communicate the intellectual excitement—and utilitarian necessity—of scientific research in an age and a country where even highly educated people usually preferred not to know. 'I cannot agree with Burke', he wrote, 'when he says that it is only our ignorance of nature that causes all our admiration and excites all our emotions.'

Scientific knowledge, Humboldt pointed out, was part of a country's wealth, a natural resource like any other: if it was not properly developed and exploited the country would stagnate and then decline. He could not agree, however, that a backward nation implied an innately inferior populace. In *Cosmos* as elsewhere he stressed his lifelong belief in the unity of the human race; and he rejected categorically the notion of superior and inferior races.

Humboldt's factual text, heavily loaded with footnotes and references, was sent in proof sheets to all the various specialists for comments and corrections before publication. In this way he aimed to ensure that what he wrote was not only accurate but up-to-date as well—a Herculean, never-ending task, especially under the circumstances in which he wrote, snatching odd moments and the late hours between trivial chores at Court. Humboldt was also particularly anxious to try and write well. No one was more aware of the weaknesses of his style than he, and he continually looked to his friend Varnhagen, whose literary judgement he respected, for advice in this matter.

> Now, my dear friend, for my request! I cannot bear to send the manuscript away without begging you to cast a critical glance over it. Be kind enough to read the opening section and write on a piece of paper, 'I should prefer—to—', without giving any reasons. But don't find a fault without helping me to mend it. And put me at my ease about the title.
>
> PS. The besetting sins of my style are an unfortunate propensity to poetical expressions, a too frequent use of participles and adjectives, and a concentration of too many opinions and sentiments into one sentence.

Varnhagen's comments were duly received and gratefully acknowledged. 'I have made use of all of them,' Humboldt told him, 'or almost all—nineteen-twentieths or more. One is always a little bit obstinate about something one has written oneself.'

Cosmos, the last great work of the last great universal man, enormously enhanced its author's reputation with the public in his own lifetime, not only in his own country but throughout Europe and America as well. Its enthusiastic reception in England, where it came out in the Bohn Scientific Library in a translation by Sir Edward Sabine's wife, particularly surprised him. The reviews were effusive in praise of both the man and his work, though some felt he had done less than justice to the contribution of modern British scientists and many were quick to point out that the man who wrote so exhaustively about the creation never once paused to mention the Creator. Thus the *Quarterly Review*:

> It is easy to say that the 'ultimate end of the experimental sciences is to ascend to the existence of laws, and to generalize them progressively'. But where is the inductive process to end? Where is the last generalization of the last and highest group of laws? The reasoning through a chain of causes must evidently bring us at last to the first cause of all—be it Necessity or be it God.

Humboldt saw his work on Cosmos *as a race against death*

It had once been said about Alexander von Humboldt that there were only three things that were beyond his comprehension: orthodox religion, romantic love and music. Certainly this was true of the first and the last; they were both social phenomena for which he had no time. His attitude to religion was quite clear: 'All religions offer three different things—a moral rule, the same in all religions and very pure, a geological dream, and a myth or legend. The last element has assumed the greatest importance.'

The murmurings of the pietists, however, in no way detracted from the admiration of the Prussian monarch for Humboldt's achievement. In 1847 he ordered a beautiful commemoration medal to be struck. On one side was a profile of Humboldt in bold relief; on the reverse, surrounded by signs of the zodiac and a wreath of tropical foliage, was a genius with a plumbline and a telescope; the Sphinx gazed down on him and electric fish swam past; above, in Greek characters, was inscribed the word which had become the symbol of an age:

ΚΟΣΜΟΣ

CHAPTER 21

The Court Democrat

In the twenty-five years Humboldt spent writing his last big book a lot else went on in his life and in the world about him. In 1840 King Frederick William III died and was succeeded by Humboldt's friend, the Crown Prince, who now became Frederick William IV, a clever and amiable man but a disastrously indecisive ruler. Humboldt had hoped at first that the new king's accession would see the end of monarchical despotism and the drafting of a new democratic constitution; but the King, in spite of the closeness of his relationship with his liberal Chamberlain, was no liberal himself and while he dithered the forces of reaction reasserted themselves in Prussia. Humboldt, who had been made a Privy Councillor, tried hard to fan the flames of liberalism at Court, and at different times achieved some success—notably over the emancipation of the Jews and (much later) the abolition of slavery in Prussia. But in the main his position was a precarious and unhappy one, and the *ultras* and the pietists at Court presented a united front against him and would have had him expelled from the country if it had not been for his special relationship with the King. 'I live', he told Varnhagen, 'in the glitter of outward splendour and in the romantic affection of a noble prince, yet in a moral solitude such as only the stunted intellects of this dour and divided country can provide—a country gradually assuming the dreary aspect of an eastern steppe.'

His social position as the Court democrat who carried the golden key of a chamberlain on his belt and the ideals of 1789 in his heart was a very peculiar one. Frederick William IV sought his company even more than his father had done. Humboldt's attendance at court was now required daily and special rooms, done out like an oriental tented encampment, were prepared for him in Schloss Charlottenhof at Potsdam so that he could sleep—and work—overnight there. Every lunch-time he was expected to eat with the King alone. Every evening he had to position himself under a chandelier and read out loud from newspapers and books while the Queen got on with her knitting. The King was furious if some other engagement prevented Humboldt from joining him at dinner, for he used his Chamberlain as a walking encyclopedia and liked to bombard him with endless questions about anything that came into his head for hours on end. Usually Humboldt had to sit up half the night rewriting the King's private correspondence, and even then he wasn't left in peace, for the King would often come alone to his room in the late hours to ask more questions. The King was genuinely fond of his old Chamberlain, though, and always ready to defend him against his critics or help him out with money. If ever Humboldt, the romantic liberal, was ill, the King, the romantic reactionary, would sit at his bedside and read to him for hour after hour.

Quite why Humboldt put up with such a regimen at his age was a question he had often asked himself. His friend Varnhagen had probably found the answer. 'Humboldt is oppressed by his multifarious occupations,' he wrote, 'but he would be unhappy without them. Society and the court have become to him like a familiar tavern, where men are accustomed to spend their evenings and enjoy their pipe.'

The christening of the Prince of Wales (later King Edward VII) at Windsor Castle in 1842. Humboldt found great splendour at the English Court, but a way of life that was natural and friendly

Humboldt, 'on the eve of an agitated but unfulfilled life', began to show signs of a weariness of the world and a despair for all human affairs. He gave up all hopes of changing the King's political views, feared war might break out in Europe, and talked again of emigrating. Almost his only source of relief were his trips to Paris and his relations with Arago. Arago was a very bad correspondent and sometimes would let a year slip by before answering Humboldt's letters. Humboldt used to implore his friend to write to him—just a few lines would do, he said, just the sight of his handwriting—and then scan the post every day as nervously as a young girl. In December 1840 he wrote to Arago:

I am longing to see you again; if my health remains good, I should like to set out for Paris in the spring and stay for some months . . . I should be happy if you would have the kindness to send me three lines. It would be enough to say: 'I shall see you arrive with the same pleasure as before.' Can you refuse me this kindness? It would be the nicest present from you for the new year.

With greater alacrity than usual, Arago three months later sent off his reply—one of the few letters from Arago to Humboldt that has survived, as Humboldt destroyed most of them: 'Apart from my family, you are beyond comparison the person I love most in the world. You are the only one of my friends on whom I would count in a difficult situation. You can have a bed at the Observatoire. You will arrive in time for my course on astronomy. My new lecture theatre is scandalously luxurious.'

Occasionally Humboldt strayed further afield. Once he nearly fell overboard from a ship taking him and the King to Denmark but luckily hit the deck instead of the sea and escaped with a bruise eight inches long. In 1842 he accompanied the King to England to attend the christening of the Prince of Wales, the future King Edward VII. The doggerel trotted out by Leigh Hunt in honour of the event—'and the genial

Frederick William IV of Prussia, a clever and amiable man but a disastrously indecisive ruler, was Humboldt's only ally at Court, defending him against his critics and helping him out with money

king with the wise companioning'—is supposed to refer to King Frederick William and his scientific adviser. Humboldt did not relish the visit and his time was so taken up with social duties that he did not even have an opportunity to visit Greenwich Observatory. He found great splendour at the English Court at Windsor, and a way of life there that was simple, natural and friendly. He hated Peel whom he thought both vain and petty, while the Foreign Secretary, Lord Aberdeen, struck him as dull and dumb. Humboldt never felt at ease in England. He found the nation as a whole reserved, formal and isolated. 'This England is a detestable country', he wrote to a friend in Berlin after a visit across the Channel. 'At nine o'clock you must wear your necktie in *this* style, at ten o'clock in *that*, and at eleven o'clock in another fashion'. He had little time for the political attitudes of the English establishment either. When Queen Victoria paid a visit to the Rhine in the summer of 1846, Prince Albert remarked to Humboldt: 'I know you show a lot of sympathy for the misfortunes of the Poles in Russia. Unfortunately the Poles deserve as little sympathy as the Irish.' He had every admiration for English scientists—Faraday, Herschel, Sabine, Darwin, and others—and they for him. But from the down-to-earth, mercantile British public, with its interest in the practical results of applied science rather than the laws and hypotheses of pure science, he expected little sympathy, and indeed received little.

In his palace in Potsdam, King Frederick William IV drifted further and further away from reality. He spent his time designing expensive Gothic ruins and drawing up elaborate plans for a pilgrimage to Jerusalem while the demands of his Prussian subjects for constitutional reform grew more insistent and entrenched. Humboldt, guardian angel of all scientists and artists, confined his influence to worthy causes, persuading the King to grant pensions, jobs and recognition to deserving men and women in need. Among the many beneficiaries was the girl-friend of his youth, Henriette Herz, who had long been widowed. When the King put Humboldt in charge of a new division of the Order of Merit, Humboldt used his position to gazette the names of some of the scientists and artists he thought most deserving of honour in his time, and his first list included the names of Chateaubriand, Ingres, Meyerbeer, Rossini, Faraday, Herschel, Berzelius, Daguerre, and Arago.

In January 1848 Humboldt returned from a visit to Paris for the very last time. Though he did not know it, he was destined never to see that city, nor his friend Arago, again. A month later revolution broke out in Paris. In March it broke out in Berlin.

Political demonstrations demanding a return to constitutional monarchy had begun in the streets of Berlin at the beginning of the month and by the 18th the King had capitulated to the people's demands and granted a constitution. However, he had failed to withdraw the troops surrounding the royal palace in Berlin and during the 18th angry crowds again filled the streets and the palace area. The troops were then ordered to clear the streets. Two shots were fired into the crowd and with the cry 'Traitors!' the people raised the barricades and the street fighting began. By midnight, however, the troops had won the battle of the barricades and were in complete control of the approaches to the palace.

The next day the King ordered the troops to be withdrawn and for a few delirious moments the people of Berlin believed they had won the day. They hurled their abuse on the departing soldiers and turned in fury on the man they held responsible for the bloodshed—the King's martinet brother, Wilhelm, later to be Kaiser Wilhelm I of Germany. Prince Wilhelm fled in disguise to London and on 21 March the King was compelled to salute the fallen fighters of the barricades and ride through the streets wearing a black, red and gold sash—the colours of the movement for a united Germany. At a rally in the palace square the crowd called for the King and then somebody shouted Humboldt's name and a roar went up for him to come forward on the palace balcony. Humboldt stepped forward, bowed silently to the crowd and then stepped back. What he thought about that moment we shall never know. He never seems to have referred to it either in writing or conversation, or if he did it has been expunged from the records. It could hardly have left him unmoved.

The following day the heroes of the revolution were buried. The 183 coffins stood on a giant catafalque covered in flowers. A bishop comforted the relatives and outside in the crowd a Protestant, a Catholic and a Jewish minister held services of dedication. The guilds carried their dead, and so did the Academy of Science, with the eighty-year-old Alexander von Humboldt, bare-headed in the chill March wind, walking at their head along the road that led to the royal palace. The King and Queen and their ministers and cohorts came out on to the palace balcony and as the procession moved solemnly by the King took off his helmet and waited there for two hours until it had finally passed. Then the martyrs of freedom were buried in a single grave and everyone went home. It had been a victory—or so it seemed—to the people.

Quite what Humboldt's position had been during those three hectic days of insurrection in Berlin has never been made quite clear. Caught half-way between his allegiance to his King and his allegiance to his liberal principles it is doubtful whether he took any more active part than has already been described. But in a letter he wrote to Arago from Sans Souci in May there seems to be little doubt where his heart lay:

My ardent hopes for democratic institutions, hopes which date back to 1789, have been fulfilled. On the bloody night of 18 March, placed between two barricades, I was attacked four times by armed men, who did not know me and who had not read *Cosmos*, who wanted to search for arms. Some groups did a little damage by breaking down the doors. I talked to them of my white hair and the sentimental drama, boringly told, succeeded . . . I continue to enjoy much affection in the lower classes of society. I have taken part in the general election in the union of artisans, but although I was proposed as a candidate for Frankfurt some time ago, I have refused to accept anything. I shall be 80 next year, and in this fossilized state I cannot begin a new career.

But by the end of the year the revolution had foundered. The King had repudiated the new constitution, the new National Assembly was no more, and the big land-

Portrait of Alexander von Humboldt by Joseph August Stieler, 1843

OVERLEAF *Humboldt in his study in Oranienburger Strasse, Berlin. Watercolour by Eduard Hildebrandt, 1856*

owners, the higher clergy and the right-wing members of the administration forced a conservative government on the people which left them somewhat worse off than they had been before.

From a Potsdam where the *ultras* now reigned supreme and a confused and broken king slid slowly down towards his ultimate insanity, a dispirited Humboldt wrote his final testimony before he turned his back on the world and the ebb and flow of history.

The year 1849 is the year of reaction. I have saluted 1789, I have been present at so many dramatic political events (monarchy, crowned republic) and now I am sad to say that at the age of eighty I am reduced to the banal hope that the noble and ardent desire for free institutions is maintained in the people and that, though from time to time it may appear to sleep, it is as eternal as the electromagnetic storm which sparkles in the sun.

'On the bloody night of 18 March, placed between two barricades, I was attacked four times by armed men who did not know me and had not read Cosmos.' *Street fighting during the 1848 Revolution, Berlin*

LEFT *Funeral of the victims of the 1848 Revolution with Humboldt at their head. Detail of a painting by Adolf von Menzel*

CHAPTER 22

The Final Years

No one was more aware of his extreme old age, or better able to take a detached view of it, than Humboldt. His letters were full of mocking reference to his gradual 'petrifaction' and he often spoke of himself, not without some pride in his longevity, as 'the primeval man'. After his eightieth birthday, which was celebrated at Schloss Tegel and attended by the King and Queen, he wrote a letter to his friend Arago in which he described, with complete objectivity, all the symptoms of his advancing years:

> I lead a dismal and monotonous life in the middle of so much hur∤y-burly. I don't have to explain the reasons for my disgust and mental malaise. My health and my capacity for work are wonderfully preserved in spite of the cold—down to 28°C—and the endless trips to Charlottenburg [the King's castle on the edge of Berlin] on duty. Only the night hours are undisturbed. Usually I work from 9 pm to 3 am. I rarely go to bed before 3 o'clock in the morning, but I sleep longer than I used to, generally till 7 or 8 o'clock. I find I don't feel any stronger at all if I sleep eight or nine hours, which would be quite possible because I can still sleep when I want to, even during the day. What I see myself losing is my sureness of muscular movement. I can stand for three or four hours on end without feeling tired, but I don't really feel safe when I reach for books from a ladder, or when I go down a very steep staircase, or when I climb into a very high carriage.

He was also hard up for money again and was being pressed to settle some old debts. His financial embarrassment probably explains why, to the puzzlement of his brother's children, who had either inherited money or married into it, he did not now resign from his official position at court—he simply needed the regular income that went with the job. Otherwise it is difficult to see how he could have tolerated the hostility that was now increasingly directed against him in court circles. His part in the events of the 1848 Revolution had not impaired his relationship with the King but it had brought down upon him the implacable emnity of the ruling conservative party and the church. He was placed under police surveillance; his flat was watched and his mail opened. 'I have become *persona non grata* in the last few years,' he wrote to a friend in 1852, 'and I would have been exiled as a revolutionary and as the author of the godless *Cosmos* if my position with the King had not prevented it. To the pietists and the *Kreuzzeitung* (the new conservative paper) I am an abomination: they would like nothing more than to have me moulder underground.'

As a result he now had to endure constant insults and humiliation at court. The extreme right-wing politicians and army generals of the *Kamarilla*, the court junta, went out of their way to make things unpleasant for Humboldt and they found a violent champion in Markus Niebuhr, a clever, influential and revoltingly ugly member of the cabinet, who made it his function to undermine Humboldt's authority by contradicting him constantly and refuting everything he said in the presence of the King. 'Humboldt', he exclaimed, 'is a superficial know-all.' To which Humboldt retorted: 'Niebuhr is a cross-eyed bug.' He began to find an almost united front closing against him at court. Whenever he held forth in his customary loquacious way over dinner the military men would disappear one by one from the table until the Queen was forced to intervene. 'But gentlemen,' she chided those who were left, 'are you so little interested in what a great man like Alexander von Humboldt has to say? Is the old gentleman beginning to be a bore?'

For some years past Humboldt had made a practice of reading aloud to the King in the evenings, mostly from biographies of scientists or from articles of a more liberal nature in the papers. But now he found it increasingly difficult to hold his audience. The young people in the court circle would giggle and talk out loud, drowning Humboldt's old and failing voice. Guests would leave the room. Even the King, who had heard it all before, would start telling jokes or wander around, noisily inspecting engravings and wood carvings. Gerlach, one of the leading members of the right-wing clique, used to sit on a small round chair, his fat bottom hanging over the sides, and pretend to fall asleep. Sometimes he snored so loudly during Humboldt's readings that the King had to wake him up. 'Gerlach!' said the King. 'Don't snore like that!'

Quite often Humboldt found himself reading his liberal and uplifting passages to an audience of precisely one—a reactionary Junker by the name of Bismarck, no less. The future founder and first Chancellor of the German Reich was in his forties then; he always appears to have listened to Humboldt with patience and politeness at these evening readings and believed that he was well liked by the old Chamberlain.

Schloss Tegel where Humboldt celebrated his eightieth birthday

He related how Humboldt was eventually replaced by a young actor who recited poetry or extracts from the latest novels. Humboldt used to try and compete with him, chipping in as soon as his rival paused for breath. Once, when he was reduced to complete silence—a most unusual condition for him—he sought solace from the cold buffet table and Bismarck was astonished to observe the old man's robust appetite as he morosely loaded *foie gras*, smoked eel and lobster on to his plate.

Outside of court, however, life was a little rosier for Humboldt and his reputation with the general public and the scientific world seemed to grow greater every day. He was recognized as 'the father and patron of the natural sciences'. Little as he cared for medals and ribbons (he preferred not to wear any when he sat for a portrait) he had been awarded almost every decoration and order that Europe could offer, including the Grand Cordon of the Legion of Honour from France and the Star of

Bismarck, Humboldt's only audience among the ultras *in the Prussian Court*

the Red Eagle (in brilliants) and the Order of the Black Eagle, Prussia's highest honours. He had been given the freedom of the cities of Berlin and Potsdam. He had been elected as member of more than 150 learned societies in Europe and America and was guest of honour at countless public occasions of all kinds, including a few which, to his own confusion, celebrated his own achievements.

His fame was as great abroad as it was at home. His portrait hung in the King of Siam's palace alongside that of Queen Victoria, Louis Napoleon and the President of the United States. In 1852 the Royal Society in London awarded him their highest honour, the Copley Medal, which Bunsen, the Prussian envoy, received on his behalf. In his address Lord Rosse, the President of the Royal Society, summed up the regard with which Humboldt was held by his fellow scientists in the twilight of his long life.

It is enough to say here that there is no one acquainted with the present state of magnetism, of zoology, of botany, of geology or of physical geography who is not aware of the extent and value of Baron Humboldt's researches. A scientific traveller of the highest order, he zealously endeavoured to advance the science of physical geography in its widest sense, regardless of toil and expense, and at great personal risk. Distant regions of the globe were in turn his habitation, and with remarkable patience and a sagacity peculiarly his own, he sought out Nature's laws under every modification of climate. The mass of facts which he has given to the world, carefully arranged and discussed, constitutes a mine of information from which cosmogenists will long continue to draw with profit, while in its vastness it will be regarded with astonishment as the work of one man.

Humboldt's reputation stood particularly high in the United States. Ever since his stay with Thomas Jefferson in 1804, when the nation was still in its infancy, he had constantly shown, in both his public and private utterances, the greatest affection for Americans and the keenest interest in the affairs of their country—the outcome of the war with Mexico, the California gold rush, the fate of the Indians, the aggrandizement of the Confederacy, Frémont's candidature for the Presidency and the issue of negro slavery concerned him deeply. In return, Americans loved him. Though he had only spent 42 days in their country they somehow saw him as a kind of founder-member of modern America, a pioneer and a hero of the West whose name was inseparably linked with those of Washington, Jefferson and Franklin. From the Atlantic to the Pacific coast Humboldt was a household word and more than a score of rivers, lakes, bays, mountains, towns and counties now bore his name. When the first trans-Atlantic steamer service between New York and Bremen was inaugurated in 1839, Humboldt became one of the principal goals—sometimes the only goal—of a never-ending stream of American visitors to Germany. All of them— college professors, journalists, engineers, portrait painters, congressmen, diplomats, young students and plain tourists—were cordially received. 'To be an American', one of them recorded, 'was an almost certain passport to his presence, and if the visitor was not ill-bred, to his favour.' Not every American, however, was properly equipped for an encounter with this extraordinary European—as the very first of them, Professor Dallas Bache, a grandson of Benjamin Franklin, discovered to his cost:

I went to see Baron Humboldt by appointment. And spent nearly two hours during which the variety of ideas and subjects was actually overwhelming and I left with a headache.

Sometimes the flood of visitors must have seemed very tedious to Humboldt. Life for him had become 'a race to death', a simile from Dante which he loved to quote. He was very aware of the short amount of life left to him and impatient to finish his self-imposed tasks—notably the completion of *Cosmos*—before time had run out altogether. 'The dead ride fast', he reminded his younger colleagues whenever they delayed sending him the data he asked for. Death itself—'the termination of the state of *ennui* we call life'—did not frighten him, and though he did not have that lust for life which appeared to him so remarkable in the unfortunate Bonpland, he did have an astonishing appetite for work and regarded every minute as precious. Which is why, in the end, his voluminous and interminable correspondence became too much for him.

In his old age Humboldt was receiving an average of 3,000 letters a year and replying to about 2,000 of them in his own handwriting and at his own expense—his postage bill alone came to about 700 thalers a year. The letters he received came from all over the world and dealt with every conceivable topic. Many of them, of course, were concerned with serious scientific matters. Others contained plans for expeditions, projects for the colonies, designs for machines, blueprints of inventions, manuscripts for appraisal, questions about airships, requests for his autograph, offers of domestic help, ideas to cheer him up, petitions to the King, letters of praise, letters of thanks, requests for advice about jobs and pensions. He was bombarded by widows and clerks, foreign kings and princesses. He was both the target of cranks and a general inquiry office. From Nebraska he was asked where the swallows went in winter (he didn't know). From both sides of the Atlantic he received letters from religious eccentrics who proposed to convert him to more godly ways. A German author, with consummate bad taste, sent him a complementary copy of his latest novel— *Son of Humboldt, or the Maipure Indian*—while an American who signed himself Humboldt wrote a filial greeting which began '*très-vénérable père*'. It was all too much. In the end he was forced to put a notice in the newspapers with a request to be left 'a little rest and spare time for my own work, at a time when my physical and intellectual powers are anyway decreasing'. It was almost too late.

The third volume of *Cosmos* had come out in 1850. In 1858 the fourth volume appeared—and at the age of eighty-nine the grand old man of European science gathered what strength was left to him to complete the fifth volume of his story of the world. His retirement from public life following the complete mental collapse of the King in 1857 gave him more time for this task, but though he was still astonishingly fit, alert and fluent in speech for a man of his age, and could still read small print without a magnifying glass, there were signs that he was fading. One day he suffered a slight stroke—what he called 'an electric storm on the nerves, perhaps only a flash of lightning'. He was getting hard of hearing, complained a lot of a skin complaint —'a milky way of irritating millet seeds' which he called 'senilitis'—and seemed to be losing one of his most precious assets, his memory. 'It is by no means pleasant', he wrote to Bunsen, 'to experience a gradual loss of the phosphorous of thought, or a loss of weight in the brain, as the new school would say. But I do not lose my courage for work.' He toiled away on *Cosmos* as hard as he could but the end, by any reckoning, could not be a long way away.

Among his friends and relatives he was now almost the sole survivor. Leopold von Buch, Aimé Bonpland, Gay-Lussac, Gauss, Rauch and Varnhagen von Ense— he saw them all into the grave before him. His most grievous loss was Arago. After Louis Napoleon's *coup d'état* in Paris in 1851, Arago was imprisoned, along with other opponents of the new régime. He did not stay long in prison but he was already a sick man and in 1853, at the age of seventy, he died, asking after his friend Humboldt, who had not been allowed to visit him, to the last. As for Humboldt's own family— several times after the death of Caroline and his brother Wilhelm, he had to attend the funerals of his younger relatives at Schloss Tegel. 'I have buried all my race', he said. He was alone.

Or almost alone. There were still his visitors—a steady flow of strangers up to his door. One November day an American traveller by the name of Bayard Taylor paid a visit to the Humboldt establishment and later described his interview in the *New York Tribune*. It remains the best account ever written of Humboldt as he was in the last days of his life.

I was punctual to the minute, and reached his residence in the Oranienburger Strasse as the clock struck. While in Berlin he lived with his servant, Seifert, whose name only I found on the door. It was a plain two-storey house, with a dull pink front, and inhabited, like most of the houses in German cities, by two or three families. The bell wire over Seifert's name came from the second storey. I pulled; the heavy *porte-clochère* opened of itself, and I mounted the steps until I reached a second bell-pull, over a plate inscribed, *Alexander von Humboldt*.

A stout square-faced man of about fifty, whom I at once recognized as Seifert, opened the door for me. 'Are you Herr Taylor?' he asked; and added, on receiving my reply: 'His Excellency is ready to receive you.' He ushered me into a room filled with stuffed birds and other objects of natural history, then into a large library. I walked between two long tables, heaped with sumptuous folios, to the further door, which opened into the study. Those who have seen the admirable coloured lithograph of Hildebrandt's picture know precisely how the room looks. There was the plain table, the writing desk, covered with letters and manuscripts, the little green sofa, and the same maps and pictures on the drab-coloured walls. The picture had been so long hanging in my own room at home, that I at once recognized each particular object.

Seifert went to an inner door, announced my name, and Humboldt immediately appeared. He came up to me with heartiness and cordiality, which made me feel that I was in the presence of a friend, gave me his hand, and inquired whether we should converse in English or German. He insisted on my taking one end of the green sofa, observing that he rarely sat upon it himself, then drew up a plain cane-bottomed chair and seated himself beside it, asking me to speak a little louder than usual, as his hearing was not so acute as formerly.

The first impression made by Humboldt's face was that of broad and genial humanity. His massive brow bent forward, overhung his chest like a ripe ear of corn, but as you looked below it, a pair of clear blue eyes, almost as bright and steady as a child's, met your own. You trusted him utterly at first glance. I had approached him with a natural feeling of reverence, but in five minutes I found that I loved him. . . .

Taylor was surprised by the youthful complexion of Humboldt's face, the absence of wrinkles and smoothness of skin. His hair was snow white but abundant, his step slow but firm, and his manner active to the point of restlessness. The two men talked about Siberia, Central Asia and the great mountain ranges of South America, about mutual acquaintances like the American author, Washington Irving, and about the pet chameleon that lived in a box with a glass lid in Humboldt's study. 'A peculiarity of this animal,' Humboldt told Taylor, 'is its power of looking in different directions at the same time. He can turn one eye towards heaven, while with the other he inspects the earth. There are many clergymen who have the same power . . . .'

> Seifert at length re-appeared, and said to him, in a manner at once respectful and familiar, 'It is time', and I took my leave.
>   'You have travelled much, and seen many ruins,' said Humboldt, as he gave me his hand again; 'Now you have seen one more.' 'Not a ruin,' I could not help replying, 'but a pyramid.' For I pressed the hand which had touched those of Frederick the Great, of Forster, of Klopstock and Schiller, of Pitt, Napoleon, Josephine, the Marshals of the Empire, Jefferson, Wieland, Herder, Goethe, Cuvier, Laplace, Gay-Lussac—in short, of every great man whom Europe had produced for three-quarters of a century.

As Taylor was ushered out, Seifert pointed out an elaborate specimen of bead-work in a gilt frame. 'This', he said, 'is the work of a Kirghiz princess, who presented it to his Excellency when *we* were on our journey to Siberia.' There was a ring and a servant came into announce a visitor. 'Ah! the Prince Ypsilanti', said Seifert. 'Don't let him in. Don't let a single soul in. I must go and dress his Excellency. Sir, excuse me—yours most respectfully.' And Seifert bowed the American out.

Humboldt's curious relationship with Seifert during the last years of his life was the subject of much speculation in Berlin society and eventually became an open scandal. Bayard Taylor was not the first visitor to notice the familiarity in the servant's approach to his master, or the degree of control he exercised over the comings and goings in the house, and there were many complaints made about his caprice in admitting callers. For the last ten years of Humboldt's life, in effect, Seifert—old, faithful but domineering—was the master of the household. Humboldt used to complain of this 'tyranny' but for the sake of domestic peace he continued to endure it—a 'penniless labourer' within his own four walls.

In the history of master-servant relationships Humboldt's situation was by no means unique, but many efforts were made at the time (and afterwards) to find some concrete explanation other than the natural dependence of the aged and infirm upon those who are younger and stronger. At one time, for example, there was a rumour, not altogether scotched even now, that the youngest of Seifert's three daughters, Agnes, was actually Humboldt's natural child, and that this accounted for Seifert's hold over Humboldt. Certainly Humboldt was quite fond of Agnes; he considered her the most beautiful and charming of the three girls and showed her paintings off to all his visitors. But that Humboldt should have sired any progeny in his later years seems improbable, especially as he had showed so little inclination towards that sort of thing in his more vigorous young manhood. A more likely explanation of Seifert's power over his master was Humboldt's everlasting financial indebtedness to him, for which there is a great deal of documentary evidence.

In spite of the success of *Cosmos*, Humboldt had for many years been virtually dependent on his annual 5,000 thalers pension from the King. This sum never proved adequate to meet his expenditure and by the 10th of every month he was usually out

Humboldt's first photograph. Daguerrotype by Hermann Biow 1847

of funds and overdrawn at the bank. Sometimes he had to ask the King for a small donation to put his account straight again and in his worst moments of financial crisis Seifert had to forgo the wages due to him, which amounted to 25 thalers a month—a perfectly normal sum for those days. It seems Humboldt owed Seifert back pay for many years and that his anxiety about providing for Seifert and his family, both during his life and after his death, placed him more and more at Seifert's pecuniary mercy. In 1841 he had made a testament in which he left all his personal possessions to Seifert and in 1855, probably at Seifert's insistence, he reiterated his bequest in a letter in which he confirmed that he had sold his Order of the Red Eagle (in brilliants)

Humboldt's niece, Gabriele von Bülow, sat by her uncle as he lay dying

back to the King for 2,688 thalers in order to pay Seifert's wages and that all his gold medals, chronometers, books, maps, pictures, sculptures, instruments, sable furs, linen, plate, beds and furniture would become Seifert's rightful property when he died.

After Humboldt's heart attack in 1857 the King had agreed to pay off his small overdraft and in the following year Humboldt finally made over all his property to Seifert by deed of gift, only retaining its use while he was still alive. A few articles, for sentimental reasons, were excepted from this last bequest—the royal cabinet orders, a portrait of Frederick William IV, a large vase with views of Sans Souci and Charlottenburg painted on it, the freedoms of the cities of Berlin and Potsdam, the Copley Medal, his notebooks and his manuscript material for *Cosmos*.

And so—penniless, possessing nothing, his own home now run and virtually owned by his valet—Alexander von Humboldt passed one more winter in Berlin, his rooms heated to nearly 80°F against the cold, as they had been ever since his return from the New World more than half a century ago. He was now quite feeble and forced to stay in bed a lot. Aware of the strength that was daily ebbing from him, he laboured unceasingly to finish the fifth volume of *Cosmos*. He had just completed his description of the granitic rocks he had encountered on his Siberian expedition when he paused. The date was 2 March 1859. For some reason he decided not to continue beyond this point but to go back and revise the first eighty-five pages of the book, adding his usual footnotes and references. On 19 April Seifert took the manuscript to the publishers. Two days later, a few months short of his ninetieth birthday and exhausted and feverish, Alexander took to his bed.

He never found the strength to leave it again and knew he was dying. The Prince Regent, the future Kaiser Wilhelm I, came to visit him and Alexander asked him one final favour—permission to be buried at state expense—and this was granted. His niece, Gabriele von Bülow, came to nurse her old uncle through his last days and sat for many quiet hours at his bedside. Beyond the window of the little alcove where he lay there were all the signs of spring and a new summer coming. He did not suffer any pain. His voice—that old torrent of a voice—grew weaker and he spoke little, though always distinctly, sensibly and lovingly. From 3 May the daily bulletins of his medical attendants announced a rapid lessening of his strength, till on the last day—his intellect as clear as ever—he was content to gaze placidly round the room. On 6 May 1859, at half-past two in the afternoon, the end came peacefully—a completely natural death, a simple running down of the biological clock. Only Gabriele and her brother-in-law General von Hedemann were at Alexander's bedside. After they had closed his eyes they found on his bedside table three scraps of paper which bore the last statement the author of *Cosmos* had ever committed to writing, a quotation from *Genesis* which read:

'Thus the heavens and the earth were finished, and all the host of them.'

*   *   *

The lying-in-state took place in the library, which was garlanded with flowers and evergreens. The Court and the people of Berlin came in great numbers to pay their last respects. The Prince Regent had commanded a state funeral and at eight on the morning of 10 May the remains were conveyed from the apartment in Oranienburger Strasse through streets draped in black and crowded with a populace in mourning. Apart from the public funeral of the March revolutionaries in 1848, it was the most imposing non-military funeral in the city's history. In front of the cortege walked four royal Chamberlains, one of whom carried a red velvet cushion on which lay the insignia of Humboldt's decorations. The hearse was drawn by six horses led by grooms from the King's stable and escorted by twenty students carrying palm leaves. The coffin was covered in azaleas and laurel wreathes; and immediately behind it walked Alexander's family—the descendants and relatives, that is, of his brother Wilhelm. And behind them, marching slowly along Friedrichstrasse and the Linden to the solemn tread of Chopin's Funeral March, came the Knights of the Order of the Black Eagle, the Ministers of State, the diplomatic corps, six hundred students flanked by standard bearers, members of both parliaments, the Academy of Science, the Academy of Arts, the directors and teachers of the university and the schools, the magistrates and the municipal delegations. Only the clergy—with the exception of the officiating clergyman and seven free-thinkers—were absent. At the Cathedral door the Prince Regent received the procession with uncovered head, and after that the bells rang out and the choirs began to sing.

The next day Alexander von Humboldt made his last short journey down the avenue of limes and along the shores of the lake at Schloss Tegel and in a ceremony of rural simplicity was laid beside his brother and Caroline in the family cemetery beneath the pines. He could rest at last.

The family grave in the park at Schloss Tegel

Bibliography

My principal source has been the writings of Humboldt himself. Apart from the South American works, which are listed separately below, the most useful of his writings have been:

Lettres Américaines d'Alexandre de Humboldt, edited by E. T. Hamy. Paris 1905.

Correspondance d'Alexandre de Humboldt avec François Arago, edited by E. T. Hamy. Paris 1907

Briefe Alexander von Humboldts an seinen Bruder Wilhelm. Stuttgart 1880.

Letters of Alexander von Humboldt to Varnhagen von Ense. London 1860.

Alexander von Humboldt, *Views of Nature*, translated by E. C. Otté and H. G. Bohn. London 1880.

Alexander von Humboldt, *Cosmos*, translated by E. C. Otté. 5 volumes. London 1848–58.

In addition, I have often consulted the two major biographies: *Life of Alexander von Humboldt*, edited by Karl Bruhns and translated in 2 volumes by Jane and Caroline Lassell, London 1873; and the standard modern work, *Alexander von Humboldt* by Hanno Beck, 2 volumes, Wiesbaden, 1959 and 1961. *Alexander von Humboldt* by Lotte Kellner, London 1963, has provided a useful view of Humboldt's achievements in the light of modern science, and Helmut de Terra's *Humboldt*, New York 1955, has shone interesting if controversial light on his personal life.

The following have also proved useful:

Hanno Beck, *Gespräche Alexander von Humboldts.* Berlin 1959.

Hanno Beck, *Alexander von Humboldt und Mexico.* Bad Godesberg 1966.

Heinrich Pfeiffer (editor), *Alexander von Humboldt — Werk und Weltgeltung.* Munich 1969.

Joachim H. Schultze, *Alexander von Humboldt — Studien zu seiner universalen Geisteshaltung.* Berlin 1959.

The South American Publications—a list of the main titles.

1 SURVEY MEASUREMENTS

Recueil d'observations astronomiques, d'opérations trigonométriques et de mesures barométriques. Rédigées et calculées par Jabbo Oltmanns. 2 vols. Paris and Tübingen 1808–10.

Nivellement barométrique. Paris 1809.

Conspectus longitudinum et latitudinum geographicarum. Paris 1808.

2 BOTANY

Nova genera et species plantarum. Described by Carl Sigismund Kunth. 7 large folio vols. 700 plates, mostly in colour. Paris 1816–25.

Plantes équinoxiales. 2 large folio vols. 144 plates. Paris and Tübingen 1805–17.

Révision des Graminées. 2 large folio vols. 220 colour plates. Paris 1829–34.

Mimoses et autres plantes légumineuses. Described by C. S. Kunth. 2 large folio vols. 60 colour plates. Paris 1819–24.

Monographie des Melastomacées. Arranged by A. Bonpland. 2 large folio vols. 120 colour plates. Paris and Tübingen 1806–23.

Synopsis plantarum by C. S. Kunth. 4 vols. Paris and Strasbourg 1822–6.

3 PLANT GEOGRAPHY

Essai sur la géographie des plantes. Paris 1805

4 ZOOLOGY AND COMPARATIVE ANATOMY

Recueil d'observations de zoologie et d'anatomie comparée. 2 vols. 57 plates. Paris 1805–32.

5 TRAVEL AND GEOGRAPHY

Relation historique du Voyage aux régions équinoxiales du Nouveau Continent, in which is included the *Political Essay on the Island of Cuba.* 3 vols. Paris 1814–25. This was published in England as *Personal Narrative of Travels to Equinoctial Regions of America.* Translated by Thomasina Ross. 3 vols. London 1852.

Essai politique sur le Royaume de la Nouvelle-Espagne. 2 vols. Paris 1811.

Atlas géographique et physique des régions équinoxiales du Nouveau Continent. Large folio. 40 plates. Paris 1814–34.

Atlas géographique et physique du Royaume de la Nouvelle-Espagne. Large folio. 20 maps. Paris and Tübingen 1808–12.

Atlas pittoresque—Vues des Cordillères et monuments des peuples indigènes de l'Amérique. 2 large folio vols. 69 colour and monochrome plates. Paris 1810.

Examen critique de l'histoire de la géographie du Nouveau Continent. Paris 1814–34.

Monochrome Illustrations

We would like to thank the Royal Geographical Society for allowing us to photograph many illustrations from books in their library and map room.

Illustrations which appear on the following pages were photographed by Derrick Witty: 23, 42, 61, 66 *right*, 72, 73, 81, 82, 91, 95, 103, 106, 116, 117, 119, 123, 134, 147 *right*, 148, 150, 154, 162, 164, 166, 178 *left*, 183, 209, 210 *right*, 212, 240–1 *below centre*, 247, 249.

Index

75171